# MEN WITH BALLS

# MEN WITH BALLS

## The Professional Athlete's Handbook

## Drew Magary

Illustrated by Christopher Brand

Additional artwork by Kevin Richards and Dan Vail

Little, Brown and Company
NEW YORK  BOSTON  LONDON

Little, Brown and Company
Hachette Book Group
237 Park Avenue, New York, NY 10017
Visit our Web site at www.HachetteBookGroup.com

First Edition: October 2008

Little, Brown and Company is a division of Hachette Book Group, Inc.
The Little, Brown name and logo are trademarks of Hachette Book Group, Inc.

All illustrations by Christopher Brand, except the following: pages 15, 35, 36, 58, 59,
87, 120, 181 and 222 (by Kevin Richards); pages 107, 151 and 158 (by Dan Vail);
pages 31 and 230 (by Drew Magary); photo on page 232 by Drew Magary.

Library of Congress Cataloging-in-Publication Data
Magary, Drew.
    Men with balls : the professional athlete's handbook / Drew Magary. — 1st ed.
        p. cm.
    ISBN-13: 978-0-316-02307-8
    ISBN-10: 0-316-02307-8
    1. Sports — Humor.   2. Athletes — Humor.   I. Title.
    PN6231.S65M25 2008
    818'.607 — dc22                                                2008014737

10 9 8 7 6 5 4 3 2 1

RRD-IN

Printed in the United States of America

# Author's Note

Certain quotes and testimonials attributed to various athletes, players, coaches, journalists, executives, and other people of note in this book have been wholly fabricated for the sake of humor—specifically, all quotes and testimonials attributed to the following persons: Gilbert Arenas, Charles Barkley, Barry Bonds, Howard Cosell, Johnny Damon, John Elway, Weeb Ewbank, TJ Houshmandzadeh, Michael Jordan, Ray Lewis, Vince Lombardi, Mike Lupica, Joe Morgan, Dirk Nowitzki, Arnold Palmer, Carson Palmer, Gary Payton, The Phillie Phanatic, Red Ruffing, Marge Schott, Chris Simms, Stephen A. Smith, Casey Stengel, David Stern, Joe Torre, Johnny Unitas, and Brenda Warner.

# Contents

# Contents

# MEN WITH BALLS

## Chapter 1

# Getting to Know You and Your Balls

## An Introduction to Pro Athletedom

**Welcome to the next level. You, sir, are a man with balls.**

In the vast realm of sports literature, there has never been a book that has taught pro athletes *how* to be pro athletes. This is a pity, for pro athletes are people who need, nay, *crave,* guidance. Yet, no one off the field is willing to provide this guidance: not their coaches (too busy watching film), not their families (too busy buying leather goods at Barneys), not even Vince Lombardi (too busy slowly decaying into the soil). I recently asked a high-profile athlete who wished to remain anonymous (it was Tracy McGrady!) to map out his typical weekday for me. This is what he sent me:

10:00 a.m. — Wake up, followed immediately by a light nap

11:30 a.m. — Egg-white omelet with multigrain toast, slice of honeydew

12:00 p.m. — Xbox

3:00 p.m. — Light snack

3:05 p.m. — More Xbox

5:00 p.m. — Hop in Town Car to be escorted to arena; play Xbox in the backseat

5:30 p.m. — Rubdown by nubile twenty-three-year-old assistant trainer while playing Xbox

6:00 p.m. — Light snack and light nap, maybe some Xbox

7:00 p.m. — Shooting drills; discuss Xbox with fellow employees

7:30 p.m. — Light nap while playing Xbox

8:00 p.m. — Play real-life game

9:00 p.m. — Halftime; Xbox

10:00 p.m. — Game over; hop in Town Car to be escorted to club

10:30 p.m. — Late dinner, drinks; some light fellatio in a semiprivate alcove

1:00 a.m. — Asleep, unless new Xbox game has arrived

Now, does this sound like the schedule of someone who has direction in life? *Pfft.* Hardly. Pro athletes need a handbook that tells them everything they need to know to maximize their potential—on the field, at the bank, and in the bedroom (or, in some cases, in the arena utility room). At long last, that book has arrived. Welcome, good friend, to *Men with Balls: The Professional Athlete's Handbook.*

You will find this book a veritable treasure trove of information and useful tips to navigate the sometimes choppy waters of athletic superstardom. For, while a career in professional sports provides you with fabulous wealth, adoring fans, and a fully stocked koi pond in your backyard, you must always be wary of its dangers. If you're not careful, you could end up in prison. Or in a bad relationship. Or in Cleveland.

You're luckier than your forebears, because you have this book to guide you. Throughout history, there have been many books written *about* pro athletes. But who, I ask you, has ever written a book *for* pro athletes? No one. And you know why? Because it would be idiotic from a marketing standpoint to write a book exclusively for a group of people who represent only a minuscule fraction of the general population, particularly since many of them choose not to read books anyway.

But let's not let a little thing like common sense stand in our way. That's for pussies.

The sad fact is that pro athletes like yourself have no idea how to handle the world they've been thrown into. The only people you have to rely on for help are other pro athletes. And many of those people, frankly, are retarded. Some pro sports leagues do offer symposia for rookies. But those presentations are long, boring, and gay. Yes, our pro athletes are sorely lacking proper education in the art of *being* a pro athlete. It's a huge gap in academia. One that must be filled with great, thrusting force. And I'm just the person to supply such force.

Who am I? I'm glad you asked. Now, I've never played professional sports in my life. On the contrary, I have a spine made of peanut brittle, and I possess all the athletic ability of Gerald Ford during the brief period he was lying in state. I have also been outraced by various stationary objects, including a lamppost, a small mound of sawdust, and renowned college basketball coach Rick Majerus.

But I have watched. In fact, I have spent more than thirty years carefully observing athletes from afar. I even went so far as to place thousands of cameras and film crews in stadiums across the world so that I might watch athletes via open-circuit television, all at considerable effort and expense on my part. And I've been known to order my camera crews to slowly "replay" certain moments in the action so that I may study athletes more closely. From all that intense field research, I have accrued a knowledge of the ins and outs of pro athletics that well surpasses that of at least any twenty-nine-year-old.

And now, I share this vast wealth of knowledge with you, the professional athlete. No doubt you've encountered your fair share of coaches during your career, a small number of whom may or may not have made sexual advances toward you. Well, I'm here to be your *life* coach, taking you through your career from its beginning to its inevitable and heartbreakingly unpreventable conclusion. I'll give you the crucial skills necessary to succeed on the field, to get paid lots of money for it, and to avoid any number of unwanted sexually transmitted diseases. Ever heard of PID, or pelvic inflammatory disease? Trust me: you don't want that shit.

Moreover, this book isn't just for pro athletes. No, it's for *aspiring* pro athletes as well—which is to say, the rest of us. Read this book, and you'll be putting yourself in the shoes of your favorite athlete, or at least a reasonable facsimile of said shoes. It's a fact: we all like to live vicariously through professional athletes. Why, I often envision myself as former pro volleyball superstar Gabrielle Reece. Then I rub my nipples in a gentle, counterclockwise motion and vigorously masturbate myself to orgasm. Good stuff. With this book, you'll be able to do the same.

As a pro athlete, you are a *man with balls*. Sometimes those balls are round. Sometimes they are oblong. And sometimes they are stitched, which is kinda nasty. You are about to become the man we all desire to be or, at least, should desire to be.

**DID YOU KNOW?**

Did you know the first black Major League Baseball player was Jackie Robinson? Seriously? You didn't know that? Jesus. You should be ashamed of yourself.

But you must use your balls wisely, lest they blow up in your face—or worse, someone else's. At long last, I have come to show you how to use those balls to maximum effect. All for the bargain retail price of $16.99. (Note: Price in Canada may vary!) You're welcome.

So let's grab our balls and get ballin', ballers.

## It's all downhill from here: draft night.

The first step in becoming a professional athlete is to be drafted into the league of your respective sport (unless you play an individual sport, such as tennis or golf). For you, the aspiring pro athlete, draft night is the greatest night of your life, a validation that everything you did in college—excelling on the field, spending a handful of hours in kinesiology class, and getting shitfaced off grape Dimetapp and Everclear outside the Delta Upsilon house—has finally paid off. Tonight is the night you become a pro athlete, the best of the very best. It's like a debutante ball, only you don't wear white gloves, and you aren't raped by your long-time boyfriend, Chad, at the end of the night. Here are some tips to make the night memorable:

**GREETING THE COMMISSIONER.** This is important. When the commissioner calls your name, do the following: stand up, hug your loved ones, walk slowly to the podium, take your jersey, shake the man's hand, hold your new jersey aloft, smile for the cameras, and leave. That's it. Do *not* hug the commissioner. I can't stress this point strongly enough. Your commissioner got to the position he's in by ruthlessly consolidating his power at the expense of friends, loved ones, and Jesus Christ. The man will *not* hug you back. He barely knows the names of his own children. Don't fuck with him. Alabama defensive end Eric Curry hugged former NFL commish Paul Tagliabue when his name was called by the Bucs back in 1993. Remember Eric Curry? Of course you don't. He's dead. All because of a hug.

**WHERE YOU'RE GOING.** It's the biggest issue on your mind: What team will choose you? Will it be Utah? Man, you really hope it isn't Utah. Utah blows. People there are creepy. One time I went to Utah and saw a nine-month-old wearing an engagement ring. How did Utah even get a team? If you were drafted by Utah, how would you make sure you got out of Utah quickly, without even having to visit? God, now you're all nervous. This Utah business is pretty fucked up.

I'm not going to lie: it's completely out of your hands. But the good news is it doesn't have to stay that way. You *can* force a trade later on. However, be warned: everyone after that will hate you and consider you something less than a man. Which, in the case of Steve Francis, is more or less justified. For ideas on places you should weasel your way out of, see page 15.

**WHAT TO WEAR.** No dilemma is more baffling than what to wear the night you are drafted. It's your chance to make a first impression on the general sporting public (actually, given the prolificacy of ESPN, it's your 1,234,987th impression). So you need to dress for the occasion.

Are you black? Then God has provided you with a brilliant canvas of a complexion against which all bright colors will pop, to use a designer term. Don't wear muted colors or earth tones. That's for pussies. I want to see you in cherry reds, electric blues, and even canary yellows. Charles Oakley can probably lend you something. And no double-breasted jackets. You know who's double-breasted? Women. You're not a woman, are you? Also, the more buttons on your suit jacket, the better. Marshall

## Getting to Know You and Your Balls

Faulk still holds the record, rocking an incredible forty-two buttons on his jacket the night he was drafted. You couldn't even see his head. Bad. Ass.

Are you white? Yeah, well, then do the opposite of what I just told you. Cracka. For more fashion tips, see chapter 10 posthaste.

**WHO TO BRING.** Bringing someone with you to draft night means that you care for them deeply, or have accidentally impregnated them. As a pro athlete, you need to arrange a support system for yourself. That all starts here. Or, depending upon whom you exclude, that all *ends* here. Here is a brief list of mandatory people to bring.

- Your mother
- Your grandmother and grandfather (mother's side)
- Your college or high school girlfriend (don't worry, you're breaking up with her later that night)
- Your best friend
- One cousin of your choosing
- Your wife and five children (BYU draftees only)
- Your high school coach (his wife is optional)

That's the list. Many athletes go well past this tally, but remember, you aren't just setting up a support system for yourself, you are also setting yourself up as *the* support system for anyone you bring. The more people you bring, the more people you have to share in your success with. Do you *really* want to bring your stepfather? I don't like the way he looks at you. He seems just a little *too* chummy, if you get my drift. Very handsy.

**CELEBRATING.** Be sure to do all your celebrating the night before the draft. Why? Because, if you are drafted high, the owner of the team that chooses you will immediately whisk you off in a private plane (complete with lacquered minibar!) to a meet-and-greet with coaches and management. That's right: they want to put you to work *immediately*. Unreal. Dicks. And if you are drafted low, you will inevitably be disappointed in where you went and will order loved ones out of the room so that you can destroy valuable objects in a frenzy of blind, uncontrollable anger. I suggest the lamp. It smashes with little effort. I also suggest swearing a blood oath of vengeance against the teams that passed you over.

Should you find yourself disappointed on draft night, fear not: you will have someone there to comfort you.

## "Wow! Cash in an envelope!" Selecting an agent.

Since you're talented enough to be a pro athlete, there's a good chance you've been dealing with agents since the age of eight. It's important that you find an agent who will maximize your earning potential. But *more* important, you want an agent who will provide you with a false sense of security in your own abilities. You want a man willing to whitewash reality for you at any cost, and to provide a twisted form of substitute love and devotion that will fill the gaping hole in your heart left over from an unhappy childhood. Is that worth a lifetime tithing of all your earnings? Shit yeah.

Now, there are many agents to choose from. You can choose an oily agent or a slick agent or even a conniving agent. Or you could go in an alternative direction and choose a family member or lifelong family friend. If you choose to go that route, take this book, close it, and slam it against your face until your eyes and ears bleed. Don't be a shithead.

## Getting to Know You and Your Balls

Take the agent experienced in shady, underhanded dealings and don't look back.

Many agents will put together elaborate PowerPoint decks that detail their long-term and short-term plans for making you a multimedia superstar. You don't need to actually read these presentations. I suggest judging them strictly by thickness.

Agents will also offer gifts or perks to persuade you to sign with them. I call them sweeteners, which is very clever on my end. Here are the sweeteners you should expect.

- Money
- Trip to Vegas or the Bahamas
- Time-share for your parents
- Pit bull or other feral dog
- Down payment on a Cadillac Escalade or other luxury SUV of equal or greater value
- Strip club membership and/or club currency
- Steak dinner (order the porterhouse)
- Concert tickets *with* backstage passes (If your agent can't get you backstage to meet Shakira, he's not connected enough. Fuck him.)
- Drugs (optional)
- VIP table at the club of your choosing, with at least two bottles of Ketel One ordered (so not optional)
- A contract hit on the enemy of your choosing

You can also pick an agent who is dead honest with you and genuinely cares for your welfare, but refuses to make empty promises. This agent's name is Jerry Maguire, and he doesn't fucking exist.

# HEAR IT FROM AN AGENT!

## I will kill for you, and then feast upon the flesh of the deceased
by Marty Battaglia, professional agent

Being an agent is my one true passion. I have no other life outside of my clients: no friends, no family, not even a dog to speak of. All I got is you, baby. It's all you, all the time. There are no barriers with me, my friend. My clients *are* my family.

And since I consider you family, I can confide in you that the truth is I rely on clients such as yourself to keep my subhuman body undead forevermore. I need your precious, precious energy. That's why, if you let me represent you, I will do anything for you. I will defend you. I will take a stand for you. I will fight tirelessly on your behalf.

And I will kill for you. Oh, yes. Mark my words.

I will kill for you and then feast upon the flesh of the deceased, which will only strengthen my representation of you. I will tear out the heart of our chosen victim, hold it aloft as a trophy of our conquest, and then swallow it whole. Because killing is the ultimate act of dedication to my clients. One I'm delighted to make. So I will kill for you. Even if you don't want me to. *Especially* if you don't want me to. That way, I can prove to you how serious I am.

## "Kansas City? Shit." Where you'll be playing.

There are forty-four North American cities (or, in the case of Green Bay, quaint little burgs) that are home to professional sports teams. And while all of these cities have ready access to alcohol and vaginally advantaged

# Getting to Know You and Your Balls

I will do anything for you, my friend. I will go to fucking war for you. No joke. I will forge a declaration, get it passed through the puppet regime of a very small Latin American nation, and formally declare war. Then, I will wage a full-on orgy of bloodshed unlike anything the world has ever seen. All on your behalf. I'll even commit war crimes. Stomping babies? You got it. Heads on bayonets? Oh, yeah. Mass shootings? That's the best part.

There's no limit to the atrocities I'm willing to commit on your behalf. If getting you that extra incentive clause means I have to create some kind of superpoison that taints the world's water supply, killing all who come into contact with it, I will do it. In fact, I even had a lab built in case such a scenario is necessary. Just say the word. Go on. Say it. Now.

Listen, any agent can get you a deal. That's easy. What you need is an agent who will go the extra mile, who will burn down cities and rend the earth asunder to get you that mandatory suite on road trips. Will your current agent do that? No. He's a pussy. In fact, I will kill your current agent for you. I will cut his throat slowly with a bowie knife and then embed the video on YouTube, to show other agents and teams that you and I, together, are not to be fucked with. That's how much I care.

Of course, this extra caring will cost you more than the standard 4 percent. Perhaps also a large portion of your afterlife. But it's totally worth it, I assure you. Just let me kill again. Please.

persons, some are obviously more desirable than others. That's why I've decided to chart them for you in order of superiority. Except the Canadian cities. I removed them from consideration because Canada, as you know, is not a real country.

I took in many factors while determining these rankings, such as weather, marketing opportunities, abundance of gated communities to protect you from the poor and destitute, real estate prices, tax breaks, social scene, fan base, media glare, leftover racial tensions that could boil over at any moment, air quality, women, cuisine, entertainment, diversity (of women), parks, traffic, lack of a gay community to threaten you, crime, and laxness of drug and prostitution laws. Now, you may disagree with these rankings, and to that I say tough shit. Write your own goddamn book.

Tear out the chart on the opposite page and keep it in your wallet or money clip. It's a handy reference guide you'll need in the course of free agency. Is it really worth the extra $100,000 a year to stay in Buffalo rather than move to San Diego? You can go a whole year in Buffalo without seeing a single partially exposed tit. Think about it.

## Deeply Penetrating the Numbers

**53** Pro athletes living in Green Bay are 53 percent more likely to die in accidents involving autoerotic asphyxiation.

## Kneel before your master: knowing your league.

There are three major professional sports leagues in North America: the NFL, MLB, and the NBA. There is also the NHL, which may or may not still exist as of this printing. Notice that each league has given itself a three-letter acronym. There's something powerful about three-letter

# THE BEST CITIES FOR PROFESSIONAL ATHLETES

| OUTSTANDING | NOT BAD | KINDA SHITTY | INTERCHANGEABLE FLY-OVER TOWNS WITH LOTS OF MALLS AND OBESE TODDLERS | SHITHOLES |
|---|---|---|---|---|
| 1. Los Angeles | 9. Atlanta | 18. Orlando | 28. Milwaukee | 38. Baltimore |
| 2. Miami | 10. New Orleans * | 19. Anaheim | 29. Pittsburgh | 39. Memphis |
| 3. San Diego | 11. San Antonio | 20. East Rutherford, NJ ** | 30. Minneapolis | 40. Jacksonville |
| 4. New York | 12. Denver | 21. Nashville | 31. Cleveland | 41. Boston *** |
| 5. Phoenix | 13. Washington, DC | 22. Raleigh | 32. Detroit | 42. Buffalo |
| 6. Chicago | 14. Philadelphia | 23. Uniondale, NY (Long Island) | 33. Indianapolis | 43. Green Bay |
| 7. Dallas | 15. Charlotte | 24. Houston | 34. Kansas City | |
| 8. San Francisco | 16. Seattle | 25. Oakland | 35. St. Louis | |
| | 17. Portland | 26. Tampa | 36. Columbus | |
| | | 27. San Jose | 37. Cincinnati | |

\* Move this up nine spaces if you plan on breaking the law
\*\* So long as you commute from Manhattan
\*\*\* Move this up thirty spaces if you're white

| ONE STEP ABOVE CHINA'S PRISON FOR ESPECIALLY TROUBLESOME DISSIDENTS |
|---|
| 44. Utah |

acronyms. I can't explain it. Would you watch a league called the NFKL? No, you would not.

These are leagues with proud histories—histories that, for our purposes, are largely irrelevant. I'm going to skip the boring crap and cut right to the vital information you need upon entering your respective league. I hope you have a highlighter on your person.

# The NFL

**Full Name:** National Football League

**Logo:** A coat of arms, featuring all-American red, white, and blue colors with stars that echo the American flag. The logo was slightly modified in 2008, presumably because the serif on the end of the *L* on the old one was just too queer.

**Founded:** 1921, as the American Professional Football Association (APFA), only to have its name changed a year later (see what I mean about four-letter acronyms?)

**Current Commissioner:** Roger Goodell

**Commissioner Fifty Years from Now:** Condoleezza Rice's cloned twin sister/daughter. As commissioner, Rice II will control all of the league's expanded holdings, including the Ford Motor Company, half of Eastern Europe, Peyton Manning's frozen sperm, CNN, the Ohio State University, and the entire Lutheran sect of the Christian Church.

**Ball:** Oblong

**Annual Revenue:** $6.4 billion

**Average Player Salary:** $1.1 million

**Guaranteed Contracts?** No. You should want to play for the love of the game, you selfish bastard.

**Skill Set Required:** Speed, lateral agility, quick recognition of formations and audibles, a deep-seated, primal urge to hurt people that can potentially spill over into civilian life should certain psychological triggers be tragically provided

**Fan Demographics:** Males, ages 18 to 45. Married. White. Two to three children. Needs regular doses of alcohol to cope with the cruel monotony of day-to-day living.

**Chick Magnet Factor:** Ten if you play quarterback. Three if you play anything else. Big men scare the ladies away.

# MLB

**Full Name:** Major League Baseball

**Logo:** A silhouette of a batter poised to hit a ball that will forever remain tantalizingly just out of his reach. It's a logo inspired by both John Keats and former Detroit Tiger Rob Deer, who sucked. Features all-American red, white, and blue colors. Baseball is often called the national pastime. The nation that moniker refers to is Cuba.

# Men with Balls

**Founded:** 1903

**Current Commissioner:** Allan H. (Bud) Selig, the first and last Jewish man to go by the name Bud

**Commissioner Fifty Years from Now:** Bob Costas III, who will be just as pretentious and disturbingly ageless as his grandfather. He will be hired as a cruel prank by owners, who will then gleefully stonewall him at every turn. He will accomplish nothing.

**Ball:** Round. Small. Hard. Stings like a bitch when you get one in the eye at age seven (thanks, Dad).

**Annual Revenue:** $5.2 billion

**Average Player Salary:** $2.5 million

**Guaranteed Contracts?** Yes. So chew all the Red Man you want. The cost to surgically remove a three-inch mouth tumor is relative chump change.

**Skill Set Required:** Quick hands, good arm, intangible feel for hitting the ball that George Will could probably drone on about for hours on end, like it's magic or something. What a douche.

**Fan Demographics:** Males, ages 65 and over. Widowed. White. Four to five grandchildren, one of whom he will inevitably drag to the ballpark, hoping to generate a spark of wonderment in the child's eyes, only to fail and become more disillusioned with the state of our nation's youth, taking his own life shortly thereafter

**Chick Magnet Factor:** Seven. Change that to a negative integer if your first name is David and your last name is Wells.

# The NBA

**Full Name:** National Basketball Association

**Logo:** Jerry West against an all-American red, white, and blue backdrop. Many people believe this is merely a silhouette of West. Not true. That's an actual photograph. I'm telling you, without the spray-on tanner, the man is whiter than an albino cancer patient.

**Founded:** 1946, as the Basketball Association of America, or BAA. The name was changed because too many people pronounced the acronym phonetically, just to be wiseasses.

**Current Commissioner:** David Stern

**Commissioner Fifty Years from Now:** David Stern. Did you really think mere death could kill David Stern? Foolish mortal.

**Ball:** Large. Round. Shape inspired by former Jazz center Oliver Miller.

**Annual Revenue:** $3.2 billion

**Average Player Salary:** $4 million

**Guaranteed Contracts?** Yes. And limited marijuana testing! They *want* you to enjoy yourself here. Please do so.

**Skill Set Required:** Wide base, excellent hand-eye coordination, court vision, the ability to make even the slightest physical contact seem a violation akin to forcible rape

**Fan Demographics:** Males, ages 13 to 30. Single. Black. Four to five grandchildren. Steadfastly believe it could be them out on that court if their middle school coach hadn't, like, played favorites and shit.

**Chick Magnet Factor:** Ten to black women. Four to white women. White women see a black man taller than 6'6" and are simultaneously curious and terrified.

# The NHL

**Full Name:** National Hockey League

**Logo:** Sort of looks like a police badge, which the league may have done intentionally, just for the delicious irony. The logo also features all-Americ— Wait, what's that? Their logo is black and silver? What pathetic, twisted Third World nation is that supposed to represent? Want to know why you're the redheaded stepchild of pro sports, NHL? Take a look at your logo, and then go get fucked.

**Founded:** 1917

**Current Commissioner:** Gary Bettman. Few people know that Gary Bettman was born without a pituitary gland and is only 3'8".

**Commissioner Fifty Years from Now:** No one

**Ball:** Round. Flat. Not actually a ball

**Annual Revenue:** $2 billion (Note: That's gross revenue. Net revenue is unavailable. Literally.)

**Average Player Salary:** $1.5 million

**Guaranteed Contracts?** Shockingly, yes.

**Skill Set Required:** Strong legs, quick wrists, an inability to recognize that pain is the nervous system's way of telling your brain that something is amiss with your body

**Fan Demographics:** Stuart Nelson of Wayzata, MN. Fourteen years old. Single

**Chick Magnet Factor:** A surprising eight. As an NHL player, your brain is a blank canvas women are often eager to work with.

You may also play an individual sport that has no league affiliation. Sports like golf, tennis, and boxing offer the freedom of individual play, along with sizable event purses. Even better, being an independent contractor athlete means that you are your own boss. Whew! No pesky coaching for you, just a domineering father who will push you to the very fringes of sanity before dying at the exact moment you need him most. It's a pretty sweet deal. After all, there's no *I* in *team*, unless there's no team.

So those are your options. Feeling settled in now? Good. Time to work. And by work, I mean play.

## Clippable Motivational Slogan!

*Winning isn't everything. Kicking your man while he's down, watching him writhe in agony and clutch at his rib cage like a little girl while you let out a slow, demonic cackle—that's also pretty sweet.*

—Vince Lombardi

## Chapter 2

# It's Not Just a Sport; It's Now a Soul-Crushing Job

## On the Field

### You don't get to play those pussies from Rice anymore: what to expect on the field.

Now that you're a pro, you're going to have to learn to adjust to the differences inherent in the pro game. It's a far different enterprise than the game you played at the collegiate level. For one, you will now be paid in real money, instead of being "paid" with a scholarship. As currencies go, American dollars are far more useful than any sort of forced learning. Especially if you studied sociology, the major for people who enjoy being useless. But I mainly want to drill down the differences in style of play here.

**SPEED.** First off, the pro game is much faster. There aren't as many slow, white assholes clogging up the field this go-round. All that juking and jiving you did junior year? That won't fool pros such as Brian

Urlacher. In fact, it's far more likely to piss them off, causing them to drive you into the ground, shredding vital internal tissue in the process. So get speedier. I suggest taking diuretics prior to game time. They really help dial up the urgency.

**EQUIPMENT.** This is most pronounced in baseball, where your aluminum bat will be replaced with a wooden bat (Note: Eighty-five percent of all incoming baseball players nickname their bat Wonderboy, until their first strikeout). The reason for this change is twofold. First off, wooden bats are less likely to injure pitchers. Given that pitchers can shatter your orbital socket with a 95-mile-per-hour heater any time they wish, this seems kind of unfair. You should be able to retaliate by nailing them dead center in the chest with a death-rope line drive. Alas, you'll just have to settle for seeing them jut out their glove to block the ball rocketing off your bat, and cowering in fear like little pussies.

The other reason wooden bats replace aluminum in the majors is for sound design. Aluminum bats go *PING!* Wooden bats go *CRACK! PING!* is kind of a weak sound. Almost fey. *CRACK!* is far manlier. It connotes the breaking of things, and that is sweet. Ask any major leaguer: *CRACK!* beats *PING!* every time. Especially if you're the late Steve Howe.

**SCHEDULE.** College schedules are notoriously padded with any number of cupcake opponents. Your Prairie View A&Ms, your SUNY-Buffalos, your Notre Dames, and your Lower Duluth Amateur Pornographer Film Scoring Institutes. Those were gimme games. Oh, sure, your college coach always told you, "Be careful of Vanderbilt! They'll sneak up on you! That number sixteen is an absolute *dragon!*" But that was all a load of shit. He knew they sucked, and so did you. Don't expect any opponent to come in and just lie down for you at this level. Unless, of course, you're playing the Knicks.

## It's Not Just a Sport; It's Now a Soul-Crushing Job

In fact, you not only face tougher, faster opponents at every encounter on the pro level, but you also have to play them *more times*. Pro schedules are considerably longer than college schedules, and that's not even counting the playoffs. There's going to be a lot of wear and tear on your body, no matter how many free deep-tissue massages and scented hot tub aromatherapies you may receive. Rookies are often said to hit what is known as a "rookie wall." This occurs when you have played the number of pro games that would constitute a full college season, only to realize you still have fifty games left to go. This is often followed by a five-minute audible groan.

The one saving grace? You don't have to attend any college classes. Not that you did before anyway, but at least now you don't have to keep up the *facade* of attending class and pretend you care about how the Revolutionary War ended. That can be pretty exhausting.

**RULES.** Pro sports often differ from the college game in terms of rules and/or timekeeping. There are some obvious ones. In the NBA, the three-point line is a couple extra feet from the basket. In the NFL, receivers must have *both* feet inbounds for a legal catch. And the PGA Tour forbids players from having any goddamn sense of humor whatsoever. Everyone knows that.

But there are some additional rule differences you may not be aware of. For instance: in Major League Baseball, it is, in fact, perfectly legal to run the base paths with the tip of your penis just barely sticking out above the waistband of your game pants. If any girls notice this, you are awarded an extra base. The NFL forbids the use of geese to distract punt returners but allows group masturbation in any bench area Cool Zone. And while hand-checking is illegal in the NBA, tickling is not. Also, were you a cross-country runner in college? You'll notice that professional cross-country running has no rules, because there is no such thing as professional cross-country running. Next time, pick a real sport, instead of gallivanting through the woods like a goddamn idiot.

## Grizzled or nongrizzled? What kind of pro athlete are you?

Not all pro athletes are created equal. Obviously, there is a big difference between, say, a Michael Jordan and, say, a Jack Haley. Jordan was a god. Haley was a towel boy who got to wear warm-up pants. As a pro athlete, you're going to fit into a certain archetype, a Shakespearean stock character, if you will. Jeff Garcia will be playing the part of Desdemona. For the rest of you, you're going to fit into one of the following categories.

**SUPERSTAR.** You are the absolute best among your peers. Not only are you an all-star, but you are better than your fellow all-stars, which makes you the best of the best of the best. This concept is even more mind-blowing after you've taken in seven bong hits. You are the rare breed of athlete that transcends your chosen sport, attracting casual fans both domestically and in important, developing foreign markets like China, India, and soon-to-be-independent-if-I-get-my-way Alsace-Lorraine. You are an icon. In fact, there's a very good chance that you are so well known that die-hard fans of your sport now resent your omnipotence and have grown to loathe your visage whenever they encounter it, which is all the time. You are a lock to make your sport's Hall of Fame one day, especially considering that losers like Warren Moon are already in there. Fans mob you. Commercial sponsors adore you. Refs protect you as if you were made of very fine porcelain. Groupies regularly scour your dumpster in search of freshly used condoms.

**ALL-STAR.** You excel among your peers and are well established enough that casual idiot fans will punch your name on the all-star ballot year after year because they've heard of you. You are considered an exceptional player, but you are not an ambassador for your sport the way superstars are. This is a good thing, because being an ambassador for your sport can be a real pain in the ass. Fans (especially children) will mistake you for some *other* all-star. Commercial sponsors like you. Refs may forgive the occasional eye gouge. Groupies will still allow anal.

**SOLID PLAYER.** You are a hardworking athlete who can make the occasional great play, but you lack the talent and the consistency to excel against players of an all-star level or higher. Try as you might, you have reached a plateau from which you can rise no higher. God, that is *so* depressing. You work all this time to get where you are, yet you'll never be as good as the very best. Look at that LeBron James, driving past you like it's nothing. He makes it look so easy. Christ, how you loathe him. If only there were a way to lure him into an abandoned parking garage, where you could stealthily mow him down with your Honda Accord, or with gunfire, or with both. Commercial sponsors ignore you. Refs ignore you. Thank God for groupies. They're the only people with low enough standards to accept you and your lesser skills.

**JOURNEYMAN.** You are good, but you aren't good enough to keep your current team from trading you to some other team that has been unwisely suckered into dealing for you. You have been passed from team to team like a bad wedding reception canapé everyone is willing to try but unwilling to finish. But your experience bouncing (or, in some cases, shuttling) around the league has become a valuable asset in its own right. You know the ins and outs of at least eight other teams, and that knowledge could prove valuable to your new team. It never does, but it *could*.

You also have a familiarity with many of the cities on the pro circuit. Other players may rely on you out on the road to know the whereabouts of good restaurants, hot clubs, or the phone numbers of various local Polish escort services. Journeymen are also called "grizzled veterans." But journeyman is a much cooler moniker. It makes you sound like some kind of nomadic vigilante who only plays by his own rules. You should carry a guitar around with you wherever you go, just for the romance of it. Fans think you still play for the other team. Refs respect you. Journeywoman groupies worship you. I suggest avoiding them. Lotta tread on those tires.

**JUST ANOTHER GUY (JAG).** Not to be confused with the Judge Advocate General acronym of the TV show *JAG*, starring the rakishly handsome David James Elliot and the fantastically bejugged Catherine Bell, JAG is shorthand for Just Another Guy. This means that you are eminently disposable. There are plenty of other players out there who play the game as well as you do, but you had the good fortune of being *nearby*. Nice work.

Being a JAG means fans ignore you unless you tell them you play a professional sport, at which point they will do a thorough Google search to verify your claim. Refs use you as a foil for their outrageous calls in favor of superstars. The only groupies you score are ones that have something egregiously wrong with at least one part of their body.

**ROLE PLAYER.** You excel at one particular aspect of your game and one aspect only: things like shooting, returning kicks, baserunning, or making flagrant elbows look innocuous. You have a particular knack for doing this one thing, but are terrible at everything else. Being a role player also means *knowing* your role, and never venturing from it. Steve Kerr tried posting up once. Michael Jordan had his pinkie toe snipped off with garden shears as punishment. You may also be known as a "specialist," which is really just a condescending euphemism. I'm good at packing a car trunk. You don't see anyone calling me an automotive compartmentalization specialist. Only die-hard fans know you. Commercial sponsors will only use you if your talent has some kind of clever alternative usage ("Morten Andersen can kick a football. But can he kick EL Fudge cookies?"). Refs cannot actually see you. And the only groupies you score are the ones who are themselves role players: dominatrices, girls dressed as Little Bo Peep, etc. Depending on your tastes, this isn't necessarily a bad thing.

**GRITTY (WHITE) OVERACHIEVER.** Subset of the role players. As an overachiever, you are notorious for your tireless work ethic. You are the first one to the practice facility and the last one to leave. You watch hours of film every night. You go hard on every play and treat practice like games. Your coach loves you and holds you up as an example to the team, saying, "The rest of you need to be more like little Ruettiger here," which will in turn force your teammates to do more work than is necessary. Within a month, they'll hate your fucking guts. I guarantee it. The gritty overachiever is often labeled by announcers as "scrappy," or "tenacious," or "a grinder," or "our last one true white hope before the physically superior black man finally crushes us in the Great Racial Holy War." Enjoy the extra attention. You worked hard for it, you annoying little white man.

**PROJECT.** You are raw (Note: All human beings are raw in their natural state). You have a huge body that you have not yet grown into, or you excel at some sort of basic athletic ability but possess no way to apply it practically. Your team will spend millions upon millions of dollars trying to make you into the all-star they envision you to be. They may even continue to try to develop you long after their plans have gone awry. But, chances are, you will end up remaining the same as you are now: a phys-

ical freak of nature who happens to be shitty. That's the way it goes sometimes. But hey, at least you suckered a few people along the way.

**SCRUB.** You suck. Stop reading this book. If a fan sees you out on the
field, he will become visibly angry at your presence. You are a blown as-
signment waiting to happen. Enjoy playing semi-pro ball in the Quad
Cities a week from now.

---

# DID YOU KNOW?

Former NFL player Tom Tupa lasted eighteen years in the league by
being a rare double role player. Tupa played both third-string quarterback
*and* punter. He also played the bugle, making him the most versatile
useless player in league history.

---

## Your playbook, now with 80 percent more confusion!

Upon being drafted by your team, you will immediately be presented
with your team playbook. It will be six hundred pages long, single-spaced,
with writing on both sides of the paper and copious notes in the margins.
Do not lose your playbook. An unpaid assistant coach spent more than
one hundred hours copying, laminating, collating, and color-coding that
thing. If you lose it, you will make him cry. And you will be fined $25.

You will be expected to have your playbook committed to memory by
the second week of training camp. By the third week, you'll need to have
memorized all the plays for everyone else's position as well. By the end
of the month, all of the plays should be second nature to you and you
should be able to school others in how to interpret the detailed workings

of your coach's brain. Coaches and fans alike will expect you to never make a single mental error. Ever. But don't worry. All it takes to master a playbook is a photographic memory and the Kasparovian ability to anticipate all probabilities for multiple scenarios and plan an endgame by instantly recalling similar plays throughout history and their statistical success rate, then calculating the correct move based upon all you've absorbed. Surely you picked up a similar skill while studying the History of UPN at Ball State. Consider this sample play:

## Split Right 48 Waggle Razor Q Butterfly Jingleheimer Schmidt Oklahoma Blue

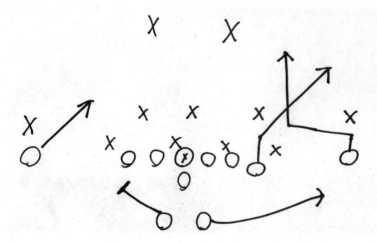

In this play, the receiver on the left is the X, or wideout. The receiver on the right is the Z, or flanker. The tight end is Y. *Split* refers to the backfield formation. *Right* refers to the side the tight end lines up on, which is the "strong" side. The *48* refers to the patterns the X and Z must run (here, a quick slant and a square in-and-up). *Waggle* means the full-back chips off the rush end and then flies up the field. *Razor* is a word thrown in to make the play sound more badass. *Q* is the flat route run by the tailback. *Butterfly* is the dummy audible call. *Jingleheimer* is the actual check-down call. *Schmidt* is the second dummy audible call used to confuse the defense as to which call is the actual dummy call and which is the real nondummy call. *Oklahoma* is the blocking scheme. *Blue* is a type of color.

Now, this is but one play. It actually has 132 different variations depending upon the formation. You'll also notice I've drawn up this play against a base 4–3 defense. This, of course, isn't how the defense will line up in reality. Chances are, they'll move all around just to fuck with you. For example, if the nose tackle shifts from a one-technique to a three-technique, the quarterback will audible to "I Right Fifty-two Motion Left Hitch Blaze R Logan's Run Macanudo Vermont." You see the difference? And, if the outside linebacker shifts outside the end into a "hip" position, the play becomes "I Left Shotgun Royal B Post Jigsaw Krull Jabberwocky Chinatown Alaska." See? It's not that complicated.

Just remember that a sport like football presents infinite strategic possibilities that no one person could ever possibly absorb, let alone comprehend. But your coaches will attempt to do so and expect you to instantly apply all of it flawlessly in adverse conditions. But you are in luck. You do get to keep a laminated cheat sheet on your wristband with every play listed in .5-point font. That should help.

Yep, you're going to fuck up. Repeatedly. Just make sure you paralyze someone while doing it.

## Because "I fucked your mother" just won't cut it: trash-talking.

Within a single professional match of football, or basketball, or even a pussy sport such as lacrosse, there is a series of battles within the game itself. And this is no team game. This is strictly a mental battle, one-on-one, between you and the man guarding you. That's right. It's time to lay a hardcore verbal smackdown on a bitch. Win this verbal tête-à-tête, and you'll have gained a permanent mental edge over your opponent. You'll be helping your team win. But more important, you'll be savaging a man's dignity and inflating your own ego in the process.

Nothing is out of bounds when it comes to trash-talking. If telling the catcher that you just stabbed his mother with an AIDS-infected needle throws him off by even one degree, then it's well worth it. Remember: aim high when you're aiming low. Consider these targets:

- His mother
- His father (especially if his father is dead)
- His wife
- His children. An underage daughter makes for an especially sensitive target, often literally!
- His sexuality
- His hometown. If he's from rural Georgia, you should have lots to work with.
- A recent injury
- A recent "trial separation"
- Appearance
- Religion, especially if he's a Buddhist or some other bullshit religion

● Grooming and hygiene. Ever smell Manny Ramirez on a Sunday? *Not* pleasant.

One thing I left out here is race. Racial taunting is only permitted in certain scenarios. Black-on-white taunting is permissible. White-on-black will almost certainly incite an angry mob. Black-on-Asian usually gets a pass. White-on-Latino is out of the question, but White-on-Sikh is allowed. And everyone can make fun of Samoans without consequence.

Remember, your goal is to shift your opponent's focus from the task at hand to you. Making him mad is just one way of doing this. You could offer him a brainteaser. For example, ask him, "Are you PT?" If he says, "No," then say, "Oh my God! You weren't potty trained? Loser!" If he says, "Yes," then say, "Oh my God! You're a pregnant teacher? What a douchebag!" You see? There's no right answer! He can't win! You have him completely out-riddled!

But the best trash talk is often highly personal. You're not gonna shred your opponent's last nerve if you're just making general insults. You need to do your homework. Check out his MySpace page. It's undoubtedly been laid out in a sloppy and careless fashion. Be sure to let him know that. Or edit his Wikipedia page to include a blatantly false fact and then tease him about that. Read his autobiography. Find out where he lives. Send a pregame death threat to his house using letters cut out from magazines and ask him, "Did you get my note? Remember, you have until three p.m. Wednesday." *That's* the kind of shit that really distracts a man.

But your pregame research is only one facet of being an all-star trash-talker. Your opponent will have done his homework as well. Even more crucial is having the perfect comeback. You need to train yourself, to sharpen your instincts for a witty rejoinder. You don't want to be the kind of guy that figures out the perfect comeback thirty minutes into the car ride home. God, that's annoying. Train your mind. Consider the following comebacks.

Soon, you'll have mastered the art of the dance. No one will dare joust against you.

Then again, why let him get a word in edgewise? You can suffocate your opponent with a steady, never-ending barrage of inane chatter (imagining you're a woman in this scenario helps). Drink lots of water before the game if you need to, but just keep talking. Forever. By the third quarter, you'll have completely destroyed his will to live. Take it from one of the all-time greats.

# HEAR IT FROM AN ATHLETE!

## You ain't got shit
### by Gary Payton

C'mon, boy. C'mon! You wanna challenge me? This isn't some JV shit you're playing now. You ain't got shit. You hear me?

YOU AIN'T GOT SHIT.

Where'd you get those shoes, you poor-ass motherfucker? Are those British Knights? I didn't even know they made British Knights anymore. Why don't you just go buy some shoes at TJ Maxx while you're at it, you bargain bin–scrounging bitch? Know who else offers the max for the minimum? Your momma.

Oh, you want personal? Oh, I can get more personal than that. What kind of Social Security number is 948-02-2301? Did you know that number is a cryptogram for YOU IS SHIT? I did. I solved that shit in my head right as I was talking. I just blew your fucking mind with puzzles. I even checked out your credit report online. Know what your credit rating is? It's Ass. That's an actual rating, too. See this printout? See what it says at the bottom? *ASS.* Who buys a scooter on layaway? With a Discover card, no less? Kiss my black balls.

I can even fuck with you in different dialects, if you like. Ever been heckled in cockney? I'm about to get all up in your skyrocket. You understand that? I can tell by the look on your Chevy Chase that you don't. Care for a foreign language lesson? You ain't *scheisse.* See that? That was German. I took lessons with Herr Ludewig in Stuttgart for eight weeks just so I could fuck with you like that. I can even fuck with you in sign language. I saw *Children of a Lesser God* twice. See this middle finger? Suck on that.

(*continued on next page*)

---

*(You start crying.)*

Oh, are you crying now?

*(You furiously deny it.)*

Shit, I've had plenty of guys get mad. But I've never seen a bitch go and *cry*. What's the matter, rookie? Are you just realizing now that you ain't got shit? Well, I'm sorry to hear that. Pussy. Would you like some Puffs tissues? I got the ones with aloe vera, just for your overly sensitive ass. Here, take this lace handkerchief. I keep it between my thighs for occasions just such as this. Only half of it is wet.

There, there. Relax. It's just a game. Everything'll be all right. As long as you remember that YOU AIN'T GOT SHIT.

---

## Showboating and the lost French art of pantomime.

In a perfect world, scoring would be its own reward. There's a certain purity to making a great play and then simply tossing the ball back to the officials. The purpose of this section is to explain to you why that sort of mentality is stupid and gay. You busted your ass all year long (in theory) to get to this point. It's your right, nay, your *duty*, to celebrate a good play in an overly demonstrative fashion. Even if it wasn't a scoring play. Even if it was just a routine play. Even if you didn't make the play but were in the general vicinity of it. Even if you only visualized the play in your mind. Regardless, you have carte blanche to go apeshit.

Remember: you aren't just an athlete. You're an entertainer now. Regular game play and the thrill of winning are no longer enough for today's ADHD-riddled masses. They demand more. They want cheerleaders to ogle. They want loud music to drown out any potential conversation. They want T-shirt cannons. They want flying monkeys. They want war veterans paraded out onto the field at the half so they can feel genuine emotion for ninety seconds. They want a show, even if you have no formal training in the dramatic arts. So, you better dance for them. Dance, I tell you!

In fact, many of today's top professional showboaters have abandoned simple dancing and gone straight into the field of pantomime. This is a field traditionally dominated by overly enthusiastic seventh-grade drama class students, but more and more pro athletes are joining the fray. When you see Terrell Owens pretending the football is a pillow and sleeping on it, or Sam Cassell running down the court jiggling a pair of imaginary three-inch testicles, you're watching classic mime techniques in the vein of Marcel Marceau, or that one dude from that Bobby McFerrin video.

Want to be like David Larible, "The Prince of Laughter"? Consider the mime routines below. They can be used to celebrate your own greatness, or to taunt the inferior skills of your opponent, or to inflame drunken fans, or, ideally, to do all three at once. Consider using a milk crate in these routines. In the world of mime, a milk crate can be *anything*.

**THE STAGGERING PENIS.** Standing with your legs a little more than shoulder-width apart, squat down halfway to the ground and mime the lifting of a very heavy concrete tube or an oaken log, placing your hands underneath. Once you have "picked it up," hold it out and pretend to lose your balance as you stagger under the mighty weight of your own monstrous appendage. Then "place" it on your milk crate. Wipe your brow and mime opening a beer. You've earned it after all that imaginary manual labor, Captain Bigdick.

**THE BREAKTHROUGH.** A nouveau twist on a classic routine. Pretend you are trapped inside an imaginary box only you can see. Oh, de-

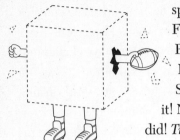

spair! But wait. You have a plan! Make a fist. Form a look of determination on your face. Play the *Chariots of Fire* theme in your mind. Now break through that imaginary wall! Smash through that air! *BOOM!* You've done it! No one thought you'd find a way out, but you did! *Très fantastique!*

**THE PHANTOM STEAMER.** Inspired by Randy Moss's performance against the Packers in a 2005 playoff game. Turn your back to the opposing team's fans. Bend over and simultaneously mime the pulling down of your pants. But keep your legs straight. This is how strippers remove pants, and it's a great ass accentuator. Squat down. Mime reading a newspaper. Strain. After five minutes, stand up. Find a cheerleader. Mime wiping your ass with her pom-pom. Do the classic "look back" at the pom-pom to see that you have wiped sufficiently. Wipe again. Watch with great joy as Joe Buck's head explodes.

**THE PARAMEDICS.** Done with a teammate over the body of an injured opponent. Pantomime carrying your injured opponent out on a stretcher, only to run into various things along the way: other players, watercoolers, cameramen, a churro stand, etc. Hilarity ensues.

**THE FRENCH PRISONER.** Imagine it's 1787. You have been held in solitary at the Bastille for one hundred days and nights with no light, no windows, and no outside contact, with only tepid water and gruel pushed through a slot for you once a day. At last, a window is opened. A brilliant shaft of light hits your eyes. You cover your eyes at first. You're so happy to see the light, yet now it burns your eyes! Oh, the irony! Soon, you adjust your eyes. Your face lights up! You mime crawling out the window to a gorgeous, sunny day and total freedom! The light! The air! Oh, the feeling that comes with being free at last! Now is the time to jump and dance and mime singing your heart out! And then, do a crotch chop.

These routines are merely a guideline. All great mimes are improv artists at heart. You must find inspiration in what surrounds you. You could mock the child with Kawasaki disease in the handicapped section by pantomiming riding in his wheelchair. Or you could unsheathe an imaginary samurai sword and wave it all around like you're in *House of Flying Daggers,* or one of those other movies that ruins fight scenes by turning them into ballet. Or you could do a live simulation of *Donkey Kong,* especially the part where Mario grabs the hammer and starts fucking shit up. It's all good.

But do take care. Someone will be judging you during your routine, and they aren't the forgiving sort.

## Integrity, my ass. Your guide to the average official.

The job of a game official is to maintain the integrity of play by enforcing all rules of the game consistently and correctly. It sounds so simple, yet you'd be amazed at how often they manage to fuck it up. Officials, after all, are human (with exception of NFL referee Mike Carey, who is 80 percent replicant). They're prone to developing the same biases as you or I, perhaps even more so, given the thankless nature of their occupation. So why not turn that to your advantage? With just a little effort, you can be a longtime beneficiary of their numerous, horrible gaffes. But to curry their favor, you must first get to know them. Here are some characteristics of the average official.

**Height:** 5'9", or one inch too short to lead a happy life

**Weight:** 185 pounds. Officials are surprisingly spry little creatures. Except in baseball. Most Major League umpires need to exit the ballpark through a specially designed gate, the one normally used for bull pen carts, professional rodeo bulls, monster trucks, and/or Joe Satriani's amplifiers.

**Salary:** Six figures. Officials are well compensated. But, given that the job entails trying to enforce rules among a group of immature men who make ten to one hundred times what they earn, officials are in essence the paralegals of the sporting world.

**Favorite Food:** Boneless, skinless chicken breast, the least confrontational of all meats

**Preferred Stance:** Slightly crouching, with his hands resting on his knees. This is known in refereeing circles as the Regulator stance.

# It's Not Just a Sport; It's Now a Soul-Crushing Job

**Turn-ons:** Silence, a flawlessly organized sock drawer, people who can whistle just by putting their fingers in their mouth, Serbian mob funds (NBA officials only), expense account reimbursements, Latin, Sam Waterston

**Turnoffs:** Happiness, jewelry, professional wrestling, chewing gum, that fucking *Forget Paris* movie, shoes that are any color besides black, trying to argue in Spanish

**Marital Status:** Married

**Children:** Two, one of whom usually has a drug habit. An official takes solace in knowing that the outcome of games is perhaps the only thing in life that he can exert some control over.

**How to Get Him to Like You:** Talking to him prior to game time or just generally acknowledging his existence, ridiculing Rasheed Wallace's bizarre gray spot, asking him about his dreams outside of refereeing (usually it's to write a best-selling legal thriller), and telling him when he's done a good job. Remember: refereeing is just like French kissing. You can get it right 99 out of 100 times, but mess up just once and everyone calls you a face-licker. Such bullshit.

**What Will Make Him Turn on You:** Looking at him wrong on a bad day, pouting (see next page), appearing to enjoy yourself, ganging up with teammates to argue a call, giggling, condescendingly patting him on the head, causing a delay of game (officials fucking hate this), doing that thing after a three-point shot where you keep your arm in the air until after the shot falls (officials *really* fucking hate this)

# HEAR IT FROM AN UMP!

## Yes, that was a strike.
## Now shut the fuck up.
by Joe Cargill, Major League umpire

STRIKE!

What? You thought that was a ball? Wow, what a shock. Yeah, I see the look on your face. You're clearly stunned by my ruling. Well, you know what? That was, indeed, a strike. Now shut the fuck up.

Aw, you're still mad. Oh, you poor thing! Perhaps you don't agree with the way I enthusiastically called that strike. My heart goes out to you. You get to make millions of dollars and give curtain calls to thousands of fans who love you more than their immediate families. Whereas I get to walk into the ballpark and have everyone throw Choco Taco wrappers at me. Boy, do I have it great! Pardon the shit outta me for actually showing some enthusiasm while performing my duty. Excuse me for taking just the slightest modicum of joy here. Did I bruise your pride? Are you hurt? Did you get a little boo-boo on your vajayjay? Let me give it a kiss to make it better.

Asshole.

We don't get to choose our passions, you know. Do you think I *like* the fact that I love umpiring so much? God, no. I wish my lifelong passion had been for bra engineering, or luxury catamaran bartending. Instead, I realized at a very early age that my one true love was to be a professional Major League whipping boy and to deal with whiny assholes like you. Every. Single. Plate. Appearance. Hooray! Lucky me! What fun it is to love something that makes me want to curl up into a very tight ball and cry my eyes out!

So guess what? I wouldn't change that call even if you gave me a life-time supply of Big League Chew. Dick.

Still annoyed? Oh, I see. You still think it was a ball, eh? Still hanging on to that idea for dear life, are you? Good thing the league gives all of us umpires a pocket-sized rule book to carry around with us! Let me just con-sult it to make sure I didn't forget rules that I've had memorized for *thirty goddamn years*. Or that the league didn't change the strike zone right be-fore your at bat!

Here it is. Rule 2.00: "The Strike Zone is defined as that area over home plate the upper limit of which is a horizontal line at the midpoint between the top of the shoulders and the top of the uniform pants, and the lower level is a line at the hollow beneath the kneecap. The Strike Zone shall be determined from the batter's stance as the batter is prepared to swing at a pitched ball."

Well, what do you know? The rule on strikes is still the same, which means that pitch that grazed the inside corner of the plate while remaining below the numbers on your uniform was a strike. And there's no replay. And my visual acuity is 20/10. Suck it.

Perhaps next time, you might actually want to swing at the ball instead of standing there like a fucking golem. Perhaps you're taking your anger out on me because you refuse to confront your own glaring pussyness. That's too bad. Let me get a string quartet to provide a soundtrack to your gripping inner struggle.

You remind me of Paul O'Neill.

Fucking loser.

# You're the best of the best, and yet you are awful: coping with losing.

Entering professional sports, you probably don't have a great deal of experience with losing. After all, you have professional athlete–level talent. That's enough to raise any middle school or high school team to championship caliber. You probably spent your entire high school career running up a 30-2 record against various tiny Quaker academies and poorly funded teams from Indian reservations. And I'm sure your college's athletic department went to great lengths to make sure that your team had a "great season": scheduling any number of lower division opponents, playing 80 percent of your games at home, playing in some bowl game that was the football equivalent of the participant ribbon they hand out at a swim meet, etc.

As a matter of fact, the entire idea of losing is slowly being phased out of amateur sports altogether. That's why the Olympics includes fencing, a sport that consists of nothing *but* losers (Fact: Eighty percent of all fencers are former Dungeons & Dragons players who took up the sport specifically to imagine themselves as dragon slayers). The idea is that sports should be a place where kids revel in the joy of participation and learn to appreciate the bonds created through shared team goals. This is a lame, stupid idea. When mankind is eventually destroyed by Google's mechanical spiders in late 2039, this will be one of the reasons why we submitted so quickly.

The result of turning youth sports into a suffocatingly nurturing environment is that professional sports have become the last bastion of pure losing in America. It's a delicious irony, especially if you're some asshole who listens to NPR. You're a world-class athlete who has reached the very upper echelon of your chosen field. Yet, now that you have arrived there, you find yourself playing for the Orioles. God can be so cruel sometimes.

## It's Not Just a Sport; It's Now a Soul-Crushing Job

It is often said that losing begets losing. Once you lose multiple games, the dreaded "losing mentality" can seep in, marked by varying symptoms such as indifference, lethargy, testiness, and, of course, impotence. Breaking out of this cycle won't be easy, but I'm going to show you how. After all, I was a loser for thirty years. I've never won a fistfight. I didn't kiss a girl until I was nineteen. And I was caught masturbating while watching *The Price Is Right* by my roommate's girlfriend freshman year. But look at me now! I'm a published author! Just like Hitler!

**1. KNOW THAT IT'S NOT YOUR FAULT.** Remember: you win as a team, you lose as a team. Which means that *all* of your teammates are at fault. This isn't finger-pointing, so much as finger-sweeping. There's plenty of blame to go around, so why not blame everyone else equally? Whatever you do, don't blame yourself. That can lead to introspection, and introspection is the sworn enemy of the professional athlete. Sure, you could have done better. But what about Tommy? And Ricky? They're the ones who *really* fucked up.

**2. SWITCH THINGS UP.** Pro athletes are notoriously ~~obsessive compulsive~~ superstitious folk. If you find yourself mired in a five-game losing streak, it should be clear to you by now that the soul patch has to go. You must do something else that will act as an effective placebo to distract your overly delicate psyche. Here are some notable historic slump busters that famous athletes adopted to help their teams get back on track.

- 1936: Joe Louis begins each fight by kissing a small marmoset, wins heavyweight title
- 1951: Ben Hogan switches to masturbating with overhand "claw" grip, wins two majors

- 1956: Mickey Mantle changes pregame shooters from single malt to blend, wins Triple Crown
- 1975: Pittsburgh Steelers hire new "team pharmacist" Jorge Tarasco
- 1986: Keith Hernandez puts away "No Fat Chicks" T-shirt, wears "Yes, Fat Chicks" T-shirt for a week
- 1988: Pedro Cerrano tells Jobu to go fuck himself, Cleveland wins pennant
- 1990: All NHL teams decide to begin growing playoff beards every year. Every Stanley Cup playoff game since has resulted in a tie.
- 1999: After being swept by the Spurs, Shaquille O'Neal decides to try caring. Three Laker titles follow shortly thereafter.
- 2008: Eli Manning moves from diapers to training pants, Giants win Super Bowl XLII.

**3. FIND A RALLYING POINT.** You need something that will bring your team closer together, usually through some sort of media-generated controversy. For instance, you could murder a longshoreman. Nothing creates an "us against the world" mentality quite like that.

**4. WAIT.** Don't worry. You'll play some other team that's having an off night eventually. And when that happens, you'll end up winning by de-

## Deeply Penetrating the Numbers

**1 in 2**

You have a 1 in 2 chance of losing any given game. And you know what? There ain't SHIT you can do about it.

fault. And nothing increases a team's confidence quite like that. Who knows, you may win enough games this way to make the playoffs.

## Everything you wanted to know about the playoffs but were too much of a pussy to ask.

While losing is more common in professional athletics, most leagues make up for it by allowing a grotesquely unnecessary number of teams to qualify for playoff participation. Consider it your reward for having to endure all that losing during the course of the regular season. Once your team has ensured a final win-loss percentage of .461 or higher, you can safely break out the Riunite on ice and celebrate! You're in, man! Congratulations!

If this is your initial playoff run, you're bound to have some questions. Perhaps these are questions of a frequent and asked nature. Fear not. The following FAQ will divulge all.

Q: **What's a "magic number"?**

A: That's the number of games you needed to win (or have the team below you lose) during the last week or so of the season to make the playoffs. This was a bigger deal thirty years ago, when making the playoffs actually meant something.

Q: **Hey, why does everything seem so much more intense in the playoffs?**

A: Because everyone is now trying.

Q: **Why is my game check so low?**

A: Because now that the regular season is over, your entire salary has been covered. All leagues offer bonus playoff pay, but it's a mere pittance compared to your regular season game check. Imagine working overtime at Wal-Mart and having your overtime pay be half your regular pay, instead of double it. And you're forced to work even *harder.* It's like that. (Note: This is Wal-Mart's *actual* overtime policy.)

**Q:** **It's 12:31 a.m. eastern standard time on a Tuesday and we're playing in New York. Why is it only the third inning?**

**A:** Ah, yes. You'll notice in the playoffs that your games start at a much later hour. Leagues do this to maximize prime-time advertising revenue. Never mind that, by around 1:00 a.m. or so, fans stop giving a shit about who wins and would just like the game to be over so they can go to bed. Playing games into the wee hours is what's in the best interest of sponsors like Lextro Body Spray. There's no better way to grow your game than that.

**Q:** **Why is my coach sucking on his Primatene Mist inhaler so often?**

**A:** Because if he loses, he'll be fired. Or he'll be kept on as a lame duck the following season and *wish* he had been fired, or at least run over by a mail truck.

**Q:** **Are those Japanese broadcasters?**

**A:** Indeed. Many international networks cover American sports during the playoffs. Play well enough here and you could become a mythical demigod in Japan, where they will then produce a twisted anime flick that depicts you as a seven-penised demon intent on destroying the world. Trust me: you're the good guy. I don't know why.

**Q:** **We won our first game, but we have to play six more. Why?**

**A:** Two of the major sports leagues, along with the NHL, have a "best of seven" series format. You must win four games against a single opponent in order to advance to the next round, and then the round after that, and then the round after that.

**Q:** **How long does this take?**

A: Fucking forever. But there is good reason for this. A five-game series, according to most league officials, is too short. There's far too much of a chance that a lesser team will win a "fluky" series and advance. Playing best of seven makes the outcome far more predictable. Which is fun!

Q: **Why is playing the Atlanta Braves so much easier now than it was in the regular season?**

A: No one knows.

Q: **What kind of champagne do they serve if we win it all?**

A: Cook's. Or Andre. Plus, there will be Appletiser for the dipshits who don't drink. Either way, that champagne is strictly for spraying and *not* drinking.

Q: **Can I dump Gatorade on my coach if we're about to win? I can't stand that asshole.**

A: Absolutely. Make sure the cooler you use has real Gatorade in it, not water. Gatorade is sticky and needs at least two cycles in the wash to clean. And make sure the cooler has lots of ice in it. Ice hurts. You may even be able to brain your coach with the edge of the cooler and pass it off as an accident. Remember: you've earned the right to torture that dick. Don't half-ass it.

Q: **What happens if we win the championship?**

A: When you win a championship, a meticulously planned sequence of events is set into motion. First, you are given a hat. And a T-shirt. You must put both on right away. I suggest putting the T-shirt on first. Trying to put on a shirt with a hat on is complicated and unnecessary. You may not break in the hat in any way, shape, or form. It must have a straight, idiotic brim, the kind a sixty-year-old Mites coach would maintain.

After you receive your new clothing, a teammate will immediately ruin it with champagne. After that, the league will roll out a dais for you to stand on. It may be tiered, with the highest tier reserved for super-

stars, and the lowest tier reserved for people like the equipment manager, the team exorcist, and Darko Milicic. Multicolored confetti will
drop.

At this point, you'll probably want to go hug your teammates, friends,
and family. You cannot do this for another three hours. First, you must
do 346 interviews for various national broadcast networks and local
affiliates. Be sure to tell them you shocked the world, even if the world
really wasn't paying much attention. After that, the commissioner will
give a three-minute speech no one listens to. Then, he will hand the
league's championship trophy to the trophy's sponsor, usually a VP at
Lextro Body Spray, who will then hand the trophy to your team's owner,
whom you will probably be laying eyes on for the first time. The owner
will then hand the trophy to the coach, who then hands it to the MVP,
who then hands it to his chauffeur, who then hands it to his friend, who
then hands it to a tiny Guatemalan woman named Inez. After about
157 minutes, the trophy will eventually be handed to you. It will be
very shiny. Savor the moment, my friend. There's nothing in the world
like it.

**Q:** **What if we lose?**

**A:** Shut up. Don't say a fucking word. Don't even look at anyone
when the game is finished. Keep your goddamn head down and walk
straight to the locker room. There, your coach will tell you he loves you
(a lie) and is proud of you (also a lie), and that you're a great group of
guys (a lie if Terrell Owens is on your team). He'll also swear you will
all be back to avenge this loss next year (he'll have a five-year deal with
Seattle by the next week). Then, he will exit the locker room for a sol-
emn, three-minute interview with Jim Gray. Then, you pack your shit
and leave. Don't shower. Don't change clothes. Just get the hell out of
there. You've already been relegated to history's discount rack. Find a
drink as fast as you can. And learn how to perform under pressure.

## That Billy Joel song was so prescient: pressure.

Superstar athletes are widely admired for their ability to thrive under intense circumstances. And make no mistake, the pressure at this level is *high*. Many people may scoff at that notion and say, "*Pfft*. It's just a game. Try paying the mortgage! That's pressure!" These people are morons. No one *watches* you try to pay the mortgage. If you default on that shit, you get to keep that shame all to yourself. No, athletes must perform at their peak with millions of people watching and judging. You think Mr. Barely Supporting His Family could handle *that* without reaching for the Paxil?

In fact, I'd argue that athletes face more pressurized situations than any other group of people on the planet. Even more than soldiers fighting a war? Oh, yeah. If you get killed during a war, you're a hero. If you survive, you're a hero. Where, I ask you, is the pressure in that? Sounds like a win-win to me. Throw in the standard U.S. military pension of $500 a year (with vision coverage!) and that's a pretty sweet deal, my friend.

Try having to make the winning putt at Royal Troon. Now *that's* a real bitch. You got everyone staring at you — fans, family, friends, TV viewers, reporters, sponsors, wildlife, ghosts, indifferent cameramen — and just waiting for you to shit the bed. Make it, and you'll be bathing in White Grenache for the next week. Miss it, and you'll find yourself teetering on the precipice of a deep psychological black hole, one very few athletes manage to climb back out of. It's the same as getting your first DUI. You're never the same. Ask David Duval, or Bill Buckner, or Scott Norwood, or Nick Anderson, or Ray Finkle: failing under pressure can destroy a man, or even turn him into a woman. You need to be able to calm yourself and phase out all distractions, both physical and mental. Visualize with me . . .

It's the bottom of the ninth inning in Game 7 of the World Series. You're down one with the bases loaded and a 3-2 count. This is it: the defining moment of your existence. You need to focus here. Stay in the present. Remember, you get paid either way, so don't freak. There's no need to think about what will happen if you fail. You don't need to visualize the *New York Post* Photoshopping a donkey's head onto your body for their late edition. That's unnecessary. There's also absolutely no reason you should be thinking about your wife leaving you. She's always been your rock. Hasn't she? There was that one "incident." But that was years ago. Let it be. You also shouldn't be visualizing having to face your father after all those years of never being good enough to win his approval. The cold-hearted bastard. What the fuck more could he possibly want? You shouldn't be thinking about that at all. It's not healthy. Stop.

Nor should you be thinking about that one chick in the third row along the first base line with the tight V-neck sweater. God, she's got a luscious rack. No! Focus! Stop looking! Man, they're big. Like two well-formed ski moguls. Oh, how you'd just like to bury your nose in those yabahoes for just a second. Take in their scent. I bet they smell like cucumbers. I wonder if she's local. If you blew the game, maybe she'd still offer you pity sex. After all, you do have an apartment with a killer view. That alone impresses most ladies. Or, if you hit a home run, you could give her a quick, playful glance as you start your trot. Oh my God, that would totally make her cream her panties. The sex could be mind-blowing.

Stop! You must again focus. This is everything you've ever wanted. C'mon, man! You're an athlete! Emptying out that melon of yours shouldn't be so hard! You know what it is? When your mind is normally empty, it's not because you tried to do it. It was just naturally vacant. But now that you have to consciously bear down and concentrate, it completely refuses. Stupid brain. If only it functioned involuntarily, like the heart or lungs.

What you should do is just start thinking about completely random shit. Like, for instance, Little Debbie Swiss Cake Rolls. They're just like Ho Hos, only they're ninety-nine cents a box! Seriously, you can't beat that. Oooh, Star Crunches! Remember those? God, they were fucking good. They were made of Rice Krispies, chocolate, and, like, crack. See, this is better. You've completely distracted your distractions. Now all you have to do is hit a 90-mile-per-hour fastball somewhere within a confined area where nine other people can't get to it.

Okay, the pitcher's winding up . . .

And here comes the pitch . . .

Curveball . . .

Oh, God . . .

Divorce, Mom, pain, Dad, tits, money, God, death, Dolly Madison Zingers . . .

*CRACK!*

FOUL BALL!

Phew! You're not out.

But now the whole mental process starts anew.

Shit.

---

### Clippable Motivational Slogan!

*In clutch situations, it's important to just relax and play your game. What's "your game" mean? Fuck if I know. Leave me alone, you little rapscallion!*

— CASEY STENGEL

## Stats are for losers. Unless your stats are awesome.

Statistics are the lifeblood of sports. They provide everyone—fans, columnists, opponents, management—with a continuous way of determining your viability as a professional athlete. It's like walking around with a performance evaluation stapled to your forehead. Isn't that fun? Statistics can even become part of your identity. For example, former Bears running back Curtis Enis is known to many around the Chicago area as Curtis Enis, the Fat Fuck Who Averaged 0.8 Yards per Carry.

General managers and owners are relying ever more on statistics to evaluate player performance. In fact, some rely on them *exclusively*. They don't even bother to watch the games, because games lie. Billy Beane once signed a catcher to a $1 million guaranteed contract because that catcher had a PARP rating of 1.786, even though Beane did not know what a PARP rating was, or that the catcher in question was a female softball player.

Stats like PARP (Performance After Resting Placidly) are part of a new generation of statistical study known as Sabermetrics. With a name like that, you might think some sort of tiger is involved, but it's not. Sabermetrics were devised by a baseball fan named Bill James. James, in a frantic effort to remain a virgin, pored over historical records from Major League Baseball and devised an entirely new means of measuring athletic performance. For his efforts, James was bumped up from fan to the level of scholar, then finally to the level of historian. Many teams even asked him for his input on personnel matters. As a result, fans across other sports have rushed to devise new statistics of their own, which is why we now have stats like VORP (Value Over Replacement Player), DVOA ratings (Defense-adjusted Value Over Average), and VO3RPLGSALHFSG (Value Over 3rd Replacement Player in Late-Game Situations Against Left-Handers Factoring in Scrotal Girth).

But there are some old-timers who do not believe statistics are at all indicative of player performance. TV analyst Joe Morgan once cast an all-star vote for Cristian Guzman because "he looked like a ballplayer," even though Guzman was batting .001 (rounded up from .0006). People like Morgan believe that athletes have certain "intangibles" that cannot be measured by statistics. It's only after you see the player play three times, Morgan argues, that you can then accurately measure his intangibles, even though intangibles by definition cannot be measured. Morgan has also gotten into many heated arguments regarding the legitimacy of the periodic table of elements. Not so clever, that Mr. Morgan.

So where does that leave you? What stats should you care about? And do they hopefully coincide with the success of my fantasy team (Britney's Rehab Sponsors) next year? Fear not. I have sorted out the critical stats you need for your respective sport. Turn the page for a detailed chart.

This chart is strictly a guideline. Chances are, you will have incentive clauses in your contract that stipulate which statistical milestones will trigger a salary bonus. Keep note of them. After all, if management wants to give you an extra $500,000 for averaging twenty points a game, then it's clear they don't *want* you to pass the ball. Right?

## Compound fractures aren't as cool when they happen to you: injuries and a guide to your body.

Injuries are any athlete's worst nightmare (a curved dagger to the rectum excepted). And it's not the physical pain that's the hard part. It's the mental aspect of it. Once you get injured, your cocksure strut and bulletproof demeanor are temporarily, if not sometimes permanently, destroyed. Getting injured means facing the mortality of your career. But, more than that, an injury is a landmark event in life that signals the end of youth. You start out this life with a perfectly functioning body. As time

## BASEBALL STATS

| IMPORTANT | KIND OF IMPORTANT | WORTHLESS |
|---|---|---|
| **Home Runs** | **RBIs** | **At Bats** (stupid) |
| | **Batting Average** | **Runs** (lame) |
| | **Stolen Bases** | **Hits** (borrrrrring) |
| | **Slugging Percentage** (if only because having a high one makes you appear to be very strong and/or sluggy) | **Errors** (forgotten a game later!) |
| | | **Doubles** |
| | **Strikeouts** (only if you're a pitcher. If you're a batter, by all means swing freely) | **Triples** (little-known fact: no one over 5'7" has hit a triple since 1937) |
| | **ERA** (this is the average amount of runs every 9 innings that are totally your fault) | **VORP** (they don't even tell you how they calculate this. What are you hiding, *Baseball Prospectus*?) |
| | **Wins** (you don't even have to pitch well to accumulate these!) | **ELO Adjusted** (no clue) |
| | **Saves** (or these!) | **PECOTA Rating** (no idea. Ask the 47-year-old dipshit keeping score in the loge-level deck.) |
| | **Innings Pitched** (or these! In fact, Innings Pitched is a shockingly important statistic. If you can pitch a large number of innings, regardless of quality, you'll be saving the ball club from having to use all the *good* pitchers, which would wear them out. Good pitchers are not meant to be enjoyed. They must be preserved, like a wheel of exceptional Gouda.) | |

## FOOTBALL STATS

| IMPORTANT | WORTHLESS |
| --- | --- |
| **TDs** (yeah, bitch!) | **Yards Per Attempt** |
| **Yards** (especially in yardage-heavy fantasy leagues … like mine!) | **Yards Per Rush** |
| **Sacks** | **Yards Per Anything, Really** |
| **Interceptions** | **Receptions** |
| **40 Time** | |
| **Vertical Leap** | **Tackles** |
| **Number Of Times You Can Bench 225 Lbs. In One Minute** | **Game Time Blood-Alcohol Level** |
| **Number Of Pints Of Fresh Orange Juice You Can Squeeze By Hand** | |

## BASKETBALL STATS

| IMPORTANT | WORTHLESS |
| --- | --- |
| **Points** | **Everything Else** |

## SOCCER STATS

| IMPORTANT |
| --- |
| **Goals** (likely zero) |
| **Assists** (likely zero) |
| **Saves** (likely zero) |
| **Yellow And/Or Red Cards** (this is the one soccer stat in which you can make some headway. Players who get carded frequently, like Wayne Rooney, often become national heroes for helping to make soccer games more eventful.) |

goes on, injuries chip away at your bones, your ligaments, your muscles, and the rest. Once that happens, you can't ever go back to the flawless, pristine body you once had, no matter how hard you rehab, no matter how well the surgery went. You may fully recover. But you get scars. You build up scar tissue inside. You lose cartilage. You change. Irrevocably. There's a finality to getting injured. It means your body has begun a slow decaying process that cannot be undone. Ever.

Jesus, that was depressing. I need to go lie down.

When you go down with an injury, lots of questions will run through your mind. *What just happened? How bad is it? Am I dead? I am not dead. Did I hear a snap? I definitely heard something snap. How long will I be out? Will I need surgery? Is morphine as awesome as I've been told? Does this mean my career is over? Will the team cut me? How long will rehab take? Will I ever get my initial burst back? Can we still afford the grand piano in the foyer? Can I still fuck? Am I a pussy if I stay on the ground much longer?*

Relax. These questions are all perfectly normal. The important thing is to *not panic*. There's a system in place when something like this happens. First off, the entire crowd will fall silent to watch you writhe in agony. Then, a team of doctors and trainers will come to your aid and ask you what hurts, and if it hurts when they give you an Indian burn in the affected area. Your head coach will come out, look at you, ask the doctor, "How's he doin'?," pat you on the shoulder, and then leave. Some of your teammates will form a small prayer circle. Then, you'll be helped off the field, everyone will clap, and you'll be forgotten for about a year or so.

See? No big deal.

A severe injury will likely require diagnostic testing, surgery, and multiple doctor visits. The good news: as a pro athlete, you get preferential treatment from the health care system. Your co-pay is only $10 ($50 if you play for the Arizona Cardinals). *And* you don't have to wait to see the doctor. Know how, when you go to a doctor's office, they make you wait for half an hour, then bring you into an exam room to talk to some assistant who you think is the doctor at first but isn't, and then they make you wait another fucking half an hour after that? Then you gotta go all the way across town just to get a goddamn X-ray? Doesn't happen when you're an athlete. You get treated like an actual human being by doctors, and that's quite refreshing.

After surgery, you'll have to endure months and months of painful rehab, which usually involves you doing a complex series of stretches and exercises using either a big red latex band or a giant rubber ball. Either way, your hands will smell like tires for hours and hours afterward. Rehab will be presided over by a perky young female assistant trainer who looks fucking tremendous in a pair of Sevens. At first, you will find her insanely cute. But, as the weeks go on, you will begin to loathe her sunny merci-lessness. You'll also resent having to spend countless hours in the training room hooked up to heat pads and stim machines. Ever read the same issue of *Outdoor* magazine seventeen times over? You'll learn.

Here are some common sports injuries you should be aware of.

**TORN ANTERIOR CRUCIATE LIGAMENT (ACL).** The torn ACL is the granddaddy of all knee injuries. It signals an immediate end to your season. The good news is that advances in modern medicine have made ACL reconstruction a relative snap. You'll almost certainly be ready to go for the beginning of the following season. After that, everyone will assume you're exactly the same player you once were. Of course, you won't be that player for another *two* years, if ever. But people will keep believing that a return to full speed is right around the corner, and teams will pay you as such. It's kind of reassuring to know everyone is so dumb.

**PULLED HAMSTRING.** Preferred injury of pussies, the pulled hamstring is perhaps the most useful injury in all of sports. A simple "tweaking" is enough to get out of practice and head straight for the whirlpool. Be sure to pull up during wind sprints and clutch it in dramatic fashion! But beware. Come back from a pulled hamstring too early, and you may reinjure it for the rest of the year. Come back too late, and everyone will *know* you're nursing it like a little bitch. A good guideline is two to three weeks. That gives you enough time to heal both your leg and your vagina.

**SPRAINED ANKLE.** A sprained ankle isn't a very serious injury. But my God, have you ever rolled an ankle? Holy fuck, it hurts. Like someone sawed off your foot and then put an acetylene torch to it. Brutal.

**TURF TOE.** Turf toe occurs when the connective tissue between your foot and toe is severely hyperextended and/or torn. It can be a very serious injury. Unfortunately, because it goes by the name "turf toe," people will think you're a real Nancy for missing any time, because they assume all you did was stub the goddamn thing. Annoying.

**GROIN PULL.** Ever been the subject of a hackneyed joke and/or lame pun? Get ready. Apparently, injuring your inner thigh is exactly the same as having something bad happen to your cock and/or balls.

**SEPARATED/DISLOCATED SHOULDER.** This is when your arm pops out of the ball-and-socket joint that keeps the arm attached to the body. Now, this may sound excruciating, and it is. But if you get the hang of it, you'll be able to wriggle out of straitjackets for money just like Riggs did in *Lethal Weapon 2*. So badass.

**HERNIA.** A hernia occurs when the lining that holds in your internal organs tears, causing your intestines to droop down into your scrotum. This can happen while lifting weights, straining while out of position, or listening to Tyra Banks speak.

**CONCUSSION.** A concussion is a bruising of the brain, often from taking a vicious hit. Bruising can vary, and diagnosing the degree of a concussion is very difficult. But the good thing is, you won't remember any of that. In fact, you'll probably be able to play the next week. Sure, ten years from now, the merest trace of sunlight will feel like a sharp knife to the temple, and you'll have mood swings that rival those of a pregnant woman during labor. But it's totally worth it to play in a handful of games you'll have no future recollection of.

**BROKEN NECK.** You're fucked. Hope you own a DVD of *Murderball* to cheer yourself up.

**SHIN SPLINTS.** What are you, a girl? Walk it off. Pussy.

# Chapter 3

# Hot Naked Men

## Teammates/The Locker Room

### "You're putting that where?" Rookie hazing rituals.

If it's your first year in the league, your fellow pros are going to want to indoctrinate you. No doubt attending college has given you a taste for massive group hazing. Now, being brutally sodomized with an unvarnished broomstick while rushing your frat probably wasn't fun. But it was a small price to pay for the handsome reward of fitting in (in this case, literally) with the other guys in your house. Besides, at least the broomstick was cylindrical! Imagine if it had been a hockey stick! Talk about a square peg in a round hole!

Hazing is a test. Sure, it's also a cruel and needless display of power born of the massive insecurities and unresolved inner anger of your new "brothers." But it is also a test. If you accept your hazing with a minimum of fuss, your teammates will see you as a reliable colleague, one who won't fold in the face of adversity. And that's a valuable bond to establish, until half your teammates depart via trades or free agency the following year. Conversely, if you resist hazing, or act like a whiny baby about having all your clothes (wallet included) doused in lighter fluid and burned to a very fine ash, then you will be seen by everyone as a big pussy. Hope you enjoy eating lunch by yourself.

So get ready for a hazing redux your first year in the pros. The first one you need to know about is **Bitch Duty**. Bitch Duty means that you are the designated gofer to all of the veterans in the clubhouse. You must carry their luggage. You must handle their deliveries. You must carry their hashish through airport security. While annoying, this is all fairly benign stuff. If Bitch Duty is the only hazing you experience your first year, consider yourself lucky. And on a losing team.

The other classic rookie hazing ritual is the **Rookie Dinner**. This is when your veteran teammates "take you out" to dinner, only to order the most expensive food and wine on the menu and then stick you with the tab. This is especially fun to do with a seventh-round draft pick, who only gets a meager signing bonus and then must fight tooth and nail just to cling to your team's final roster spot. You should see him start to freak out when he considers the possibility of having to split the tab equally, even though all he had was a panini and a mineral water, while everyone else at the table ordered five-pound lobsters and solid bricks of foie gras. Then, when he finds out he has to pay for the whole thing, he *completely* loses his shit. Man, does he get pissed! It's priceless stuff.

Lugging bags and paying for dinners are not exactly extreme forms of hazing. There are, as you might suspect, more severe initiation rituals. The first of which is the **Jump-In**. This is when you stand in the middle of a circle of teammates and then each one "jumps in" to the circle to beat you senseless, often with some sort of foreign object. This mimics the hazing techniques of many inner-city street gangs, those great trailblazers of modern American fashion and social trends. Tight end Cam Cleeland was beaten with a sack full of coins by his fellow Saints in 1998.

But instead of taking his subdural hematoma like a man, he went screaming to the media about it. What a little snitch.

The Jump-In is usually followed by the group **Insertion**. The number of times you will be penetrated and the objects that will penetrate
you are strictly TBD. I suggest you close your eyes really hard and sing
nursery rhymes to yourself. Everything usually turns out all right after
that.

You also may be called on to do the obligatory **Rookie Cross-
dressing**. Being forced to dress like a woman totally makes you gay, and
your teammates will be more than happy to point that out to you. You
may briefly become confused about your own sexual identity as a result
of this, but I assure you this is a common occurrence, and nothing to
worry about. Unless you're gay. (See the end of this chapter.)

Other types of hazing exist and will vary by both team and region.
You may have your hotel room bed short-sheeted. You may have lye
poured down your throat. Some light bukkake may take place. It really
depends on where you are, and just how bad your karma is. If you already have a wife and/or children,
I suggest sequestering them until
your rookie year is over.

Once that rookie year is finished, you will have the chance
to become the hazer, rather than
the hazee. It's your opportunity
to continue the horrendous cycle
of peer-to-peer abuse, and it's a
great feeling to scar someone else's
psyche for a change.

# DID YOU KNOW?

The most accomplished
hazer in pro sports history was
Hall of Famer Ty Cobb, who
plugged an astounding 132
assholes as both a player and
a manager.

## Unwritten rules of the locker room. Now in written form!

In all sports, there is a code of conduct among denizens of the locker room. This code needn't be written down. Everyone on the team instinctively understands it. But, in case you went to Florida State, and drawing logical conclusions is something that often proves troublesome for you, let's not take any chances.

**WHAT HAPPENS IN THE LOCKER ROOM STAYS IN THE LOCKER ROOM.** You will likely forget most of these rules, and indeed the majority of this book. But do *not* forget this rule. All jokes, confessions, fights, and torrid love affairs that occur between teammates are not to be spoken of outside the confines of the locker room. Ever. You don't go talking to the media about it. Or your wife. Or your pastor. Or Larry King. You deal with that shit *internally*. Do not involve outsiders. The whole point of playing on a sports team is to experience all the thrills of being in the Mafia without having to commit any actual crimes. Even though you may indulge in that anyway. So don't go fucking up the fun for everyone else.

**ONLY STEAL TOILETRIES.** Stealing from teammates is wrong. Former Yankee Ruben Rivera once stole Derek Jeter's glove, no doubt to take in its fresh, cedarlike scent. He was immediately cut by the Yankees and stoned to death by crazed Bronx-dwellers as a result. So don't do it. The lone exception? Toiletries. Help yourself to all the Pantene you like.

**NEVER DISCUSS CONTRACTS OR MONEY.** Did the guy next to you just get a $50 million extension? It never happened. Don't even joke about it. Even when you're joking about money, you're not really joking about it. You're just expressing your extreme jealousy in a more palatable fashion. Your teammate can read between the lines. He knows you're really saying, "You dick. You don't deserve that kind of cash. WHEN THE FUCK IS MY MOTHERFUCKING PAYDAY COMING?" Just let that elephant in the room keep stomping around and shitting all over the place.

**ONLY THE TEAM CAPTAIN MAY TOUCH THE STEREO.** At the beginning of the season, each team designates a team captain. The team captain gets a *C* on his jersey, plus a fancy hat with an anchor on the front. Team captain responsibilities include leading the team out onto the field, presiding over team stretches while counting in a very loud and husky voice, applying eye black to everyone's face, and organizing involuntary voluntary off-season hill-running sessions. But the real prize of captaincy, the real reason your captain kissed all of that coach ass, is control of the locker room stereo. Only the team captain may touch the stereo. If your captain is black, you should expect lots of hip-hop. If he's white, you should expect lots of heavy metal. Or country music. Or, if you have the misfortune of having a captain who likes Kid Rock, all three.

**NO WIFE-SWAPPING UNTIL AFTER MIDSEASON.** If you and a teammate have decided the grass is better shaved on the other side of the fence, you are not allowed to officially switch families until after the all-star break. You need that full half-season to make sure that you're doing the right thing. Trading wives as if they were chattel is not something one does lightly. Oh, sure, it's a fun idea as a lark. But you're gonna want additional time for that frivolous idea to take an unexpectedly dark and serious turn. Those extra couple months will also give you time to ensure that you're trading for the *right* wife, and not some cold fish.

Also, if you trade wives, you must also trade children. No exceptions there. Don't worry. Your new "daughter" will soon learn to grudgingly accept your twisted little experiment-gone-horribly-awry.

**DO NOT MENTION YOUR TEAMMATE'S SUBPAR PLAY UNLESS HE BRINGS IT UP.** If he wants advice on how to break out of his slump, rest assured he will come to you. Unless you happen to be Joey Harrington. No one goes to Joey Harrington if they want to improve. He blows.

**DO NOT MENTION STREAKS.** If you mention a streak to your teammate, you'll cause him to *think* about his streak, knocking him out of his groove. Many people know that Joe DiMaggio hit safely in fifty-six consecutive games, a hallowed record in baseball. What few people know is that the Yankee Clipper's hitting streak would have gone *seventy-eight* games had bench player Red Ruffing not sidled up to him in the clubhouse on July 16, 1941, and said, "Hey, Joey D! That's one kickass hitting streak you got there!" DiMaggio's streak ended the next game. Later on, DiMaggio took out his anger with Ruffing by occasionally beating Marilyn Monroe and never tipping a waiter again for the rest of his life.

## A time to kill: motivating your teammates.

Motivation can be difficult for the professional athlete. After all, you're at a better point in your life now. Back in your college days, you were hungry, eager to prove you had what it took to make the pros. You were desperate. Urgent. You had a dream, and a single-minded drive to see that dream through. And now, you've realized it. You made the big-time and now have an incredible salary and lifestyle to show for it. What, exactly, is there to get up for anymore? It's funny how, when your dreams come true, they stop being dreams. I'm pretty sure that last sentence was lifted from a Hilary Duff film, but I can't confirm it.

It's up to you and your teammates to motivate yourselves. This won't be easy. It's not like back in high school, when you had a veritable surplus of late-puberty testosterone coursing through your system that could spike instantly at the sight of a bare midriff. And there's no token teammate with cerebral palsy to play for. That kid wasn't good enough to make the pros.

Fortunately, I, a fully untrained life coach, am here to help. Now, I was a terrible athlete. I was third string, and even when the backup was injured, the coaches would move another player *out of position* so that I would not be able to get onto the field to fuck things up. But what I lacked in agility, and looks, and talent, and speed, and coordination, and reflexes, and general usefulness, I made up for in my astonishing ability to get fired up for games I had absolutely no chance of playing in. How? By devising a killer motivational speech. I've never shared this speech with anyone. After all, it's not exactly stirring coming from a human traffic cone. But coming from you? *Magic.*

Be sure to recite this speech while listening to Ennio Morricone's "The Ecstasy of Gold" or watching the first forty-five minutes of *Full Metal Jacket:*

Men.

*(Always start off your speech by saying, "Men." It reinforces the gender status of everyone in the room. Also, start softly. And seated. You want to build to a crescendo here.)*

Men, this is a special day today. This is the day we find out how we'll be remembered. How do you want to be remembered?

*(Leave a pause here so everyone can reflect on that point.)*

Do you want to be remembered as strong?

Do you want to be remembered as a hero?

Do you want to be remembered as someone who rose to the occasion?

How do you want to be remembered?

*(See what I did right there? I repeated the initial question over again! This is known as a "refrain." I'm totally gonna do it again. Watch.)*

How do you want to be remembered, men?

Do you want to be remembered at all?

Maybe you'd like to be forgotten.

Maybe you'd like to fade into history, to fade into the shadow of those assholes across the field.

Maybe you'd like everything we've gone through together up to this point to go to waste.

All the early morning lifting.

All the tape sessions.

All the things Coach *(your coach's last name here)* taught us.

Is that what you want?

*(Classic reverse psychology. Everyone in the locker room will get crazy pissed off. Now rise. Rise!)*

Do you want to be forgotten like that?!

To shuffle off this earth without leaving an indelible mark?!

Is that what you want?! IS THAT WHAT YOU FUCKING WANT?!

*(Start crying.)*

I FUCKING DON'T!

How do you want to be remembered?!

Do you want to be remembered as men?!

Remembered as winners?!

*(Start throwing around shit. If there's a chair nearby, stand on it.)*

Remembered as the kickass motherfuckers who went out onto that field, took the game to those fucking worthless pieces of shit, AND FUCKING RIPPED OUT THEIR GODDAMN THROATS?! I ASK YOU: HOW DO YOU WANT TO BE RE-MEMBERED?

*(Everyone will now proceed to go apeshit.)*

I SAID: DO YOU WANT TO BE REMEMBERED AS CHAMPIONS?!

*(Everyone will respond in the affirmative.)*

DO YOU WANT TO FUCK SOME SHIT UP?!

*(Everyone will again respond in the affirmative. Cue up "Shut 'Em Down" by Public Enemy on the locker room stereo, provided the captain gave you permission.)*

THEN LET'S GO! LET'S FUCKING FIRE IT UP, MOTHERFUCKERS!!!!! FUCKING BRING IT IN!

*(Everyone brings it in.)*

FUCKING WIN ON THREE! ONE . . . TWO . . . THREE!!!!!!!
WIN!!!!!!!!!!!!!!!!!!!!!!!

Oh, man, I am ready to run through a brick wall right now. Granted, this speech may be more effective before, say, a championship game as opposed to the last game of a nine-game West Coast road swing. But hey, that's what snorting Dexatrim is for.

# Why you're in Detroit: traveling.

Business travel might be the most annoying part of being a professional athlete. Maybe you're with a New York team and have the good fortune of playing most of your road games against nearby teams from the many cities that are tightly bunched into the Northeast Corridor. But if you play for Seattle, you are fucked. No matter what, you'll be traveling on weekends and holidays. You'll be taking chartered red-eye flights and be expected to take the field six hours later. And when you arrive, the airport limo may occasionally be three minutes late. This is the quiet suffering that fans don't see. Maybe if they knew what it was like to travel forty-five days every year in exchange for millions of dollars and five months off, they'd appreciate you a little more.

**PACKING.** Road trips can last upward of ten days, and even longer if you play baseball and are in the middle of a divorce proceeding. So it's important to know what to pack. Be sure to bring two bags with you on every road trip: a folding bag for your suit (turn the jacket inside out to prevent wrinkles!) and a rolling suitcase. I suggest buying Tumi luggage. It's expensive, but nothing moistens a hotel lobby groupie's panties quite like the sight of Tumi luggage. Having expensive luggage lets people know you have expensive shit *inside* your luggage. That's well worth paying $1,000 per piece. And if you buy Vuitton luggage, you are legally allowed to walk into the hotel naked from the waist down.

**AIR TRAVEL.** If you play for big-revenue teams like the Mavericks or Redskins, you'll be boarding a private, team-owned jet to fly to road cities. The jet will include first-class seating, satellite television, a fully stocked bar, a four-star restaurant, a crepe station, a fully operational health club, two hospitals, and a petting zoo. If you play for small-revenue teams like the Clippers or Royals, you'll be flying AirTran. Sorry. Be sure to bring your own food, or else you'll get the standard team "dinner" consisting of a day-old turkey sandwich, Humpty Dumpty potato chips, and a can of Veryfine Cran-Raspberry Cocktail. AirTran will also provide Shasta and unsalted pretzel nubs.

**MEALS.** You'll be given a union-mandated food stipend for road trips, usually around $200 a day. It's not much, but it should be enough to just barely get by.

**BUS TRAVEL.** Regardless of the length of your trip, you will find yourself on a team bus at some point. The team bus is used for road trips of two hours or less, and for shuttling you from the airport to the hotel and back. When you board the bus, go immediately to the back. Only kiss-asses sit at the front. Your coach will sit at the very front of the bus. The only person he will make chitchat with is the driver. Trust me, he has more in common with the driver than he does with you. So don't talk to him unless you like your casual conversations awkward and stilted. Your team bus and team plane have specific departure times that your coach has noted on his detailed trip itinerary. Your coach spent hours overthinking this itinerary, so do not test him by arriving late. If you arrive late, your team bus will leave without you and you will be fined and suspended for a quarter. Unless you're really good, in which case you can show up whenever the fuck you want.

**HOTEL ACCOMMODATIONS.** When you arrive at your hotel, you'll be assigned a room. Certain superstars have suite clauses in their contracts that guarantee them a deluxe suite to themselves on the road (complete with champagne-glass Jacuzzi). But if you do not have such a clause, you'll be sharing a standard room with a teammate. Veterans usually get to choose their roommates. But if you are a rookie, you will be matched with someone via a pairing system that is as poorly designed as the one that determines female freshman roommates at Middlebury. If you are clean, your roommate will be a slob. If you like to go to sleep early, he'll be a night owl. If you're in favor of fair trade, he will be against it. But you can probably survive this unpleasant circumstance so long as you adhere to a few simple rules.

**ROOM ETIQUETTE.** First, always tie a sock on the doorknob when masturbating. And make sure it's a sock you haven't "used," if you catch my drift. Second, always bring a travel edition of Connect Four. You aren't just connecting checkers when you play that game. You're building relationships that will stand the test of eight to twelve hours. And always bring your own alcohol. You and your roommate may have nothing in common, but years of watching romantic comedies has taught me that people can overcome their differences and really bond if they get stone-cold shitfaced off margaritas and dance around to James Brown together. No matter where you're from, alcohol is the social glue that brings us together in a sloppy, forgettable, and disingenuous fashion.

## "In Russia, we like to shoot basketballs *and* Chechen rebels!" Being an international player.

As we Americans grow ever fatter and more sedentary, we must increasingly rely on importing foreign players to play our games *for* us. Soon leagues will consist of nothing but foreign-born players, hired mercenaries from another part of the world paid to represent your preferred locality. I can't wait. If you're a talented expatriate from a former Soviet republic that is constantly teetering on the brink of anarchy *and* you have a neck beard, chances are you'll find yourself playing on our side of the pond at some point. In which case: *guten Tag, Comrade!*

As an international player, it's important that you assimilate into American culture as quickly as possible. Don't expect your teammates to adapt to you. This is America. The world adjusts to us, not the other way around. It's much easier that way. Oh, and don't bother staying in contact with your family back home. They're so lame now. Do they even have running water in Haiti? Losers. Our shallow and depraved pop culture will be all the family you'll need. Some quick notes on what to expect depending upon your country or region of origin.

 **EUROPE.** Yes, I know what you're thinking: *Wow, the play here is so physical!* I know. It's gonna be a bit of a culture shock from the world of European sports, where each player is granted a three-inch imaginary force field that no opponent is ever allowed to enter. You'll also notice that flopping is discouraged here in the United States (unless you play for the Spurs). I know you're used to soccer. Or, as it is known over there, football, or the beautiful game, largely because all the players remain so clean throughout the contest. But we don't give a fuck about that sport here. So don't bother lying down and flopping around like a freshly caught marlin should an opposing player gesture toward your general vicinity. The refs won't have it. Should you grow to miss some of the comforts of your home nation, don't fret. We Americans are sure to have a bastardized version of whatever it is you crave. Jonesing for one of the morning cappuccinos you enjoyed back in *Italia*? No problem. You can grab one at Starbucks for a mere $8. Yes, it *is* supposed to smell like vanilla syrup!

**AUSTRALIA.** Get ready for a whole lot of American women (a) testing your accent to make sure it isn't fake, and (b) throwing themselves at you once they realize it isn't. Seriously, milk that accent for all it's worth. I was born in Australia, but I only lived there for one year. Oh, if I had just lived there long enough to pick up that accent, or at least long enough to justify affecting it. Holy shit, would I have gotten some serious trim. Fuck. See, Australians are exotic enough to entice American women while also providing the comfort of being just as lazy and obnoxious as American men. Best of all, you live a hemisphere away. If you dump an American woman, the flight to Sydney is too long and expensive for her to stalk you. Bonus points if you live in Perth. That place is farther away than Andromeda.

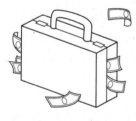

**SOUTH AMERICA.** Is your family still back in Venezuela? Are you out of your goddamn mind? They'll be in the hands of rebel kidnappers by sundown. Do you really want your family hauled off to an undisclosed holding pen in the jungle for eight months while you bargain for their freedom? Seriously, get them on a fucking plane. Once the details of your contract hit the press, they'll be a riper target than Hayden Panettiere.

**DOMINICAN REPUBLIC.** No need to assimilate. You've got at least three fellow Dominicans on your team. Don't even bother trying to learn English. In fact, don't even bother to acknowledge the white people in the clubhouse. What's the point? They're all more or less alike. Go ahead and look right through them when they wave hi. The same goes for your

manager. You've had the same swing since you were eleven months old. Where does this *maricón* get off telling you you've got a hitch on your follow-through? Is not right.

**CUBA.** The first thing you'll notice once you get off your raft is that America has roads that are *paved*. Pretty sweet, eh? Many Cuban athletes come to the States with the intention of using their newfound fame and fortune to improve living conditions back in their homeland. But they soon realize that Castro will never die, that the proletariat is too low in morale to start a revolution, and that cigars, in reality, taste like shit. They never go back, and neither should you. Defect. In fact, have a press conference announcing that you are defecting. You'll feel just like Ramius in *The Hunt for Red October.* It's pretty cool. Oh, and vote Republican. Cuban immigrants always vote Republican. Why? No one knows.

**RUSSIA.** No doubt your hockey team paid one hefty sum to the *Mafiya* for your rights. Just remember: at any time, the *Mafiya* can tell your team, "Oh, sorry, the rights fees have doubled. In fact, they have tripled." There really isn't anything you can do about this. Just continue drinking your homemade potato vodka and pray they don't come to claim their "prize." At least your girlfriend is smokin' hot.

**JAPAN.** Like Dominicans, there is no need for you to assimilate with your fellow American teammates. For one thing, you will be completely disgusted by their work ethic and complacent attitude toward life in general. So you won't want anything to do with them. You'll be surrounded by a cadre of eager young Japanese reporters ready to transcribe your every word. So go ahead and hang out with them. Together, you can discuss how America embodies the very antithesis of Japanese culture, which prizes hard work and loyalty above all else. Then you can hop on the Internet together and order all the necessary Japanese underage pornographic serial comics (for you) and ridiculous amounts of brand-name merchandise (for your twelve-year-old niece, Mayuko). When speaking through your interpreter, be sure to have your translated words sound exactly like the dialogue from *Ran*. And drop your last name. It'll make you that much more mysterious, even though in reality you're just an aloof dick.

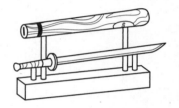

**AFRICA.** The first thing you'll notice about America is that most of the murdering here is performed by civilians and not the police (except in New York City). Be sure to adopt an American-sounding nickname that has nothing to do with your given name. Ndebe can become Sam in a snap. Many American fans and journalists will marvel over your polite demeanor and genuine kindness. Well, no shit. You just left the Sudan. People from the Sudan tend to perk up a bit when they get air-dropped into a kickass town like Chicago. Be sure to bring your white professor legal guardians to every event. Your American dad will be beyond psyched to have a pretend son who has the athletic ability to notch three sacks in a single game.

Many African athletes use the majority of their earnings to invest back into the destroyed areas of their homeland. Some, like Dikembe

Mutombo, go back for months at a time to help build roads, hospitals, and more. These are athletes who know that you don't help people simply with money or photo ops, but with lots of time and hard work. So when Bono asks you to talk about Africa at Coachella, tell him to go eat a bag of shit.

**CHINA.** There is only one prominent Chinese athlete playing in America today, and that is Yao Ming. But soon, China's practice of selective breeding will pay off in spades. As part of this future wave of Chinese athletic and economic dominance, you'll be counted on to bring glory to the Communist party. And to murder any Chinese girls under fifteen months old. This won't be a problem, as in the future all Chinese people will be genetically engineered by the government to feel no human emotion. Fraternizing with your American teammates will be discouraged, and a very small tracking device will be inserted under your toenail so that the government can follow you at all times. Try not to think about this while masturbating.

No matter where you're from, you should usually make a token effort to try to enjoy things that are uniquely American. Our athletes will pay you back by feigning interest in things from your home country. It's all about trying to find common ground, failing, and then pretending that you succeeded for the media. In the end, you'll own five hip-hop CDs you don't like, and your American counterpart will discreetly head to the loo to throw up the shabu-shabu you prepared for him. And that's what diplomacy is all about.

---

### Clippable Motivational Slogan!

*Deh haffe flugenblugen! Schnell! Weiss ausche! Nien mit schnitzengruben! Ich bin dingelhoffer! Scheisse! Tisheldecke!*

—DIRK NOWITZKI

---

## "I'm gay! After I retire!" Being a closeted athlete.

Even though an estimated 10 percent of the human population is homosexual, an astonishing 0 percent of athletes are gay. How are we to account for this amazing phenomenon? Could it be that pro athletes are so manly they don't qualify for gayness? Possibly. I know I've never made love to one, despite many valiant attempts.

But a more realistic explanation is that there are many homosexual athletes out there who choose to keep their sexual orientation (direction: gay) hidden from teammates. If you're afflicted with "the gay" and are unsure as to what to do about it, relax. This handy FAQ will answer all of your questions.

**Q:** **How do I know I'm gay?**

**A:** We all start off heterosexual, of course. But if your mother coddled you as a child, you're well within the danger zone of becoming a gay little firecracker. Here are some early symptoms of gaiety:

- Bossiness
- Unreal level of self-absorption
- Bally's Total Fitness membership

- Beginning 90 percent of your sentences with "Okay . . ."
- Referring to jeans as "denim"
- Tricking straight people into supporting gay rights by declaring it Denim Day when everyone wears jeans every day anyway
- Love of sangria
- Affinity for placing your hands on your hips
- Well-groomed eyebrows
- Affinity for cock

**Q:** **Should I come out to my teammates?**

**A:** Good God, no. You need to repress that gayness far down into the depths of your psyche. In fact, you need to go in the opposite direction. Submerge your own identity and put up a false front of overly aggressive masculinity. Get drunk. A lot. Brag about all the hot chicks you banged. Do lots of grilling. And, at least once a month, order a male hooker to your apartment, pretend to like him (and, if you do like him, pretend that you are pretending to like him), kiss him once, and then beat the ever-loving shit out of him while crying your eyes out. Your teammates will adore you.

Or get married and have children. Nothing takes your mind off your true sexual orientation like marrying someone you don't love and then producing offspring in order to lock yourself into a horrible, unhappy life forevermore. It keeps you super busy.

**Q:** **But why can't I come out?**

**A:** Because your being gay serves as a distraction to the rest of the team. Your teammates need to remain focused. They can't be sitting around thinking about the fact that you're gay, and that you might like them, and that you might be staring at them in the shower, and that you might nail them to the bathroom floor when no one is looking. It'll cause them to lose their concentration. All so that you can be yourself. Now, don't you think that's being a bit selfish? You should be ashamed of yourself, which shouldn't be hard for you. Closeted gays are excellent at self-loathing.

Look, you won't be playing ball forever. Once you retire, you'll be able to go on an epic, yearlong man-binge that would make your average New Jersey governor cream his jeans. You'll move to Chelsea, shack up with four crazy new friends, join a gym, get a new wardrobe, hit the clubs every night, and overcompensate for lost time by becoming almost cartoonishly gay. You'll become so promiscuous, you won't be able to tell when one hot, sweaty, gay sexual encounter ends and another begins. Then you'll grow disillusioned with the superficiality of the whole gay scene, taking less and less joy from all the nonstop, anonymous fucking. Then you'll get hooked on Zoloft and consider going back to women for a bit. Then you'll move to Napa and become an olive farmer.

Sound fun? It is. Right now, you're the only guy on your team with something to look forward to after his playing days are over. Why spoil yourself now with the occasional clandestine handicapped stall BJ? Save yourself.

**Q:** **I have a boyfriend who is pressuring me to come out. What should I do?**

**A:** Of course he wants you to come out. The media has been dying for a gay athlete to come out for ages. The *New York Times* already has a special sixty-page commemorative section ready for press. All they have to do is stick in your name. *Vanity Fair* will have Annie Leibovitz at your house within an hour. MTV will promise you a two-hour *True Life* special. Gay rights are one of the last causes left for the media to champion. Everyone else's civil rights — blacks, immigrants, criminals, hunters, suspected terrorists, children, pornographers, Klan rally marchers, dolphins, the paparazzi, pederasts, online stalkers, gamblers, Linkin Park fans — have already been well established. You're all that's left, baby.

They'll turn you into an icon. Like Jackie Robinson, only *fabulous*. So of course your special friend would like to be a part of it all. He was disowned by his family back in Montana for coming out. You're his karmic reward for decades of sullen family meals. He's got ulterior motives. And he still wears Benetton. Dump him.

**Q:** **What do I do if a teammate finds out I'm gay?**

**A:** Keep cool. Many teammates will be surprisingly discreet about it so long as you aren't "in their face" about being gay. In other words, don't be gay around them. Never bring up your gayness to them. Don't talk to them about some great date you had. That will cause them to envision you fucking another man, which will in turn trigger blind hatred. Don't mention it. And do everything to keep a low profile. This will send them the message that "Hey, I'm gay, but I'm doing everything in my power to make sure that fact doesn't ruin your day." They'll appreciate the gesture.

Unless the teammate who finds out is Evangelical. He'll douse you in kerosene and light you aflame within an hour.

**Q:** **Who are some gay athletes I can turn to for advice?**

**A:** All current gay athletes are, of course, still firmly locked in the closet. But, as a card-carrying insider, I have come to learn the names of several athletes who dabble in the homoerotic Dark Arts. And I'm quite confident that I can divulge their names to you here without any fear of legal reprisals whatsoever. Like ███████████. He's gay. And remember ████████████? Gay as an Audi TT. And ███████████ is totally gay. Man, is that ███████████ gay! He's so gay, you turn gay if you accidentally bump into him.

Ooh! Ooh! You know who I found out was gay recently? ███████████. You wouldn't have guessed that, right? Guy is totally into bondage and domination. Really wild stuff.

███████████ is gay, of course. He's one of those "hide behind

# HEAR IT FROM A CLOSETED ATHLETE!

## Being a closeted athlete is hard, especially when you love cock as much as I do

by ███████████

As a closeted homosexual, I can't enjoy being a pro athlete as much as most people would. Other guys in the locker room joke all the time about going out and having sex with all these girls and stuff. It bothers me, because it's such a culture of intimidation. I hate my teammates for making me feel like I have to suppress this enormous part of my identity. But I'm also envious of them because they're able to lead a normal, all-American sort of life. I feel so ostracized. I guess, in many ways, that's why I lash out at teammates to the media and do all that showboating on the field. If I alienate myself from teammates with my actions, then my homosexuality becomes less of a reason for my not fitting in. Does that make any sense? I suppose that sounds foolish to you. But how can you understand what I'm going through?

You see, being a closeted athlete is hard, especially when you love cock as much as I do.

Man, I love cock. I love all kinds of cock. I love little white cocks, big black cocks, wrinkled old cocks, fresh young cocks, freckled cocks, hooded cocks, unhooded cocks, hairy cocks, shaved cocks, cocks that are semideflated after an orgasm, Indian cocks, pointy cocks, rigid cocks, Taiwanese cocks, curved cocks, straight cocks, clay cocks made in a pottery class, smelly cocks, glassy cocks, soapy cocks, etc. I love them all, and with an uncommon amount of zeal. And I'm surrounded by them every. Single. Day. (*continued on next page*)

## Men with Balls

Do you understand how hard that is? Imagine loving Chinese food, working in a Panda Express, and being unable to touch any of the orange chicken. It's that kind of hell. Why should I have to hide my love of cock from the world? Cock is my passion. It's the first thing I think about in the morning and the last thing I think about or suck before I go to bed. Yet I'm surrounded by this oppressive culture that constantly treats cocklovers as something evil or less than human.

Frankly, I think it's just immaturity. If the fact that I dream of one day lining up a group of black and white male slaves to create a giant cock organ makes you uncomfortable, I say get over yourself. Grow up. ████████████ used to clip his toenails in the locker room. It was disgusting. But I held my tongue. You know why? Common courtesy. My love of cock should be treated the same way.

Alas, it probably never will. And that's a shame. Imagine how much more confident, how much better I could be if I were simply allowed to be myself. Imagine how many gay athletes out there are being held back because a bunch of dipshit homophobes are too insecure to handle the idea of a gay teammate. We could win Super Bowls. Then I could have all the cock I wanted. That's the way it should be. Hate the player. Don't hate the gay.

I love me some football.

I love me some cock.

Why can't I love me some both?

Jesus" gays. ████████████ is gay, though he doesn't realize it yet. And ████████████ is also super gay. Quiet, bookish, excellent ball control: he's a textbook gay. Super nice guy, too. I heard he's a really great cook.

Yes, there are many gay athletes out there, but don't even think of going to them for advice. They've got problems of their own, and

# Deeply Penetrating the Numbers

**1,032** An estimated 1,032 active professional athletes have had a homosexual encounter. Here's a percentage breakdown of that number by sport:

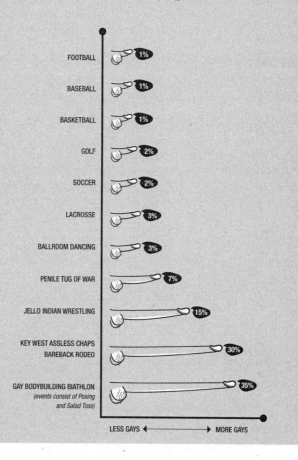

FOOTBALL — 1%

BASEBALL — 1%

BASKETBALL — 1%

GOLF — 2%

SOCCER — 2%

LACROSSE — 3%

BALLROOM DANCING — 3%

PENILE TUG OF WAR — 7%

JELLO INDIAN WRESTLING — 15%

KEY WEST ASSLESS CHAPS BAREBACK RODEO — 30%

GAY BODYBUILDING BIATHLON
*(events consist of Posing and Salad Toss)* — 35%

LESS GAYS ◄————► MORE GAYS

they don't need you snooping around. Unless you're good at rubbin' and tuggin'.

**Q:** **I play for the Browns and I absolutely cannot stand these drab uniforms. What's a girl to do?**

**A:** You just have to suck it up for now. Don't be such a fag.

## Chapter 4

# They're Like Bosses, Except They Like Hitting You

## Coaches and Management

**Because life wasn't meant to be enjoyed:
your guide to the average head coach.**

Your head coach is a tireless taskmaster who spends only five seconds savoring a victory before going back to sucking all the fun out of your sport until it is no longer a sport, but rather an endless, grueling death march. It's no wonder fans and media alike adore him. What a fun-loving free spirit is he!

The modern head coach or manager is a different animal from years past. He isn't involved in as much hands-on coaching and strategic planning as you might expect. In fact, you may barely see him during the week. Be grateful for this, because he can be a moody prick. His responsibility is to delegate work to an army of assistant coaches, and then to painfully micromanage each one of them as they do that work. A head coach is also responsible for structuring practices, coordinating travel schedules, managing communications between staff, handling press relations, and commissioning his own portrait. When you think about it, he's kind of like an event planner. I bet that Bill Belichick could plan one killer business luncheon. With sandwiches from Così and Orangina and everything.

Your coach is also in charge of handling the requisite mental coddling of athletes. The twenty-first-century pro sports team comprises multiple players who believe they are the centerpiece of the franchise, including you. The head coach's job is to dupe all of you into believing that this is the case, while simultaneously getting you to play unselfishly without even knowing it. Tricky? You bet!

But a good head coach knows how to pull it off by massaging your ego. How? First, he brings your ego into a serene, candlelit room. Then, he puts on a very relaxing Enigma record. Then he sprays a fine eucalyptus mist into the air. At this time, your ego will start to feel very loose and relaxed. Then, he oils up his hands real good and rubs your ego all over, starting at its core and then branching out to its furthest extremities, including the portion of your ego that helps suppress your love of Nora Ephron films. Then, after a brief pause, he turns your ego on its back and furiously pumps it up and down until it becomes engorged and finally achieves full release.

Needless to say, Phil Jackson is excellent at this. Andy Reid? Not so much.

All coaches today face an inescapable catch-22. In order to win a championship, a coach must win your respect. But in order to win your respect, he must have won a championship. In fact, he must have won many of them. After all, Barry Switzer won one Super Bowl. And we all know Barry Switzer has an IQ below room temperature.

In order to gain the respect necessary (not a lot, just enough) to get you to play to your potential, all head coaches fall into two distinct camps:

the **Disciplinarian**, and the **Player's Coach**. Disciplinarians, or "hard-asses" in the common vernacular, are coaches who try to earn your respect by being complete and utter dicks. Typically raised by a drunken father in a rural portion of Pennsylvania, disciplinarians enjoy taking their sad, isolated childhood out on you by constantly questioning your commitment and riding your jock like a stray crab. But, should you do something extraordinary, the disciplinarian will show a mild form of approval, such as an ass slap or a quick nod. The idea here is to get you to believe that you can, through hard work, melt the disciplinarian's heart and get him to love you. It's sort of like *Jane Eyre,* and you're the jailbait governess. So fucking hot.

Player's coaches, also known as "spineless pushovers," believe that they can win your respect by treating you like a man. Considering that most athletes live in a state of suspended adolescence, this is not a well-thought-out strategy. The player's coach will offer positive reinforcement, leave his door open at all hours, play pranks, take you white-water rafting, set few curfews, and carry about as much authority as a substitute homeroom teacher. He may also have a candy dish in the office. Get there early in the day and you can probably snag a handful of Snickers Minis. Norv Turner is widely praised by players for his frequent candy-dish refills.

Disciplinarians are typically hired after player's coaches have been fired, and vice versa. Some coaches try to cross over between disciplinarian and player's coach. If the players are threatening to mutiny, he may take a softer approach. If the players become unruly and start lighting random fires around the locker room, he'll try to crack the whip. This approach never works. Players respect consistency. If your coach is an asshole, he should *always* be an asshole. If he's a bleeding-heart pussy, he should *always* be a bleeding-heart pussy. Never the twain shall meet. If your coach tries to play Bad Cop/Different Kind of Bad Cop, feel free to take the rest of the season off. That guy's a lame duck and he knows it. Fuck him.

If you're looking to impress your head coach in order to get more playing time, I strongly suggest never asking him about his family. Your coach has been married for thirty years to a wife he mentally abandoned twenty-nine years ago. He also probably has three or more children, all of whom are complete train wrecks. A much smarter approach is to pepper him with questions about strategy and what you need to do to improve. Most coaches are, at heart, teachers. Which means they like being real fucking know-it-alls.

Your coach woke up at 3:00 a.m. after falling asleep at 2:00 a.m. on a cot in his office with his hand on the DVD player remote. Why? So he could try to absorb more information about your sport than any other person on Earth. He does this even though research has shown the brain can only take in so much information in a single day, and without proper rest, intensive work can be counterproductive. So, if you want to kiss his ass, make him feel that all of that needless effort was worth it.

He'll appreciate it when your owner fires his ass three weeks into the season.

## DID YOU KNOW?

The average tenure of a professional head coach or manager is 10.2 months. Hate your coach? The good news is that he'll be out the door shortly. The bad news is that Larry Brown will be replacing him. And man, is that guy a ballbuster!

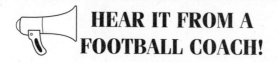

# HEAR IT FROM A FOOTBALL COACH!

## I will control you with my mind
### by Bill Belichick

Hey, *(your last name).* Over here. Yeah, you. Come here.

I want you to drink this.

What is it? It's uh . . . a supplement. It contains vital electrolytes. You need it. It's good for your circulation. Look, just fuckin' drink it or I'll cut your ass.

*(You drink it.)*

Okay, good. Feel okay? You don't feel faint, do you? I'm gonna try something, okay? I want you to relax. I'm going to concentrate really hard, and I want you to let me know if you feel anything.

*(He scrunches up his face real tight like he's having a bowel movement. You involuntarily move into a three-point stance.)*

Ahhhhhh! Good. Good, it worked on you.

I've been studying principles of nanotechnology for about seventeen years now. Right when I began coaching the Patriots, I had a breakthrough. Together with a team of Danish engineers, I was able to create robot microbes that control bodily movements based upon my brain waves. We even designed them to reproduce on their own. What you just swallowed was a mixed solution containing 4 moles, or $6.02 \times 10^{23}$, of these microbes. Don't worry. They're relatively harmless. What they'll do is embed themselves in your muscles and cause them to flex at my command. For example, JUMP!

*(You jump.)*

*(continued on next page)*

See? Pretty fuckin' cool, right? Now stand on your toes like a really jacked ballerina.

*(You stand on your toes like a really jacked ballerina.)*

Nice. Try not to fight my commands. This is a beta version of our latest upgrade. If you try to fight them, they may turn against your muscles, colonize them, and begin devouring them. And then you're no good to me.

Now, I'm not gonna use this technology for anything weird. I'm not gonna have you shoot the queen or anything like that. But I needed to develop a technology that eliminated freelancing and ensured that you did everything I told you. After all, I am not the world's most charismatic fellow. When I was in Cleveland, no one listened to me. I had no presence. I spoke in a horrible monotone that acted as a sort of audible Sominex. And I smelled a bit off. I needed something that would cut out any mental mistakes players would make and completely satisfy my freakish thirst for control. And these little bastards have done the job quite well.

You might be wondering how I can control the movements of all eleven players on the field at once. Well, the answer again lies in nanotechnology. I've had trillions of these nanobots implanted into my cerebellum. This hood hanging in the back of my sweatshirt helps hide the deformed growth caused by the implant. See?

*(He shows you the growth. It is the size and shape of a large mango, and has hair, teeth, and a single eyeball.)*

## They're Like Bosses, Except They Like Hitting You

Don't look into the eye. You may become lost forever. Again, that would make you no good to me. Jasper here—that's what I call him—helps me simultaneously coordinate the movement of all the players on the field. And with this Power Glove *(he dons a lacrosse glove covered with thin wires and metal plates)* I can make the nanobots that reside in your spittle fly into the bodily orifices of our opponents. Once there, I can make them do all sorts of naughty things. One time I made Zach Thomas bite off his own ring finger in a fumble pile. That was fun. I've also equipped them with very small cameras so that they can fly into our opponents' eye sockets, turning them into unwitting double agents for our cause. I don't spy on anyone. They spy on themselves. You should see the MILFs some of them bring home.

Anyway, glad you're part of the team. From now on, all of your bodily movements will be recorded into the database back at CentComm and placed on a large visual graph. If you would like to see this graph, it will cost you 20 percent of your base salary. Sorry, that's team policy. In the meantime, I wouldn't walk through any airport metal detectors if I were you. The nanobots don't like it.

Now run wind sprints until you vomit.

*(You run wind sprints until you vomit.)*

Good.

# HEAR IT FROM A BASEBALL MANAGER!

## Good job, everybody
### by Joe Torre

*(claps hands)*
Good job, everybody. Nice job. Good job out there. Really nice job.
*(pats you on the ass)*
Good job. Way to hustle.
Want some sunflower seeds?
Attaboy. Good job.

---

## "You're like the more athletic, better son I never had." A guide to your team owner.

There are ten things you need to know about your owner, and here they are.

**1. HE IS RICHER THAN YOU ARE OR COULD EVER HOPE TO BE.** Did you ever wonder where that $375,000 game check you get every week comes from? No, it didn't come from the magic money pixie, as Rickey Henderson may have told you. Your owner is the megarich superfuck who deigns to pay you your little pittance every year. He's got a yacht that's worth six of you, and he owns gated compounds on each of the seven continents, along with a starter colony on Mars. Think the Pegasus is just a mythical creature? Wrong, bucko! He's got a stable of them in Nepal. He may be watching you from the sky on his winged steed as you read this.

The average owner is at least a billionaire. Consider how rich that is. If your owner took a $1,000,000,000 check and put it into a regular savings account at a local bank at a lousy 2 percent annual interest rate, he'd have more than $800,000 a month to spend and still keep his billion dollars. Is that the very definition of fuck-you money? Why, yes, I believe it is.

Most of today's owners earned their fortune by being pioneers of industry. Some, like Mark Cuban, earned it during the first dot-com boom. Others, like Home Depot founder Arthur Blank, realized that Americans crave an airplane hangar–sized warehouse of home improvement products with no store directory, a parking lot that resembles the third stage of Armageddon, and, from what I can tell, no store employees on hand at any time. Either way, the average owner has stockpiled the kind of cash that goes beyond obscene and makes the American Dream seem even further out of a normal man's reach. It's the kind of money that makes even millionaires feel inadequate and unhappy. It's a nice place to be.

**2. HE IS ECCENTRIC.** You don't become a billionaire and remain a normal person. It just doesn't happen. I strongly urge you to avoid looking at your owner's toenails, or asking him what he keeps in that turret sticking out of his mansion. You don't want to know what he does with his spare time. He's got a lot of it, and he's got a lot of strange ideas that society wouldn't approve of. Ever reanimate your dead father? One owner has. Stay away.

**3. HE IS SHORT.** Your owner didn't become rich by being happy. By being 5'6" or shorter, he carries around a chip on his shoulder the size of

Mama Cass. He hopes that the financial stature he has attained will compensate for the physical stature he has always lacked. But the hard truth is that nothing makes up for being pocket-sized. Your owner will always resent his pathetic, halfling physique. That's why, as we speak, he is constructing a series of underground concentration camps, where he hopes to imprison and murder all the Tall Ones. By 2026, they'll be dead, and he'll be the tallest man on Earth! Who's laughing now, huh? WHO'S LAUGHING NOW?

**4. HE IS NOT BLACK.** He is very white. He may blend in with the wall occasionally. So be aware. Don't bad-mouth a guy who's got a complexion perfectly suited to indoor camouflage.

**5. YOU ARE HIS TOY.** Remember that Richard Pryor movie? That's you. The rich man pays you to run and jump. So run and jump, piss boy. And if he wants to put you in an inflatable Wonder Wheel and roll you down a steep hill, you let him. You're his property now, so you'd better get used to it. Your owner may also ask you to attend a key party and give his wife the good, hard reaming she's always begged for. It would be unwise to turn him down.

**6. WHEN YOU SPEND THREE QUARTERS OF A BILLION ON SOMETHING, YOU CAN DO WHATEVER THE FUCK YOU WANT WITH IT.** In the old days, most team owners bought the team, then happily turned over all of its operations, including personnel decisions, to "football people" or "baseball people," who were then given carte blanche to do as they pleased. The idea was that team owners were too inexperienced to buy a team and then actually become involved in it. So owners paid people who got to experience all the enjoyment of running a team with none of the expense of having to buy it.

But sometime around the early nineties, owners stopped being dumb. They realized that, since they were the ones who paid so much money for a franchise, they were in a position to exercise some semblance of authority. This has led to a boom of hands-on owners. Hands-on owners are owners who eschew hiring traditional general managers and do all the fun stuff like making draft picks and personnel decisions, while bringing in cap gurus to handle payroll and the other boring, administrative bullshit no one wants to do. Hands-on owners will also grope any female employee within a five-foot radius.

**7. HE GOT RICH BY BEING A CHEAP BASTARD.** You don't get rich by spending money. Your owner grew up dirt poor and understands the value of a dollar, which is why he's so reluctant to share one with anybody else. He may be paying you a grand salary, but know that his blood boils every time he has to sign that check. If he could pay you in loose kidney beans, he would. Following Bill Belichick's example, many owners have already taken exploratory steps to replace live players with highly skilled androids by 2029. Did you really think Tim Duncan was from the Virgin Islands? Fool! He's their first prototype. Next time you play against him, look closely at his left arm. You will see *ASIMO* stamped just above the crook of his right elbow. When no one is looking, Duncan has been known to sprout helicopter blades and fly away.

Evidence of your owner's pettiness can be seen elsewhere if you look closely enough. If he was forced to pay for a portion of your home stadium, it's probably made entirely of particleboard. And that cooler in your locker room? It's filled with nothing but Sam's Club drinks. Ever drink a twenty-two-cent diet cream soda? Don't.

**8. HE'D LOVE TO COACH YOU IF COACHING WEREN'T SUCH A SHITTY JOB.** Your owner probably dreamed of buying the team and then coaching it to multiple titles. Then he found out that coaches work 140 hours a week and barely have time to eat a hot meal. Now, instead of coaching the team, he prefers to coach it in his imagination, then to undermine your real coach at every conceivable turn. Many owners subvert their coach's authority by signing players the coach doesn't like, or reversing team rules he has implemented, or drawing obscene graffiti on the coach's office door. If you think your coach and your owner are at odds, remember: your owner is the one who owns the team. He's the one who will always be here. Side with him. It is often said that coaches are hired to be fired. This is 100 percent true. All fans dream of firing the idiot coaching their team, and your owner is the one fan who gets to really do it, which is why he enjoys doing it again and again and again.

### 9. HIS FAMILY IS COMPOSED OF NOTHING BUT FUCK-UPS.
Team ownership used to be a family business. A team was handed down from father to son, or nephew, or son-in-law, or anyone but a woman. But the proliferation of estate taxes and forked-tongued lawyers has made that sort of tradition obsolete. Your owner's immediate family consists of two or more siblings who have no speaking relationship, a wife who will soon inherit the team and run it into the ground, and a series of nephews and grandchildren who all have no-show jobs at the team complex. Jobs like Team Enthusiasm Coordinator and Director of Awareness. None of these relatives will show even the slightest trace of motivation or initiative. Your owner would never let his prized possession fall into the hands of these feuding idiots. So, if your owner is old and infirm, take note. Those two queers from Google could be sweeping in any day to buy you.

### 10. HE WANTS TO BE YOUR FRIEND. You'd never be friends with someone like your owner under normal circumstances. He's a loser.

## Deeply Penetrating the Numbers

**1″** The average owner loses one inch in height per decade as a result of the hunchbacking process.

That's why he bought your team in the first place: so he can hang out with coolass athletes like you and feel like one of the guys. So humor him. Go to dinner with him. Play poker with him. Join him in a game of Homeless Kickball. He'll be more apt to keep you around, no matter how badly you suck.

## HEAR IT FROM A COMMISSIONER!

### I see you have taken up the rather distressing habit of leaving your jersey untucked
by David Stern

Oh, hello. Please, come in. Have a seat. Were you waiting long? My deepest apologies. Oh, the jade dragon statue? Yes, I picked that up in Beijing last spring. It was a gift from the prime minister. Dates back to the eighth century. Do you like it? I think it's quite striking.

Can I get you something to drink? I can have Kitty get you a fresh
*(continued on next page)*

Deer Park if you like. We also have San Pellegrino if you prefer your water with gas. No? There's also a Starbucks across the street. Then again, I guess there's a Starbucks across every street now, isn't there?

*(laughs disingenuously)*

I also have a lovely 1962 Armagnac in this antique Baccarat decanter. But, given the early hour, I don't think it would be appropriate to partake. Don't you agree?

*(You nod.)*

Good. I'm glad you agree. Well, I'd hate to waste any more of your time. This shouldn't take long at all. Please, please sit. No, come closer. Don't worry. I don't bite. Young man, it's come to my attention recently that you have taken up the rather distressing habit of leaving your jersey untucked during game play.

Now, why would you go and do a thing like that?

I'm sorry to say that it's a league rule that players must have their jerseys tucked in at all times during the course of a game. This rule isn't merely a suggestion. It's something we took great care in instituting many years ago. It's not something we made up for you to simply ignore, now is it? We have these rules for a reason, you know. They're important. Now, they may not be important to you. Obviously, you have demonstrated that they are not. But *we* find them to be quite critical. After all, we take our image very seriously. It impacts more than you might think: our fans, our corporate sponsors, and even our international interests.

But I'm assuming you didn't know that. I'm assuming you just wanted to make a personal statement. I understand your naïveté. It's somewhat endearing. But we can't have you brazenly flouting our rules anymore. I can forgive the occasional loose jersey. Sometimes, Bruce Bowen will tug at it and it will become untucked inadvertently. Oh, what a tenacious defender that young man is! Like a very fierce malamute!

That I forgive. But this . . . this . . . *flagrant* display is simply unacceptable. Now, I could fine you $275,000 for this, as is customary. But I'm not sure that would really get my point across, would it? No, I don't think it would. Perhaps a more direct approach is necessary. Vito? Spider?

*(Two very large men grab you and strap you to a giant steel table. The ceiling opens to reveal a complex series of razor-sharp blades rotating at an incredibly high speed.)*

Ingenious, isn't it? I call it the Lacerator. It was designed by a disgruntled former engineer at LA Gear. The blades are placed precisely where the nerve bundles on your body are at their highest density. Feel free to scream. We soundproofed the walls after using it on Roy Tarpley many years ago. Like you, he was a habitual miscreant who thought the rules didn't apply to him. Funny how no one ever hears from Roy anymore. I do wonder where he went. Oh, yes, I know where he went. Right into the pen of starving wild boars below that very table you're lying on.

Pity.

What's that? You want me to show mercy? I'm afraid it's far too late for that. I didn't see you showing any mercy for our sartorial policies. No, I'm afraid the only way to teach you . . . *is to kill you.*

*(The blades lower.)*

Go ahead, beg all you want. I've heard it all before. We got through forty-three inches of Charles Barkley's flesh before we finally struck vital tissue. Oh, how he screamed. To this day, it still brings me such delight.

Oh, you know what? I'm feeling rather charitable today. You seem to have learned your lesson, haven't you? Stop the Lacerator, boys!

*(The blades stop.)*

You're a very lucky man, did you know that? I'm not usually so forgiving. Don't ever forget it. Next time, tuck in that jersey, okay? Or else it won't just be you on this table. It'll be you and someone you love. You got me?

*(You nod vigorously.)*

Good. Now get out of my fucking sight.

## By exploiting you, they're showing they care: unions and collective bargaining.

Fifty years ago, pro athletes were treated no better than common share-croppers. Free agency didn't exist. Athletes were drafted by one team, paid whatever their team decided to pay them, and forced to drink water tainted with strychnine. But soon athletes formed unions and success-fully bargained for huge salaries, free agency, and extremely lax drug testing. Now that your union has achieved all of its original goals, you might be tempted to ask whether it has outlived its usefulness. Don't. You'll be knifed in your hotel suite if you do that.

The purpose of your union is to represent you, the athlete, during the collective bargaining period. Should your union and the owners fail to reach an agreement, one of two things will happen. One: you will go on strike, which is when players voluntarily stop working (or in this case, playing) to force the owners' hand. Two: the owners stage a lockout, which is when the owners refuse to pay players or let them play in order to force the union's hand. This is not to be confused with a lock-in, where you and five friends lock yourself in your dorm room until the keg is kicked. That's *way* cooler. The important difference between a strike and a lockout is that a strike is the owners' fault, and a lockout is even *more* their fault.

Your team, along with every other, has a player representative des-ignated to act as a liaison between you and the union. This is not a pay-ing gig, unless you count the tens of thousands of dollars he gets from illegally skimming the union's pension fund. Should a strike or lock-out occur, he will talk to you from time to time to give you updates and answer any questions. Here is a sample conversation you two may have.

**You:** When can we start playing again?

**Your Rep:** Our hope is to get you back out on the field as soon as humanly possible. But I'm afraid that, right now, we're at an impasse.

**You:** But how am I supposed to feed my family, especially my morbidly obese son?

**Your Rep:** It'll be tough, but we all need to dig in and get ready for a long holdout. I hope you've saved up some of your money.

**You:** You're shitting me, right?

**Your Rep:** *(laughs)* Yes, of course. We have an emergency fund set up to pay each of you during the strike. You'll get $10,000 a year.

**You:** What if they get replacement players?

**Your Rep:** Ha! No fan's gonna accept replacement players. Do you really think Americans will accept a *substitute* Michael Olowokandi? Don't be a fool.

**You:** How did this impasse come to be?

**Your Rep:** We made an offer to the owners, and they countered with an offer that was unacceptable. So talks broke off.

**You:** But what was unacceptable about the offer? Can I see it?

**Your Rep:** No. Mind your own goddamn business.

**You:** But what if the owners never make a suitable counter-offer?

**Your Rep:** Don't worry. They will. How long can a billionaire hold out while one of his many tertiary income streams runs dry? Those fuckers are bound to crack.

**You:** Are we gonna march?

**Your Rep:** What is this, *Norma Rae*? Hell no, we aren't marching. Marching requires physical exertion, which is just like working. The whole point of a strike is to *not* work. Know who likes marching? Nazis.

**You:** I'm not sure I can take this. What if I *(gulp)* cross the picket line?

**Your Rep:** Well, that depends. Do you like having your cleats shat in?

**You:** No.

**Your Rep:** Do you like your wife receiving threatening phone calls in the dead of night?

**You:** No.

**Your Rep:** Do you like being regularly assaulted with a tomahawk?

**You:** No.

**Your Rep:** Then you won't be crossing the picket line, now, will you?

**You:** No, sir.

**Your Rep:** Or whining like a little bitch to the media?

**You:** No, sir.

**Your Rep:** Listen. As I said, we're doing everything in our power to get you back on the field. We plan to meet with the owners again next month for another round of negotiations.

**You:** But why next month? Why not now?

**Your Rep:** Because shut the fuck up, that's why.

As you can see, your union provides an invaluable service during the stressful moments that come with labor strife. Rest assured, they will fight tooth and nail to win an agreement that will, in no way, be noticeably different from the previous deal to anyone except those who negotiated it. If you are a bottom-tier player who lost a precious chance to earn whatever income you could during your limited window of opportunity to play at this level, you may not feel like you won much of anything. But trust me: you did. You totally won. That sense of victory should help you ease into your new job at the toothpaste factory.

## "This is such bullshit!" Why you got suspended/benched.

All head coaches have a doghouse to which they banish players who have greatly displeased them. You might think a coach's doghouse is some kind of metaphor, but it is not. Your coach has a real doghouse, complete with a clear, thick plastic flap and a food dish filled halfway with a flavorless mixture of ground beef and rice. This doghouse is located right behind the team complex next to the grease-recycling dumpster. Here's an artist's rendering:

Once banished to the doghouse, you must sleep there until your coach unlocks the gate and drags you out by the scruff of your neck. If you bark, your coach will kick you and talk to the owner about having you put down. It's not a fun place to be. While you are there, you will have been officially benched or suspended for "conduct detrimental to the team."

What is conduct detrimental to the team? Here's a quick rundown of typical offenses.

**YOU TALKED BACK TO A COACH.** Coaches despise even the slightest challenge to authority. A hearty "Fuck you!" to him during seven-on-seven drills will always cost you a game. But there are more subtle challenges to your coach that may also anger him, sometimes even more so. For example, if you walk up to your coach and say, "Hey, Coach, I noticed that Tony Romo occasionally telegraphs throws by patting the ball. Is that something we could exploit?" *BOOM.* You are fucking *gone,* my friend. What did you think, your coach didn't already notice that? You trying to make him look stupid? You think you can draw up a better game plan? That is insubordination at its most insidious, and your head coach isn't going to stand for it. He didn't spend two decades toiling through bullshit jobs in the MAC and Big 12 just to have his strategy questioned by some rogue newbie who plays by his own rules! To the pine with you, Johnny Rebel! That'll learn you. That'll learn you good.

**YOU BITCHED ABOUT MANAGEMENT TO THE MEDIA.** After a loss, your coach will happily spend three hours in a press conference bashing the shit out of your play until your family watching at home bursts into tears. But if you publicly question him or the decisions of management, you are crossing the line. Don't you see? When your coach berates you in the press, he's doing it to make you *better.* What's your excuse? So what if management held a fire sale to clear cap room and eliminated free car service from the airport? You don't go outside the family to talk about that. That's petty. Management would prefer it if you just quietly bitch about it to teammates until an irreversible mood of indifference and cynicism takes hold of the entire locker room. That's the proper way to do things.

**YOU SUCK.** All bad pro athletes have a hard time coming to grips with their own shittiness. But, if it makes you feel better, you can always say your coach had an "agenda" and remain ambiguous about it. People will just assume he's a dick. No one will suspect you're actually allergic to humility and objective self-analysis.

**YOU GOT IN A FIGHT WITH A TEAMMATE WHO IS BETTER THAN YOU.** Coaches love fights. It makes them think you've got fire and that you love to play. They never consider the idea that the guy you got into a scrap with is a fucking dickhead who slept with your niece and had it coming. In fact, 99 percent of all practice fights have nothing to do with competitive spirit and everything to do with pure, unadulterated rancor. Most coaches will let a fight slide, unless you happen to get into a fight with a superstar. Superstars are a coach's meal ticket. Fighting him means potentially injuring him, which means your coach will see the downfall of his entire career flash before his eyes—the injury, the resulting malaise, the mailed-in second half of the year, the firing, the lost championships, the lost Hall of Fame bust, the lost stint as a retard analyst for ESPN, the new job as an assistant at Lehigh. Putting that vision in your coach's mind will ignite a white-hot fury you don't want any part of. So lay off the franchise player.

**YOU SKIPPED PRACTICE.** You can't skip practice. Coaches hold practice sacred. It's their only chance to boss you around. Once you're playing a real game, you can do whatever you want. You deprived your coach of a precious opportunity to feel like a big man, and he will bring the hammer of Thor down on you for it.

**YOU WERE LATE TO PREGAME WARM-UPS.** Pregame warm-ups usually consist of some light stretching, light running, and talking with players on the other team about where to meet up once the game is over. It's a calm, relaxing time to hang out and gather your thoughts. Skipping the pregame warm-up usually merits a one-quarter suspension from your coach, giving you an extension of your pregame warm-up, which is a really nice gesture on his part. And you still get paid as if you played a full game. So relax and enjoy!

**THE COACH IS NEW AND HAS AN IRRATIONAL HATRED OF YOU.** New coaches are always eager to replace incumbent players with "their" players: players they personally brought in. If you were hired by your old coach and continue to play well after his departure, your new coach can't take credit for finding you or making you good, and that won't do. You also may be a victim of the dreaded Ex-Boyfriend/Dead Son Syndrome, in which your coach is constantly comparing you to an all-star player he once coached at your position. He'll do everything in his power to make you similar to this favorite player of his. He'll make you study tape of this player. He'll make you change your mechanics to mimic this player. And he'll make you wear Skin Bracer, just like ol' Smitty used to. In the end, he'll hate you all the more because, no matter how hard you try, you can never be this player. Unless you were to undergo some sort of facial reconstruction surgery. Would you at least consider it?

**YOUR COACH IS PLAYING MIND GAMES.** You can do everything right and your coach may still find fault with you. It's his way of maintaining the upper hand in the relationship. In many ways, he's just like my ex-girlfriend, who was a total cunt.

**YOU ARE A TEAM CANCER.** Team cancers, also known as malcontents, are players who disrupt the delicate intangible known as team chemistry. According to every sports column ever written, team chemistry occurs when a majority of players on a team like one another and share a common team-oriented goal. Never mind that any team can fit this description and still be terrible. And it's not like everyone at Microsoft likes each other. That company is worth billions of dollars. Do you really think it has anything to do with whether or not the sales department goes bowling every Thursday? Fuck and no.

Regardless, your coach enjoys propagating the myth of team chemistry, because then, if your team has it (and it may, by sheer luck), then he will get credit for perfectly orchestrating the natural human relationship dynamics of your locker room. But he can't do that if you're the one asshole on the team trying to turn guys against each other. So cut it out. You'll never be as ruthlessly effective as real cancer anyway.

**YOU ARE GAY.** See previous chapter.

---

### Clippable Motivational Slogan!

*A successful coach needs a patient wife, a loyal dog, and a great quarterback. But if you don't have a wife, the dog can usually pull double duty.*

— WEEB EWBANK

## Chapter 5

# "Don't You People Have Homes?"

## Fame and Fans

### "I love you AND I hate you!": a guide to the modern fan.

It has been said that Americans are obsessed with sports. I don't know where it was said, or who said it. But, for the sake of my straw-man argument, let's just say someone said it somewhere. I personally consider this obsession a healthy thing. You see, sports serve as a distraction from all the serious issues in our lives, like war, God, family, and proper nutrition. Sports let us forget about that stuff for a while and, in many cases, successfully phase it out completely. After all, if India and Pakistan decide to engage in all-out nuclear conflict, do we really want to know about it? Much better to freak out over shit like Nick Swisher's batting average. It helps keep things in proper perspective. Sports are an escape, a chance for fans to get away from the stress of everyday life and enjoy an entirely *different* kind of stress.

As a pro athlete, you serve as a proxy for the unrealized athletic dreams of the people in the crowd. They are coming to cheer you. But the real truth is that they have come to watch you and imagine themselves as you. So when you play well, the fans like you because you are making their alternate universe selves look good and helping them get some hot alternate universe pussy after the game is over. If you fuck up, then you're just ruining the dream. And that won't do. So when you hear fans booing, remember: they're not booing you, they're booing themselves *through* you. It's called displacement. Look it up.

Your margin for error with today's crowd is slimmer than ever. Being a fan used to be easy. You could walk to the stadium in your bowler hat, throw down half a shilling for a box seat, and kick back with a Coca-Cola that had real cocaine in it. Not anymore. Seeing you in person now means sitting in traffic for God knows how many hours because the new stadium was stuck in some shitass suburb without proper infrastructure surrounding it. Then, fans have to negotiate the parking lot, where a fifteen-year-old parking attendant directs them to the farthest corner of the field even though there are clearly available spaces closer to the stadium. They can see them! They're *right fucking there!* No wonder they resent you. You get valet service. Fucker.

There are three kinds of fans out there today: **Casual Fans, Avid Fans**, and **Die-hard Fans**. Casual fans are the ones who take periodic interest in your team, usually depending upon your winning percentage, or if you have a catcher the girls positively swoon over. Casual fans also go by the derogatory term "bandwagon fans," and are sneered at by avids and diehards. But this is a spurious mentality. You see, bandwagon fans are the people who make sporting events special. It takes something truly amazing to make some fair-weather asshole fan like your mom say, "Wow, that Darren Jeter is pretty darn good!" The most exciting sporting events are the ones that reach out beyond the

standard fan base and manage to capture the interest of people who don't even like your sport. Without these people, sports lose their transcendent quality. So when you see some douchebag Cowboy, Yankee, Red Sox, or Laker fan walking down the avenue, be sure to thank them for extending sports beyond its normal reach. Yes, they are fucking losers I'd like to see dragged behind a semi and then doused with tar. But they do serve a purpose. Remember that when they're talking on their cell phones in the front row during the last two minutes of a playoff game.

Avid fans are fans who follow your team and all local teams with the utmost devotion while maintaining a semblance of balance throughout the rest of their lives. As ticket prices grow, these fans are becoming rarer and rarer, though they are evident in places like Busch Stadium, Dodger Stadium, Qwest Field, and a handful of others. But if you aren't playing in any of those places, you are fucked. Because that means your stadium is likely to be filled with diehards.

Die-hard fans are fans who are unhealthily obsessed with your team and you personally. Worst of all, die-hard fans are actually *proud* of this obsession, and are happy to tell anyone nearby about it. Sports are just about the only obsession people are willing to tout publicly. You don't see people wearing jerseys proclaiming their love of stamps, or young boys, or Andrew Lloyd Webber. Society would shun these people, and rightfully so. But die-hard fans are given a free pass. Why? *Fear.* These are the crazy, drunken motherfuckers who throw bottles and shit on the field. Do *you* want to be the one to tell them to stop? Me neither.

But look on the bright side. At least you aren't playing in Europe. Think the diehards here are out of their fucking gourds? The fans over there *premeditate* their stabbings. They even wear scarves, they're so batshit insane. And these are soccer fans we're talking about. Imagine how worked up they'd get over a *real* sport.

Because they pay for tickets, buy merchandise, and squander their money in other ill-advised ways, die-hard fans are the ones who help pay your salary. And you can be quite certain that they will never, ever let you forget it. But don't take my word for it . . .

---

# HEAR IT FROM A DIE-HARD FAN!

## You fucking suck!
by John Fleischmann, longtime season-ticket holder

Hey, *(your name)*!!!!!!
You fucking suck! I pay your fucking salary, cockface!
*(gives friend high five)*
FUCK YOU!!!!

---

## "Let's see *you* try it, prick!" Dealing with heckling.

During the course of your career, some people will boo you for poor play. Why do they boo? you might ask. Fans boo you so that they can feel superior. After all, you've been blessed with God-given athletic ability, something every man yearns for. You probably breezed through high school and were voted Homecoming King. I bet you were one of those cool kids that got invited to all the house parties every weekend. I bet you even got laid when you were fifteen or younger. Christ, how I would have loved that to happen. I'd have been so much more confident if I had just been able to lay some pipe back then. Instead, I stayed home on weekends and fucked my sheets. Did you know I had to resort to making love to a peach once when I was thirteen? True story. I got a peach, hollowed it out, microwaved it, and stuck my ding-dong right in it.

> **DID YOU KNOW?**
>
> Did you know John Fleischmann pays your salary? Well, don't you fucking forget it, or he'll dump a Miller Lite that's 30 percent backwash right down your shirt.

Did you ever have to do *that*, Mr. Athlete Man? Bet you didn't. I bet you had it made. I bet you think you look so cool out there on the field, don't ya? With your spiffy uniform and rugged good looks. Well, I got news for you, buddy! I'm a person, too! You think I'm just gonna take your impossible perfection lying down? HELL 2 DA NAW! BOO! BOOOOOOOO!!!

See? I've just taken out a lifetime of sexual frustration on you by belittling you for your performance. And I have to say, I do feel quite better. Thanks!

It probably won't bother you anyway. If you played for a school like Duke or Notre Dame, you're already well accustomed to fans hating your guts. Most pro athletes excel at blocking out distractions and focusing on the task at hand. Your job is made easier by the fact that most antagonistic fans have about as much creativity with words as Avril Lavigne. "Go fuck yourself" tends to lessen in impact the 9,000,000th time you've heard it.

Still, there are times when fan heckling can get to even the best of us. I'm going to play out a few hostile situations for you and show you the proper way to respond. These scenarios can happen on the road, or even at home games, where the fans can be *real* dicks.

**SCENARIO #1:** A close relative of yours, let's say your dad, has recently died, and a nearby fan has decided to hit too close to home. He shouts, "Hey, asshole, how's your dead father? Oh, yeah, he's dead! How's it feel to be fatherless, daddy's boy? DEAD DAD!"

*Your Response:* Take out a pen during a stoppage in play and transcribe the taunt word for word. Then, in the postgame press conference, read it aloud to the media. Hometown columnists hate the fans and love to portray them as drunken sociopaths. Your dead father just bought you two solid weeks of sympathy coverage. Tell him when you visit his grave!

**SCENARIO #2:** A drunken fan throws something at you.

*Your Response:* Fans usually throw things because of a poor officiating call. So grab the nearest official and use him as a human shield. It's a win-win for everyone. If you get struck by a flying object, your response can vary depending upon the object thrown. If you get mad because someone threw a marshmallow at you, you're a pussy and deserve it. If the object in question was a battery (fans in the know use nine-volts, which are effective for breaking skin and scratching corneas), be sure to note what the fan looks like and the exact seat he's sitting in. What's that? You don't have time to note all of that? Don't worry. That fan is a season-ticket holder and the nephew of a team sponsor, so you'll be seeing him again next week regardless of his behavior.

**SCENARIO #3:** Fans en masse taunt you about a lascivious Internet rumor (see chapter 8). You know, like that thing about you peeing on girls.

*Your Response:* Stop peeing on girls. That's nasty.

**SCENARIO #4:** Fans en masse taunt you about a recent arrest or drug problem.

*Your Response:* Develop a strong Christ complex. Explain your actions through a wide range of subtle excuses and defensive postures. You'll love having an excuse to become even *more* arrogant after you've made a terrible lifestyle choice.

**SCENARIO #5:** A fan taunts you by calling you by your ridiculous given name and not by your sporty, cool nickname. If you're Chipper Jones, that means hearing chants of "Lar-ry! Lar-ry!" But you don't just hear it once. No, that one fan has to shout it during the whole fucking game, every game. He chants it so incessantly, it becomes a kind of aural waterboarding. Two hours in, you find your heart beating in lockstep with the horrible chanting. Soon, you want to give up on life entirely and succumb to the traumatizing emotional numbness. You are forever changed by man's limitless appetite for cruelty. Life will never taste as sweet as it once did.

*Your Response:* Find your parents and slap the shit out of them. No one deserves to be named Larry. That's a silly name.

**SCENARIO #6:** A drunken fan has decided to storm the field and attack you!

*Your Response:* Take just a second to savor this moment, my friend. It's such a rare occasion when you can beat the living shit out of a fan with cameras present and be completely justified in doing so. Pin that white trash down and go to town. Don't let up until you can feel his sinuses caving in. That lets you know the damage is permanent!

Remember: you can only attack a fan if they come onto the field and attack you. If you go into the stands, you'll be suspended and branded as an out-of-control lunatic. It's not worth it. Unless you get in at least one solid uppercut. The high you get from destroying another man's jaw can't be topped. I've tried.

I know what you're thinking. "What about racist fans, like all the ones in Boston?" I'm glad you asked.

## Racism, hate mail, and death threats: they work for you!

Being a famous athlete means having racist white people hate you (if you're black) and having racist black people resent the extra attention paid to you (if you're white). If you're Asian or Hispanic, you'll find that most people are indifferent. Sorry, but it's true. Blacks versus whites is far and away the best rivalry in the world of racism. For its history and sheer bitterness, it can't be topped. If you need proof, just consult my handy Racial Rivalry Heat Index on the next page.

Many people will bad-mouth racism and tell you that it is an "evil thing." But these people fail to understand the practical aspects of racism. Yes, racist people are bad. Even your grandfather. But racism in and of itself is the greatest all-purpose coverall available to the professional athlete. Racism acts as a giant DETOUR sign that leads people away from things like, say, your terrible performance on the field. People will always ignore an ill-timed dropped pass if there's a chance to run and gawk at whatever giant racial bonfire has been ignited nearby. Smart athletes use racism to their advantage, and so can you.

How? Let's say you scored a touchdown and decided to perform the

# HATEROMETER

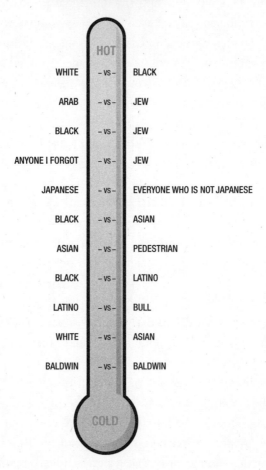

| | | |
|---|---|---|
| WHITE | – vs – | BLACK |
| ARAB | – vs – | JEW |
| BLACK | – vs – | JEW |
| ANYONE I FORGOT | – vs – | JEW |
| JAPANESE | – vs – | EVERYONE WHO IS NOT JAPANESE |
| BLACK | – vs – | ASIAN |
| ASIAN | – vs – | PEDESTRIAN |
| BLACK | – vs – | LATINO |
| LATINO | – vs – | BULL |
| WHITE | – vs – | ASIAN |
| BALDWIN | – vs – | BALDWIN |

Staggering Penis (did you take notes from chapter 2?) in the end zone, earning a fifteen-yard penalty that allows the opposing team to get close enough on the ensuing drive to convert the winning field goal at the end of the game, knocking you and your team out of the playoffs. Let's also say that you are black, or at least burnt umber. This is just the kind of selfish, me-first type of play that really gets dormant racists fired up. The next day, you walk to your mailbox and receive a poorly worded letter from an anonymous writer with a mailing address in Tennessee (75 percent of all death threats are postmarked from Tennessee), which reads:

U FUKING PIECE OF BLACK SHIT. U THIN YOU'RE SO FUKING GREAT. WE SHULD HAV FUKING KILLD U LIK THEM INDIANS AND I HOPE U FUKING DIE AND FUK THE JEWS 2

Your first inclination might be to throw this letter away. Don't. Keep it. Study it. Take note of the all caps. Racists love to write in all caps to let you know they mean business. And the spelling errors? Those are just a sign of the incredible passion with which this letter was forged. Also, notice that the racist has made sure to insult three ethnic groups even though you have nothing to do with two of them. He was going to write a manifesto one day, but since he writes so infrequently, his letter to you is pulling double duty. And racists always like to refer back to a time of racial oppression, to try to put you in your place. All in all, this is one *extremely* racist letter, one I myself would never, ever write, nor allow to be published in any sort of printed form. I can't even think thoughts that awful.

Letters like the one above are not trash. They are absolutely priceless. What better way to get people to sympathize with you, or to prove that everyone really *is* out to get you, than with this letter? Just one racist letter is all you need to tar all your critics with the same brush. Make the letter public and people will not only have compassion for you, they'll also veer way off course and start talking about big-picture shit that has absolutely nothing to do with you. Is showboating part of the black culture that white people don't understand? Are rules against dancing a way for the white man to continue to repress the black man's spirit during modern times? Is Don Imus a total fuckhead? Who cares? The important thing is that you used that little letter to ignite a racial debate that allows anyone, no matter how idiotic, to spout an opinion in a never-ending back-and-forth debate that has no possible resolution. You're off the hook!

And what do you have to thank? Racism. In fact, in the long run, your little episode has ended up doing more good than harm. After all, if it weren't for racism, would we ever seriously discuss race? Think about *that*. No, it takes a good ol'-fashioned racial controversy to get us Americans talking about issues of race and inequity in our society. If there were no racism, we'd never have to confront all the terrible damage racism has wrought upon the world. And that would be a tragedy.

Racism isn't just a diversion, it also works as a tremendous motivator. Consider this: if it weren't for racism, would Jackie Robinson be the legend that he is today? Sound kooky? I think not. If we had been a perfectly integrated society back in 1947, then Jackie Robinson wouldn't have had to endure all the terrible, racist catcalls he received from the stands. He wouldn't have gotten a single death threat, or even an ominous postcard. Without racism, Robinson never would have gotten the chance to show off the fiery dignity for which he would later be so revered. Hell, he wouldn't have even been the first black ballplayer! Jazzy Bones Harrison would have been. Think about what we would have lost. Robinson would have been just another ballplayer in a perfect social utopia free of prejudice and injustice. And that would be terrible. Jackie

Robinson was a great baseball player, but racism made him even better! It made him a pioneer! An icon!

Nothing will fire you up like a good racist taunt. I remember seeing *Mississippi Burning* once and wanting the American South napalmed out of existence. And I'm not even black! And I still feel the same way today! Racism is the best natural catalyst to help get your competitive juices flowing. There's no better adrenaline rush out there. Imagine hitting a home run. Now, imagine hitting a home run in Fenway, where they throw Sambo dolls at any black player who walks into the park. How much sweeter is it to shut those annoying fucking Massholes up once and for all?

That's racism working for you. You should send that guy in Tennessee a box of chocolates.

(Note: If you found this section racist, please mail any death threats to my home address: 15 Cherrydale Terrace, Merkin, CT, 06781. If you could send it prior to my book tour and include a handful of anthrax spores in the envelope, I would appreciate it.)

## "Sign this, asshole." Autographs and fan encounters.

The proliferation of Applebee's restaurants in this nation has created a massive demand for sports memorabilia. Restaurant decorators are in desperate need of autographed pictures, jerseys, game balls, shoes, and anything else to distract patrons from wondering what part of the chicken was used to make the boneless buffalo wings. That means everything you touch from now on turns to gold. Or, if you suck, fine pewter.

You may think signing autographs is a nice thing to do for fans. You'd be wrong. Remember: that fan asking you for your signature just paid $350 to see you play. He isn't looking for a memento. He's looking to get back in the black. Or worse, he's a professional collector. Is he wearing a plaid shirt and pleated khakis with white socks? Does he have visible dandruff? Oh, yeah, he's one of them.

The average sports memorabilia collector starts off as an aspiring serial killer, only to discover he lacks the requisite evil genius to lure teenage girls into his '87 Dodge van (with curtains on the windows!). Now he has his eyes trained on you, the pro athlete. He'll do anything to add you to his list, including harassing you wherever you go, regardless of what or whom you are doing. The autograph hound will use a variety of disguises and even send his children out in an effort to get you to sign. Yes, he has children. Incredible! For this reason, you should only sign autographs for children who have no visible adult guardian present. Baltimore is littered with kids like this. It's a great town for parental neglect.

The problem with avoiding autograph seekers altogether is that normal fans will find you mean and standoffish. In the case of Patrick Ewing, this is deadly accurate. But if, unlike Ewing, you aren't a total prick, you might want to pick a few select places to give the people what they want: an autograph they can sell on eBay for pot money. Places like next to the stands during pregame warm-ups and charity functions are a good choice. Make sure you bring a large bottle of Purell to kill all the peasant germs.

You need to do this periodically so that fans will have a good experience with you and tell others about it. It especially helps if your public image is suffering. Give an autograph to a fan and he may say, "You know, I know Michael Vick once slaughtered dogs for sport, but he was really cool when I met him!" It's amazing how one nice gesture can really sucker people like that.

On the flip side, being rude to fans can cost you. Sure, at the ballpark they'll chant your name in fawning adoration, but if you're rude to them in a moment of weakness, they will never forget it. In fact, they'll tell other people about it. As many as they can. Did you know there's a blog called garygaettiwouldntsignformesofuckhim.blogspot.com? Now you do. Word gets around.

When signing, always be sure to include your jersey number, plus a brief message to the fan in question that incorporates some sort of cliché from your chosen sport ("Dear Mikey, your mother can give me strokes anytime! Love, John Daly"). Your signature should be fluid and distinctive. This will be hard to master, since you are part of the generation raised on computers and have handwriting that resembles an EKG monitor. Check out some of the signatures below for a good guide on how to sign.

(John Elway)

(Gilbert Arenas)

(Barry Bonds)

Dear John,
Don't ever ask
me to sign a
golf ball again.
It's too fucking
small.

(Arnold Palmer)

*Chris Simms*

(Chris Simms)

X

(Johnny Damon)

One last thing: you can refuse an autograph request if the fan does not have a pen. Even kids. If they can't be bothered to remember a goddamn Sharpie, fuck 'em.

- - - - - - - - - - - - - - - - - - - - - - - ✂

### Clippable Motivational Slogan!

*Remember: we're in this business for the fans. Largely because they're so easy to bleed dry. God, I just fucking hate them so MUCH.*

— MARGE SCHOTT

# HEAR IT FROM A MASCOT!

## I don't think you understand just how fucking hot it is in here
### by The Phillie Phanatic

I'm a mascot. Yes, I know you find this inherently funny. I get paid to wear a ridiculous outfit and then go and start pretend fights with umpires. I get why people don't take me seriously. I get why people find it humorous when a five-year-old comes up and head-butts me in the nuts. Ha ha. Hysterical. If it weren't happening to me, I'd laugh too. I know you pros don't think that my job is all that difficult compared to yours.

But I don't think you understand just how fucking hot it is in here.

I'm not kidding. Being inside this outfit is like landing on the surface of Venus. I mean, look at this thing. Fucking look at it. It's made out of 90 percent Styrofoam and 10 percent regenerated cellulosic fiber. Just screams breathable, doesn't it? MRI machines are less constrictive than this god-awful piece of shit. I smell like a tackle box when I take it off.

Don't get me wrong. I think it's bullshit that baseball players have to wear gray polyester pants in the summer. That doesn't look like fun. But dude, I work in a fucking coffin. You have a dugout to go to for cooling off. You get a bench to rest on. Shit, you even get free Gatorade. Me? I gotta stay out on the field in the sun the whole goddamn game. And field temperatures in Philly can hit 120 in August. Do I get water? Do I even get ice chips to suck on? No. Sometimes I hallucinate. Just yesterday, I saw Jimmy Rollins turn into a Creamsicle. That shit ain't right.

(*continued on next page*)

And, on top of that, I have to *dance*. That's right. I have to remain in constant, gyrating motion during the course of the entire game. If I stop once, just once, everyone in the crowd boos and throws peanut shells at me. It's as if they're shooting at my feet. Oh, and I can't take my headpiece off either. No, no, we'd hate to ruin the magic for little Johnny out in the stands, watching the game with his father on the one weekend a month Daddy has visitation privileges.

And God forbid I fart in this thing. Seriously, one time I farted in the first inning of a game of a doubleheader and nearly died of methane poisoning four hours later. This thing is like a fart incubator. Farts can't leave here. They can't disperse into the air like a standard fart. Even the most innocuous "Psst! I got a secret!" fart has punishing long-term staying power here. I served in Iraq and was subject to numerous germ warfare drills. And it never got as bad as the shit that goes on in here.

I can't even scratch my nuts. Yeah, I see you guys grabbing your junk during the game. Christ, how I'd love to do that. Half the game, my balls are stuck on the roof of my taint. What sweet relief it would be to just pry them off and let them hang back down. But no, if I scratch my balls, suddenly I'm some perv who wants to molest kids. Jesus. None of these people have had to walk around for two hours squeezing their own testicles between their legs with every alternate step. They have no idea what kind of suffering I go through in here. None. I hate them.

## Because sports alone aren't that interesting: gamblers.

For the average fan, the problem with being emotionally invested in a team is that emotional investments have no tangible payoff. Yeah, your home team winning a championship is a nice feeling. But let's face it: you gotta wade through a whole lot of shit just to get to that one moment. It

## "Don't You People Have Homes?"

Even if I could scratch my nuts, I can't. There's a sixteen-inch layer of padding directly in front of my crotch, and I'm wearing gloves. A little nut scratch does nothing for me. I gotta retract my arm out of the sleeve and then go down into the outfit to hit pay dirt. But then I got my right arm hanging limp on the costume, and then people stare at me like, "What's wrong with Mr. Phanatic's arm? Did he have a stroke?"

There's more. See this horn? You think that's where my mouth is, right? Wrong! My eyes see out of it. That's right, they put the eyehole at the end of a very long tube at the center of my face. Why not just fuse my pupils together and be done with it? I've now named all the pores on the bridge of my nose. This one's named Jim.

I don't even know why the Phillies have a mascot. Kids are terrified of me. What kid isn't going to shit his pants at the sight of a green space alien with blue eyebrows rushing in to give him a hug? I may as well carry a cleaver around with me wherever I go.

So when you see me dancing out there, just remember: I may not be a pro athlete like you, but I am an athlete. A big, green, sweaty athlete who needs to rub his entire body with prescription Certain Dri prior to each game. Remember that I'm constantly on the verge of pulling a Korey Stringer out there. Be nice to me. Take pity. Pat me on my poofy tail. I need the support. And fresh towels.

can take years of suffering through any number of pointless regular season games and entire seasons of rebuilding. And, even then, it's never a guarantee your favorite team will win it all. Especially if that team is the Minnesota Vikings. Fucking Vikings. There's only one thing that can make the eternal wait somewhat tolerable: the excitement of losing money.

# Men with Balls

Why do sports fans gamble? It's a self-esteem thing. If a fan places a bet on a team and that team wins, he gets to fancy himself a genius. He can even tell people of his little victory and offer gambling advice until he becomes as insufferable as Sarah Jessica Parker, which is what all gamblers do. You, the professional athlete, get to experience the glory of winning games at the highest level of competition. Gambling is a fan's way of becoming indirectly involved in the outcome of a game, and then experiencing a seedy, bastardized version of that glory. And what better way to try to mimic the thrill of winning a Super Bowl than by placing a $10 wager on it at the MGM Grand sports book, then watching the game in an overcrowded, smoky lounge surrounded by eighty-year-olds who are hoping to die before facing the next month without their lost Medicare stipend? It's a pretty ingenious line of thinking.

The other purpose gambling serves is to get fans excited about games they otherwise wouldn't care about. Remember, the reason for being a sports fan is to distract oneself from having to think, or from having to live life. By gambling on more sports, fans have an excuse to *watch* more of them, thereby blocking out an even greater portion of the real world. And this is good, because the real world is fucked up.

Now, most gamblers lose. Big. Most of them accrue a pile of debt that not only bankrupts them but also bankrupts the family members who try to bail them out. But if you think that stops a gambler from being a smug asshole, you're wrong. Extremely wrong.

You see, the more a gambler loses in cold hard cash, the more he gains in supposed gambling experience. This is why you'll hear gamblers say things like, "Four and a half? *Pfft.* Vegas clearly has no clue how to set the line for this game." They have no better feel for gambling than you or I. But that lost money allows them to *pretend* that they do, to pretend they've actually learned something to change the outcome the next go-round. And that's all that matters. Vegas has long thrived on people dumb enough to believe they can outsmart Vegas. And, as long as morons roam the Earth, it will continue to do so.

During your career, you may be approached by bookies and gamblers looking to wrangle useful betting information out of you. You can usually spot one of them from a mile away. Is he wearing a baseball hat pulled way down? Are his fingernails chewed down to disgusting little nubs? Does he have psoriasis? Bingo. That's a gambler.

Nothing like Kenny Rogers described, is he?

Don't give him any information. You could be violating the most sacred rule of your league, which is to never become involved in gambling on your sport. Everyone else can gamble on your sport, but you cannot. Why? Because you could ruin the integrity of your sport, which would, in turn, ruin the integrity of *gambling* on your sport. If gamblers knew your sport was fixed, they'd stop watching it, which would hugely impact league revenues. Your league can't afford to have you gamble on games when they have so much invested in fans who gamble on games. You'd be breaking the circle of trust.

Many players have given their reputations a black eye by colluding with gamblers. The 1919 Black Sox conspired to rig the World Series and paid a heavy price. They became the most notorious team of all time and even had movies made about them. Hell, no one remembers the 1919 Reds, who actually won the Series. The 1919 Black Sox became true immortals. You don't want to have that happen, do you? Look at Shoeless Joe Jackson. The guy had *no shoes,* for fuck's sake. Nor do you want to end up like Pete Rose, who was banned from baseball both for gambling and for having persistent, terrible BO. It's best if you avoid the whole gambling scene altogether. You don't want to know about stuff like parlays and vigorishes anyway. That's a douchebag's vocabulary.

Besides, traditional sports gambling is becoming a thing of the past. Fantasy sports are the real wave of the future.

## A more interactive way to not be active: fantasy sports.

The beauty of fantasy sports is that they render real sports all but irrelevant. That's why they're called "fantasy" leagues. Sure, real leagues like the NFL are cool. But imagine a league called the League of Extraordinary Bearfuckers, with teams like Fred's Cornholio, Stuart Scott's Lazy Eye, I Heart Vag, The Eskimo-Raping Shitheels, and John Cafferty & the Beaver Brown Beaver. *That's* the league fans like me fantasize about. And fantasy leagues help make that fantasy a *real* fantasy!

Fantasy leagues superimpose an entirely new game over the game you currently play. Instead of rooting for their home team to win, fans can now root for your kicker to kick a field goal of forty yards or longer, while also hoping that your running back is held to sixty yards or less. Don't you see how much better that is than just rooting for normal games? By creating an entirely fictional sport dependent upon the arbitrary statistical results of a real sport, fans have an opportunity to become even more divorced from reality. Take me. I rarely answer to the name Drew Magary anymore. My preferred identity is that of HotCarl76, and that's far more rewarding. HotCarl76 owns a football team. Drew Magary owns three tracksuits and a ColecoVision. He's also a peachfucker. Who would you rather be?

Fantasy sports do present one problem for you, the player. And that is that fans have become even more emotionally dependent on your on-field performance. The average fan loves to bitch that he could run your team far better than current management. The problem with fantasy sports is how often they prove that fan wrong. There's a real danger here. Many fans have mundane lives, but if they can maintain the illusion that they are smarter than the general manager of a professional baseball or football team, that's enough to sustain their existence. If it turns out they can't even run a goddamn fantasy squad without it sinking to the bottom of the ocean, what hope is there in life? Disappointment can transform into homicidal tendencies so easily.

In fact, you'd be surprised at how fantasy leagues help turn fans into even bigger assholes than management. They'll be far quicker to place blame for any failure squarely on your shoulders. They'll be more eager to trade or cut you. And they'll happily bad-mouth you to anyone within fifty feet. Thought Bill Polian was a ballbuster? He's nothing compared to me. If I see Shaun Alexander in an airport, I'm gonna fucking stab him.

By performing poorly, you're messing up the idyllic imaginary life of many fans. You're killing the fantasy, so to speak. And the psychological ramifications of that can be bloody and horrifying. So, if a fan walks up to

## Deeply Penetrating the Numbers

# –$578,903

The cumulative lifetime winnings of the average professional handicapper total –$578,903. They are called handicappers because their bookies have handicapped them.

you in the parking lot and says, "I need some TDs out of you this week, my man!" you'd best run. Run as far the fuck away as possible. That guy will gut you like a fish if there's no one else around. And if you're Daunte Culpepper, who followed up a thirty-nine-TD year in 2004 with just six TDs in 2005, I have to say you deserve it. You worthless bust.

## Chapter 6

# The Best and Worst Part of Athletic Superstardom

## Women

### They love you for you, conditionally! Know your woman!

For you, the pro athlete, a woman can often be a ticking time bomb. Unfortunately, I mean this as a metaphor, and not in the literal sense. If women actually detonated, there'd be no problem. Provided you aren't in the area at the time of the blast. But, in reality, dealing with women is the trickiest part of your new life. There's a delicate balance here. On the one hand, you want to extract as much sweet, delicious poontang from your exalted status as humanly possible. On the other, you want to avoid any long-term consequences resulting from such encounters, including bad relationships, unwanted offspring, low cash flow, surprise bouts of syphilis, etc. If you do it right, you'll have George Clooney's life. If you fuck it up, you'll have Brad Pitt's life, complete with seventeen undisciplined children and a cyanide pill as your only way out. Which women out there will take the least bucks for your bang? Here are some examples.

**HOOKER.** The great thing about hookers is that, unlike normal women, all the costs involved are clearly stated up front. You don't have to buy a hooker a canary yellow diamond necklace if you get caught screwing around with a different one. You're paying for sex instead of paying for everything *but* the sex, and that's a huge cost savings in the long run. Plus, they'll do whatever you ask. You don't have to spend weeks trying to introduce the idea of anal. They're cool like that.

The other thing hookers offer is discretion. No hooker who wants to keep her client base is going to go blabbing to the press about all your bizarre sexual proclivities. Do you enjoy bringing random immigrant grocers into your sexual encounters? Best to entrust that sort of thing to a hooker. The only loose lips they have are the ones below the garter belt.

The problem with making love to a hooker is that it eliminates the joy of acceptance. Speaking personally, there's no better turn-on than someone legitimately wanting to have sex with me. It engorges the ego and the penis simultaneously. Getting a hooker also means missing out on the thrill of the hunt. It's never a legitimate score you can brag about. And I find that 98 percent of the joy of sex comes from being able to brag about it the next day.

Should you wish to procure a hooker for the evening, simply hang out in your team's hotel lobby. Hookers follow the rules of supply and demand. Hotel lobbies are full of athletes, businessmen, and government officials who are in constant need of coldhearted, anonymous sex. If, for some reason, this fails, consult the back section of your town's local free progressive newspaper. Find the hooker that best suits your needs, and call the number listed. Ask for "full bodywork." In hooker lingo, this means intercourse. Yay, intercourse! And always double-check for penii to make sure you didn't get a she-male by accident. Happens all the time. LaWanda, if you're out there, I apologize for kneeing you in the groin like that.

**GROUPIE.** Groupies fall into any number of subcategories. You've got your skanky hos, your Fly Girls, and any number of three-hundred-pound women hanging outside the arena in outfits the size of a linen coaster. It's tough distinguishing hookers from groupies. After all, both are whores in a sense. The thing that sets groupies apart from hookers is that groupies will have sex with you for free the night you meet them. That certainly makes them alluring, but they aren't giving themselves to you just because they like you. Groupies have motives that will remain unclear to you until *after* you have slept with them. Some will simply want to brag about having sex with you. It's a way of boosting their superficial self-esteem, while deep down doing the exact opposite. Other groupies will hope that a sexual encounter with you is a first step on the road to a potentially lucrative divorce and/or paternity suit.

If you're going to take the plunge with a groupie, I recommend doing it on the road and away from the hotel room in which you currently reside. When you are finished, burn any evidence of your sexual encounter to destroy any leftover seminal residue. And I suggest leaving immediately when you are finished. Most groupies do not pass the Morning Test. In fact, by the morning, your groupie will probably look like a prairie dog that got run over by a semi. It's like Chili's: "Get in. Get out. Get on with your life."

**STRIPPER.** Why have sex with a regular woman for free when you can pay to watch a stripper? Strippers and athletes go together like Carnie Wilson and pancake batter. Hell, Pacman Jones sacrificed his entire career because he couldn't give them up. Smart move. Yes, there's nothing quite like walking into a strip club and spending $20 every fifteen minutes to have a stripper tell you about her dream of one day working with animals, then staggering out at 3:00 a.m. to go jerk off in a back alley. Strip clubs truly are magical places, where you can mingle with any number of asshole junior analysts from Morgan Stanley while maxing out your credit card on $50 hamburgers and $500 dry humps in the VIP lounge. Shangri-la, I tell you.

Strippers are smart, savvy women who know how to charm a man without actually having sex with him. So tread lightly. That girl grinding against you in the corner booth doesn't actually like your shirt. She's just delivering one of the many tip-inducing compliments she learned at l'Académie Strip-Teaseuse in Quebec. She, in fact, fancies herself an ultra-postmodern feminist: a woman who combines smart business sense with a smoking hot body to earn a cool $5,000 a night giving you a wicked case of blueballs. She enjoys having power over you. It's her way of asserting her female dominance for the brief period during the day when she isn't being sexually harassed by the club owner or being accused by her bounty hunter boyfriend of being a no-good whore. It's the kind of women's lib Gloria Steinem always dreamed of.

If you want to date a stripper, you have to put yourself on equal ground. Never hit on her in the club. It'll make you look weak and creepy. *Trust me*. Never works. Instead, buy her a shot and ask her if she'd like to hit a club after her shift is over. Once out of the club, she'll shed her professional superficiality and engage you with her normal, female superficiality. Turn on the charm from there and you're in for a night of real, nonpantomimed sex.

If you're lazy and want strippers that double as hookers (and who doesn't?), I strongly suggest catching a flight to Montreal. Strippers there will do the pas de deux on your beignet for a mere pittance.

# The Best and Worst Part of Athletic Superstardom

(Note: Clip out the above section and bring it in to your local strip club before 3:00 p.m. to receive $3 off the $20 nonalcoholic beverage of your choice.)

**ACTRESS/MODEL/SINGER.** It's easy to get a date with an actress, model, or singer. Simply have your agent contact her agent, and then give *OK!* magazine a call and sell them the photography rights for your intimate evening out. There's no more spontaneous way to meet someone.

But beware! An actress is a career woman who will only couple with you as a means of enhancing her celebrity profile. A famous woman can always increase her Q rating by fifty points simply by nailing another famous man. You're a résumé builder for her: a stepping-stone to an even higher echelon of celebrity. And no amount of attention will ever be enough to satisfy her undying need for the spotlight, or bring her absentee father back. Once she has a chance to hook up with someone who's more famous than you, she'll happily kick your C-list ass to the curb. Not so much fun to be on the other side of Relationship Control Tilt-A-Whirl, is it? Like Tony Parker, you now occupy a level of importance in your woman's world somewhere between publicist and handbag.

**JAILBAIT.** Is she over eighteen, or over twelve in Louisiana? Are you sure? Buy a black light and scan the shit out of her driver's license. You wouldn't believe what kids can do with computers these days. Also, does she twirl her hair and snap her gum a lot? Does she spend the majority of her time text-messaging? Does she like Maroon 5? Is her bed surrounded by nothing but Pound Puppies and a golden picture frame that says "Daddy's Little Girl"? Did R. Kelly hit it? Was Mark Chmura at the same party where you two met? Abort! Abort! Abort!

**FEMALE ATHLETE.** Does she play tennis or beach volleyball? Nice. That's a real nice job. The great thing about dating female athletes is that you two will be able to relate to each other on a professional level. Hell, you can even work out together. And chicks who work out are *hot*. Especially if they wear those little spandex hot pants and do those little lunge exercises and holy shit my pants just exploded. The problem with dating a female athlete is that girls who are way into sports are far more annoying than girls who don't give a shit about them. Don't believe me? Just you watch. Don't say I didn't warn you. Enjoy having nothing to enjoy by yourself.

**NORMAL, SANE WOMAN.** Sometimes, you hit the jackpot and encounter a lovely, normal woman who loves you for the person you are. She's gorgeous without being haughty about it. She challenges you, but only because she genuinely believes in your potential. She even cooks. The truth is, the majority of women out there are perfectly well-adjusted, wonderful people. The problem is that you have become so conditioned to distrust and objectify women thanks to this section that you will find a way to mess it up. Serves you right, pig.

> ## DID YOU KNOW?
> The average woman uses three times more words per day than the average man. Therefore, I strongly suggest you avoid average women.

## From a thousand feet away, they don't look like transvestites: cheerleaders.

Almost every pro football and basketball team has a group of cheerleaders (except for the Packers, due to the scarcity of attractive female Wis-

# HEAR IT FROM A GROUPIE!

## Damn, you look fine
### by Shanna Franklin

Oooooh!

My, my, my, my goodness.

Damn.

You look fine, boy.

Yeah, you definitely had it goin' on out there. Runnin' and jumpin' and flexin' that little tushie of yours. You like what I'm wearing? I wore it just for you tonight. It's not easy getting into a dress made entirely of vulcanized rubber. Yeah, I saw you looking at me in the stands. What, you think I can't see? Ha ha! You're feisty. I like that.

*(bites lip)*

Mmm.

Shit.

Listen, baby, why don't we go somewhere and talk? Just you and me. How about that empty stairwell over there?

*(takes you to empty stairwell and rides you like a carousel)*

WHOA. Seriously, hold up. That was so fucking *real*. I've never felt like that before with anyone. *Anyone.* Baby, that's only the beginning. There's so much more I can do for you. You want more? You want *all* of this?

*(You nod.)*

Call me the next time you're in town, baby.

*(You call the next time you're in town.)*

*(continued on next page)*

Holy shit! Oh my God, you make love like no other, baby. Can you see my legs shaking in these thigh-high pleather boots? My legs don't shake like that for no one else. Swear. To. God. You're different. You're special. Do you think I'm special?

*(You nod.)*

Tell me there's no other, baby.

*(You tell her there's no other.)*

You want more of this?

*(You nod.)*

Well, you just gonna have to wait. I don't give it out like Halloween candy. I'm a lady, you know. I'll see you soon, baby.

*(Two months later)*

Baby, I got something to tell you. I'm pregnant. And I'm having the baby. Don't try and talk me out of it. Go ahead and try and talk me out of it. Go on. Try. HOW DARE YOU TRY TO TALK ME OUT OF HAVING THIS BABY? I thought you were special, and now you want to go runnin' like a little punk bitch? Why don't you stand up and be a man? No, no, no, see, a real man would be loving, and supportive, and would provide for his family. Oh, yes, I am family now. I'm as much family to you as your mama. Don't you turn away from me! Don't you walk out that door!

*(You walk out the door.)*

*(Two months later)*

I miss you, baby. Can't we just be friends? No pressure. No sex getting

consinites). Why baseball doesn't have them is unknown. If any game could *benefit* from the presence of large-breasted remedial nursing students dancing around in outfits the size of a Wet-Nap, it's baseball. After a forty-five-minute inning, everyone could use some titties. Even the children. But smart ideas have never been baseball's forte, so you'll have to do without if you're a big leaguer.

in the way of things. I'd just like to see if we can have a good relationship. You know, for little baby *(your name)* Jr. Do you like that name? I named him after you. C'mon over, baby. Let's see if we can work things out.

*(You come over and have sex.)*

What'chu mean, you have to go? No, no, no, we are *here* now. We are in this. *You* are in this. Don't you walk out that door, you gutless mother-fucker!

*(throws lamp)*

*(Four months later)*

What'chu mean, YOU GOT ANOTHER GIRL PREGNANT?! Well, who the fuck is she? Did she name her child after you like I did? She did? Well then, you got yourself one big confusing-ass problem then, don't you? I'm not changing the name. And we're getting married. Oh, yes we are. Or would you like me to go on *Oprah* and tell the whole world you ain't noth-ing but a fuckin' dog?

*(You get married.)*

Baby, I'm so happy. We're gonna have a great life together. I'm gonna be a great wife. I'll stay home, take care of the kids. We'll get old and sit on the porch together, laughin' at our grandkids. It's gonna be so magic. Baby, I love you. Do you love me?

Do you?

No?

GET THE FUCK OUT OF THIS HOUSE.

Now, for the rest of you, your cheerleading squad may have some sort of empowering, euphemistic nickname to disguise its true purpose: the Knicks City Dancers, the Laker Girls, the Jacksonville 65 Percent Meth-Free Jazz Hands Ensemble, etc. Don't be fooled. If it's female, and it's allowed to roam temporarily on your field of play, then by God it's a cheerleader. They are meant to be ogled creepily. So feel free to ogle away. Be sure to stare one or two seconds longer than is normally appropriate (appropriate ogling time being 1.8 seconds). They're used to it.

In recent years, many teams have increased the sex appeal of their cheerleading squads in order to sell calendars, swimsuit videos, and videos about the making of the first swimsuit video. Of course, the cheerleaders receive no royalties from the sale of these products. But they do help serve an important altruistic purpose: to create a team-branded mental archive of fresh masturbation material for fans of all ages.

Cheerleaders are an interesting breed. Yes, they're way hot, especially when encased in a two-inch layer of high-gloss enamel foundation/body glitter. But they also make *fabulous* drug mules. And, above all, they love themselves some pro athlete manmeat. You, my friend, have something every cheerleader wants: a one-way ticket out of earning minimum wage, living in a group house, and being trapped in a career of semisexual indentured servitude. Being a cheerleader means having to train twelve hours a day to perform three forty-five-second dance routines that no one will pay attention to, then spending the entire off-season shuttling between any number of hotel sales manager conferences and Bar Mitzvahs. So it's understandable that they might want to latch on to you and hold on with the grip of a thousand starving condors.

But beware! Most teams discourage fraternizing between employees (see your team's "Don't Shit Where You Eat" educational pamphlet, located in the lobby of your practice facility). Technically, you and your team's cheerleaders are both employed by the team, which makes dating a risky endeavor. This might seem odd, since you train in separate areas. And you never actually work together. Nevertheless, cheerleaders are off-limits. Sure, it's tempting to offer them a bump of coke to let them suck you raw. But you should refrain. You don't want to break up with someone who also has an ID pass to the locker room.

If you must flirt with cheerleaders, be selective. Most cheerleading squads have a similar makeup. There's the head cheerleader. She's the one shrieking directions to all the other girls and looks ten years too old to be a cheerleader. Avoid this woman. You don't want to know how she got to the top of the cheerleading "pyramid," so to speak. Lots of passive-aggressive behavior involved.

Try to aim for the freshest faces on the squad. They're the ones who exhibit genuine enthusiasm and have yet to realize that being a professional cheerleader does not make one a celebrity. Go ahead and give them a quick smile from the bench. If they smile back, you may be in for a solid season and a half of high-quality eye-banging, give or take (the average cheerleader squad turnover rate is four months). This in itself can be quite fun. You can even involve them in your showboating mime routines. Chad Johnson once faked proposing to Cincinnati Ben-Gal (yes, that's the name of the Bengals cheerleaders) Daphne in a 2005 game against the Colts. You know he totally hit that later on.

You may also find yourself flirting with a lesbian cheerleader. To this, I would again caution you. In February 2006, witnesses said two members of the Carolina Panthers cheerleading squad were having smoking hot girl sex in a Tampa nightclub bathroom. Sounds arousing, right? I suggest not exploring the story any further. The picture in your mind is so much hotter than what the Smoking Gun dug up.

## How to make love like a pro.

Now that you're a pro, you'll find that expectations in the bedroom are as high as the ones you encounter on the field. Like fans, women will enter into congress with you expecting to be positively dazzled. They'll have plenty of preconceived notions of what bedroom relations with you will be like: a stunning display of sexual acrobatics that leaves no position or orifice unexplored, with trumpets blaring and Chinese firecrackers bursting in the background, and maybe Phil Rizzuto appearing in a cameo. That's a big fantasy to live up to, given the general difficulty of simply maintaining an erection. So I suggest getting your female counterpart drunk. I mean, totally fucking blotto. If she can't remember anything, then she can't remember that banging you was about as special as having Ramen noodles for dinner.

But let's say you're going out with a girl who isn't all that into drinking. First off: what a tightass. Second, you need a plan to ensure that you're performing some serious penile sorcery when the clock strikes mating time. The key is variety. I've gathered positions and techniques inspired by some of the biggest names in sports to get your ladyfriend screaming like a Tom Jones audience member. And now, I present them to you in this handy and somewhat titillating study guide. As Abraham Simpson said, think of me when you're having the best sex of your life.

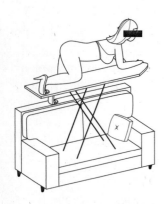

**THE YAO MING.** First, place an ironing board on a chair or a sofa. Then, using heavy twine, lash the structure together to make a crude scaffold. Place your partner atop the structure and have at it, doling out gracious compliments as you go.

**THE BILL PARCELLS.** Lift gunt. Insert yourself. Release gunt. Repeat as necessary.

**THE KOBE BRYANT.** Bend partner over couch or credenza. Finish. Flee Colorado.

**THE BRIAN BOSWORTH.** Sit your woman down on the bed. Tell her she's in for the ride of her life. Dim the lights. Turn up *The Best of Otis*

*Redding.* Retire to the bathroom and return in your finest silk robe. Pop open a bottle of Veuve Clicquot. Fall asleep.

**THE MARK FIDRYCH.** Have mind-blowing sex the first time out and terrible sex every time thereafter.

**THE DAN MARINO.** Take your partner to dinner at the finest Japanese restaurant in town. Ask for the *omakase* dinner. Shock your ladyfriend by being conversant in Japanese with waitstaff. Take her to a four-star Broadway show. Establish an incredible rapport. Talk about your dreams. Share an embarrassing story or two. Make her laugh a surprising amount. Take her home. Tell her you had a really great evening. Lean in for a kiss. Get the door slammed in your face. Repeat for seventeen more dates.

**THE ANDRE AGASSI.** Make love to your woman on a bed, on the carpet, on the bathroom tile, and on a beach. Declare yourself a master of all fucking surfaces.

**THE KEN GRIFFEY JR.** Bring your woman to the very precipice of an earth-shattering, lip-quivering orgasm. Pull up with a cramp. Blame the hotel room massage staff. Try again at the Waldorf-Astoria with the exact same results.

**THE ALEX RODRIGUEZ.** Ask her if she orgasmed. Continue wondering what you did wrong.

**THE PHIL MICKELSON.** Get cocky during intercourse and attempt the notoriously difficult "Rodeo" maneuver. Get bucked off your partner, fall off the bed, and shoot your load out a window, shattering the windshield of a nearby helicopter, which then plummets into the middle of the freeway, killing everyone on board, along with numerous innocent motorists on the ground. React with a dopey, shit-eating grin.

**THE BABE RUTH.** Point at her vagina. Insert penis. Bring her to orgasm in three seconds. Light a cigar. Eat a hot dog.

**THE ALLEN IVERSON.** Start making love immediately. When she asks you about foreplay, give her a look of disgust.

**THE '86 MET.** Bring partner into bedroom. Lay her down gently. Tell her to close her eyes. Bring midget, Girl Scout troop, and panda bear into the room. Kill the lights. Crank Foghat at the highest volume possible. Take out bullwhip and can of Reddi-wip. Snort line. Put on Indian headdress. See what happens.

**THE CURT SCHILLING.** Nail her. Blog about it.

**THE TED WILLIAMS.** Bring her to orgasm. Spend the next eighty years lecturing everyone within earshot about how you were able to do it.

All of these techniques will help you establish a solid reputation as a freewheeling dynamo when the lights go out. You should be able to parlay that sexual goodwill into increasingly hot and freaky encounters with any number of attractive partners. With any luck, you'll amass so much sexual experience that you'll cease being a normal human being and transform into a soulless stalker constantly in search of the next fresh body to use for depraved, empty acts of pleasure. Regular sex simply won't be enough for you. You'll develop all sorts of bizarre fetishes and masochistic tendencies to compensate for the lack of real emotional love and support in your life.

It's the kind of life every man dreams of. Provided, of course, that you're single and able to do all these things. You *are* single, aren't you?

## What? You married your high school sweetheart?

You idiot! How could you do that? You've known you had potential professional athletic ability since you were a preteen. Yet you still married little Stacy Jo anyway? You jackass.

Oh, you love her? Well, of course you love her! No shit, Romeo! Ninth-graders will fall in love with anything! One time a girl in my class helped me pick up my pencil box after it fell out of my bag. I stalked her for the next three years. Love at that age isn't *real*. It's far too spontaneous and natural. You're an adult now, buddy. Love should be a calculated emotion that fluctuates depending upon certain matters of practicality. Don't you know how the real world works, you naive little child?

Have you even been to Miami yet? Good fucking Lord. The women there are so hot, they had to fill the rest of the city with gay Cuban men just to ease the sexual tension. And you got married without even paying a visit? Idiot!

Some of us depend on athletes for good vicarious living, you know. Some of us might be stuck at home with the kid all day, in desperate need of hearing sordid stories about cocaine-fueled orgies and baby-oil-filled wading pool excursions. You can't just ruin our fun like that, you fucking dick. Okay? It's not right. What about *my* needs? What about making sure *I'm* happy by going out and engaging in a pattern of self-destructive behavior that I can admire from afar while still retreating to the stability of a loving family at the end of the day? Ever think about that? Huh?

I can't believe how selfish you are.

You know what's gonna happen, don't you? You're gonna be surrounded by single teammates who are sexually active and vocal about being so. They're gonna tell you shit you won't even begin to fathom. Ever nail a Hawaiian Tropic girl on the diving board at the Shore Club? Well, they have. And they'll be happy to tell you all about it. Does Miss "I Sent You Care Packages All Through College!" do that? Good God, no. So enjoy wasting the best part of being a pro athlete. I hope your good Christian marriage and fifty years of bland, missionary position intercourse are worth it.

Asshat.

## Deeply Penetrating the Numbers

# 10,000

Basketball legend Wilt Chamberlain claimed to have slept with more than 10,000 women. What you may not know is that Chamberlain also had intercourse with well over 500 men. Chamberlain was not gay, nor was he bisexual. These were simply men who ended up getting fucked in the crossfire.

## "You're what?" How you knocked that girl up.

Wondering how it is that someone you've known for a grand total of one hour can come to play a critical, unwanted role in the rest of your life? Well, did you know that pro athletes are more prone to impregnating women than men in any other profession? It's true. And it's not just because athletes are often irresponsible and lack good judgment. No, physiology also plays a vital role. Let me show you just how God creates those little bastards we call children, and why you're more vulnerable to having them than most.

As an athlete, you possess a penis much larger than the average man's. As such, there's a good chance that your monstrous appendage could, in fact, penetrate the cervix and deliver sperm right into the fallopian tubes of your conquest. This gives your sperm an incredible head start in the marathon race to reach a woman's egg. Now, instead of having to go cross-country to get some hot membrane-penetrating action, your boys are just a hop, skip, and jump away. This detailed, anatomical diagram shows you the depth of your penetration:

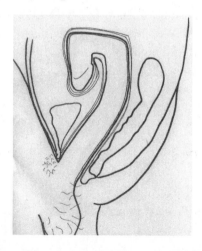

If your penis is even bigger than the one depicted here, there is a chance that you could skewer your sexual partner completely, like a human corn dog. Once your boys hit pay dirt, there's no going back. You couldn't talk that girl into an abortion even if you convinced her you were Satan himself. Prevention is the key. And you know what that means: birth control.

Now, the most effective form of birth control out there, obviously, is the **birth control pill.** Birth control pills are easily identifiable. They usually come in a circular blister pack and are located on top of your lady's dresser. No doubt you've dialed the pills around once or twice just for shits and giggles, pretending like it's some kind of kickass submarine depth-charge dial. This blister pack is embossed with a graphic design that looks similar to the chick on the Emmy statue, back arched and head tilted toward the sky. It's a design that communicates a woman's temporary freedom from the punishing lifelong agony of childbirth and child-rearing. You'll also find a corporate yet feminine name for the drug somewhere on the pack, such as Yasmin, or Juvistop, or Babykill.

The pill is touted by many as being 100 percent effective. The only problem, of course, is that you have to rely *on the woman* to take it. Which makes it all but worthless as a dependable contraceptive for you, Mr. Potential Lifelong Benefactor. So what other forms of birth control are there that *you* control? Well, that **IUD** you bought doesn't work for dudes. Trust me. I gave it a whirl. Not fun.

In fact, most every form of birth control is dependent upon the woman for its application. The pill, the **patch**, the **diaphragm**, the **injection**, the **custom-built vaginal bear trap**: all are subject to the whims of a woman you probably do not trust. Shit.

What does that leave? Looks like you're stuck with the good ol'-fashioned **condom**. The condom, while annoying, does have its benefits. Sure, a condom makes sex feel like a handjob from Madge the Palmolive woman (Look, Madge! I soaked!). But it does help protect you from nasty infectious diseases like AIDS and more. I suggest you keep a three-pack of condoms on your person at all times, even while bathing. Also, be sure to pre-tear each wrapper for easy access and less fumbling. And no flavored condoms. If you haven't figured out yet that those are for the gay community, you may be beyond help. And no neon condoms either. Sure, it's fun to imagine yourself as some sort of sexual Darth Vader, but more often than not it just makes your dick look silly. And sex is not supposed to be silly.

But whatever you do, use that condom! If you don't, your big fat cock is almost certain to be used as God intended it, and not as *you* intended it. The result?

## Only eighteen years to go: how to handle pesky baby mommas.

More than 60 percent of athletes have baby mommas, with NFL running back Travis Henry accounting for 40 percent of that 60 percent. Your baby momma is not only an incredible pain in the ass, but she's also part of a group of people solely responsible for the decline of American global hegemony as we know it. It's true. I skimmed over it in a Pat Buchanan book once. You see, the steady erosion of American values and the treasured American can-do spirit can be traced directly to the steady rise in single-parent families. Without a father to guide them, many children lack the love and support to develop into smart, responsible members of society. And who are these single parents recklessly raising children without a gentle, caring dad around? You got it: baby mommas. They not only harass you, but also hurt your child by failing to provide any sort of useful father figure. And that is tragic.

Try as you might to avoid your baby momma(s), dealing with her (them) is inevitable, especially if you lacked the foresight to rig a court-ordered DNA test. You're locked in now, just like Tom Brady. What will the monthly phone call from your baby momma be like? Read below for a glimpse into your future. And remember: don't call her. She'll call you!

> *(phone rings)*
>
> **You:** Uh, hello?
>
> **Baby Momma:** Is this you?
>
> **You:** Uh . . . no. It's not me. This is . . . uh . . . Priest Holmes.
>
> **BM:** I know it's you, so you can quit faking it any time now.
>
> **You:** Oh. Oh, it's you! I'm sorry. But I've been getting lots of sales calls from Verizon recently, and I've been trying like heck to discourage them.
>
> **BM:** Why can't you just return my calls? Am I really so horrible that you have to avoid me at all costs?
>
> *(five minutes of silence)*
>
> **You:** I'm sorry.
>
> *(five minutes of silence)*
>
> **You:** So, how's little Jimmy doing?
>
> **BM:** Johnny.
>
> **You:** Johnny! Yeah! How is the little chip off the old block?
>
> **BM:** He misses you.
>
> *(five minutes of silence)*
>
> **BM:** He's growing up fast, you know.
>
> **You:** That's great. That's really great.
>
> *(five minutes of silence)*

**You:** Is he, like, walking and stuff?

**BM:** Oh, yeah! Walking. Talking. We went to the zoo yesterday and he absolutely *loved* it. And I took him on this carousel that was also there. At first, he was a little scared, but then he really got excited and started bouncing up and down on the horse and . . . *(you drift off into a sexual daydream about another person for the next twenty minutes)* and when we got back from Albany, I think he was happy to be home. It's nice to get out of the house, but then it's always nice to come home. You know? Hello? Hello?

**You:** Oh, hey! Yeah! Yeah, animal crackers are great.

**BM:** Jesus, you weren't even listening. Honestly, I don't know why I bother calling.

**You:** Oh, I *know* why you're calling.

**BM:** You know, that is such a typical remark. I didn't even bring that up. In fact, not only do I have to bust my ass raising our child *alone,* but then I have to jump through hoops every month just to get you on the goddamn phone so I can beg for a lousy $1,500. Which, by the way, doesn't even begin to cover the cost of day care, or diapers, or health insurance . . .

**You:** Hey, you're lucky I can pay you that kind of money. A lot of baby daddies out there aren't professional athletes. It's nice to have a man who brings home the bacon, isn't it?

**BM:** Your last check bounced. Ass.

**You:** I told you, I have a very lucrative real estate invest-

ment in the Florida Everglades. Lot of liquid cash
tied up in that.

**BM:** Listen to me. I can't afford to have a lawyer
chasing you around. It's cost me more than I've
received back from you. I'm tired of this. I'm
begging you, from one human being to another, to
help us. Please. You have a separate life. I get it.
You don't want to be part of this? Fine. That's your
decision. But at least give your son a chance to
have a good life. Please?
*(ten minutes of silence)*

**BM:** Hello? Are you there?

**You:** Can you run that back by me again? The reception
in the casino is going in and out.

**BM:** Oh, goddammit.
*(end of call)*

As you can see, those baby mommas can get awfully dramatic. I'd say
you handled it well.

## Because no penis is an island: your guide to cheating.

Some athletes decide to bite the bullet and live with their baby
mommas, or, as normal people call them, wives. Let's say you decided to
do the right thing and went and got yourself married. Good for you. I
happen to be married myself. In fact, I'm a loving and faithful husband,
and I am a devoted father. I'm like this because I've found it profoundly
rewarding on a spiritual level to have a caring, trusting family unit. But
let's be honest. It ain't like I'm flooded with alternative options. You, on
the other hand, have any number of salacious, tawdry affairs at the tips of

your fingers. There's no reason you can't go out there and cheat on your wife repeatedly for my vicarious enjoyment. Remember: you owe me.

In fact, if some of the more uneventful episodes of *The Sopranos* are any indication, you can even get your wife to subconsciously agree to your constant betrayals. How's that, you say? Hey, women aren't stupid. (Cameron Diaz excepted.) They know full well the temptations that face you, the hardworking athlete, out there on the road. But many women are willing to let the occasional dalliance slide in exchange for certain "lifestyle requirements." And here they are. Please note that there are many of them. You pay for a hooker in more ways than one!

- SUV
- Sports car
- Labradoodle
- New piece of jewelry every month with at least one three-carat precious stone (opals don't count)
- Personal massage therapist she will have an affair with for seven years without you knowing or even suspecting
- Fifty new pairs of shoes a month
- $50,000 a month in "flash money"
- House for her parents
- $90,000 for interior designer who will spend $1 million on expensive shit to get your home spotlighted in *Architectural Digest*

That's merely the tip of the iceberg, but you get the idea. If there is money to be spent, your woman will find a way to spend it. Her mind is constantly awhirl with new and creative ways to fritter away cash. Just consult the handy diagram on the next page for a detailed spending cycle.

In exchange for all that loot, you and your wife will come to an unspo-

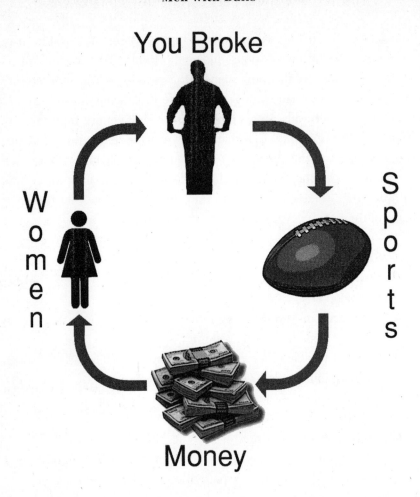

ken but tacitly acknowledged "agreement" about where you go every Tuesday night. She knows you aren't out playing poker. And you know that she knows that. And she knows that you know that she knows that. It's amazing how much you can communicate by simply not talking.

This is not so much living a lie as it is living without truth. After all, if you never mention that you banged three hookers on your last road trip, and she never asks about it, is there really a problem? Did it even happen? I say no. Your wife will learn to accept your cheating so long as it's never "in her face." That means you should make love to your mistress(es) at least three rooms away from your bedroom, preferably while your wife is out taking the kids to school. And always be discreet. Never go out in public with other women or be photographed with them. If there's anything your wife hates more than adultery, it's having to face all the pitying glances at the country club the next day. So, if you can't keep it in your pants, at least keep it away from a camcorder. Do all that, and you can expect a long marriage completely devoid of happiness. Mazel tov!

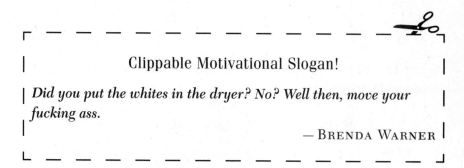

### Clippable Motivational Slogan!

*Did you put the whites in the dryer? No? Well then, move your fucking ass.*

— BRENDA WARNER

## Chapter 7

# A Study in Anchors

## Your Friends and Family

### They're not just family, they're codependents: your entourage.

An entourage serves two purposes. If you grew up without much in the way of family, an entourage can act as a surrogate family, minus the unconditional love, life education, and smartly established boundaries. Or, if you have a rather large family to draw on, having them in your entourage is an excellent way of pitting them against one another for your affections.

Either way, having an entourage means having a large group of people eager to do the menial tasks you no longer have time for. All they ask for in return is to live with you rent-free for an indefinite amount of time, a Bank of America Visa card with no spending limit, and whatever sloppy seconds you don't feel like banging that night. It's a symbiotic relationship: you care for your family and friends, and they pretend to care for you. There's no shortage of important roles for your loved ones to inhabit.

**1. CHEF.** Most athletes hire their moms to be personal chefs. After all, no one cooks like your mom, except fifty million other mothers. If your mother does not live nearby, it helps to appoint a friend who knows how to cook or, failing that, how to order and pick up from Baja Fresh. A personal chef will not only cook and clean, he will also make sure that you are getting the proper nutrition necessary to reach your maximum performance. For dinner, expect grilled chicken and three pounds of boiled asparagus seven days a week. The rest of the house gets pulled-pork sandwiches, waffle fries, and Dr Pepper. Sound unfair? Tough shit. You're the one who wanted to be an athlete.

**2. DRIVER.** No doubt you went out and leased yourself a fleet of expensive automobiles before even signing your first contract (see chapter 10). But why go through the hassle of actually *driving* those cars?

That's for suckers. Make a friend or cousin your personal chauffeur and you never have to worry about drinking and driving again. They'll do all the drinking and driving *for* you.

**3. BARBER.** There's nothing like heading to the corner barbershop, engaging in some witty banter with Cedric the Entertainer, flirting with that oh-so-feisty Eve, and then paying $18 for a three-second haircut. Hiring a friend to be your barber allows you to duplicate that unique neighborhood experience in the privacy of your own home. Your friend doesn't even need a degree in cosmetology. Anyone can give you the Number 3 cut. Don't mess with a proven winner. You can also hire your niece to frost your tips. You can pay her in Twizzlers.

**4. IPOD LOADER.** You don't have time to rip every single CD in your collection onto your laptop and then transfer it to your iPod or iPhone. Besides, that's nerd shit. Hire that one friend of yours that graduated from correspondence school to do it for you. You can also have him download new music for you through illegal file-sharing software. I suggest using BitTorrent. It allows you to steal music in bulk, which is much cheaper than regular stealing. That's how baseball players amass such huge Staind collections.

**5. PRIVATE SECURITY.** Eighty-five percent of all entourage members are hired as bodyguards. You'll find that your friends will be more than happy to handle all your private security matters, including shooting intimidating glances at autograph-seeking children, roughing up that one asshole who looked at you funny, and destroying photographers' equipment. Many of them already have a great deal of experience in these affairs, so take advantage. You can also make like Tiger Woods and have your overzealous caddie double as your bodyguard, which can be a real savings. Make sure your bodyguard likes to wear sunglasses indoors and has little to no experience handling firearms. That way, when he's shooting into a crowd, he's more apt to miss people.

**6. DRUG FETCHER.** If you choose to do drugs (and I support you wholeheartedly on that), don't get your hands dirty by procuring them yourself. Get a friend to pick up some of that sweet, lovely construda for you. You'll be keeping your name clean. More important, it'll keep you safe should a deal go awry. Let your friend be the one who gets tied up by an angry, coked-out Peruvian distributor, who then pulls off his nipples with a pair of pliers. You don't want that happening to you. Way better if it happens to Ed.

**7. FEMALE EVALUATION AND COMMUNICATION.** Hitting the town? The very best nightclubs have a VVVIP section waiting for you. This is the section that is cordoned off from the VVIP section, which is in turn cordoned off from the VIP section, which is in turn cordoned off from all the New Jerseyites on the main dance floor. This section consists of one small table for you and your friends to crowd around while trying to talk over techno music being played at 130 decibels. It's a real good time. The problem is that you need someone to scope out the other areas of the club for attractive women and then bring said women to you. You need a friend with a keen eye for large breasts and tight asses. I'm available if need be.

**8. MAID.** This one's tough if your mom or wife is not available. All of the above jobs can be enjoyable at one point or another. Unless you have a friend who is a meticulous German, no one in your entourage will be interested in cleaning toilets, vacuuming, washing dishes, and doing the laundry. Especially while wearing a French maid outfit, as any smart boss requires. It's shitty, demeaning work no American citizen likes to do. I suggest hiring a day worker. Failing that, do nothing. I spent most of college pissing into Snapple bottles when our toilet broke, then chucking them out the window. It's not as bad a way to live as you might think.

**9. PERSONAL ASSISTANT.** The most important role in your entourage is that of personal assistant. You need one person who is willing to do important things like file your taxes, pay your bills, arrange your schedule, and pick up your dry cleaning. You must trust this person implicitly. Hire someone even the least bit disloyal and you'll get screwed over just like Sigourney Weaver did in *Working Girl*. Fucking Melanie Griffith. Your wife or mother can assume this role. This is the ideal situation, since it does the most to hinder you from acting like a grown man. But, if your wife or mother balks at the idea, you need to find a qualified, trusted assistant. I suggest hiring a pathetic lackey who worships you and, despite knowing you will treat him like complete shit, will happily settle for just being near you on a daily basis. I hear Ahmad Rashad is available.

**10. PATSY.** If you get in trouble, it's good to have someone in your inner circle who's willing to take the fall for you. Anyone in your entourage can be a useful patsy, but you should always choose someone who you never really liked to begin with. Every athlete has a friend like this. If you're a female athlete, you have nothing *but* friends like this. Singling out your one annoying friend for blame is a win-win. You'll get off scot-free, and you'll rid yourself of the jackass once and for all. The look on his face when you throw him under the bus, having realized that all those years of friendship meant less than nothing to you? Priceless.

Together, the above employees form your inner circle, a group so tightly knit as to be all but impenetrable, unless you happen to come across a real smooth talker. Remember, you can boot anyone out of your circle at any time: for talking to the media or for generally displeasing you. It's always good to remind them once in a while that none of them is safe. It helps reinforce your control over all of them, which is what healthy relationships are all about.

## Deeply Penetrating the Numbers

# 76

The average athlete discovers 76 "new" relatives upon turning pro. Damn you, classmates.com!

## Friend and criminal since childhood: bad influences.

No matter where you grew up, you probably have a couple childhood friends who turned out to be bad seeds. Shit, I grew up in the lily-white, upper-middle upper-class enclave of Wayzata, Minnesota. Didn't stop me from making friends with miscreants who liked egging sailboats, deliberately smashing bottles of black cherry New York Seltzer, and making crazy secret trips to Dunkin' Donuts at 5:00 a.m. Rebellion knows no tax bracket, I tell you!

Here's why folks like you and me are so prone to hanging around with bad influences: because having an evil friend is a really good time. No matter how many people he shoots, or how many dancers he assaults, he'll always have a good story to tell. You can't put a price on that. Your sociopath friend will also let you share in the sordid thrill of his wild, out-of-control behavior. He'll say all the things you can't say. He'll punch all the people you can't punch. He'll snort all the things you can't snort. In fact, you could argue that without him around you'd have to do all those things yourself just to make up for it. Why do you think players from the Portland Trail Blazers used to commit so many crimes? Think about it. The only way you can find any danger in that fucking town is by eating a bad oyster. Sometimes, you gotta make your own adventure.

But times change. You're a grown-up now. You have to be responsible. And being responsible means cutting off all contact with any childhood friend who threatens your earning potential. Real men don't remain loyal to old friends in trouble. Real men turn their back on them forever in a heartbeat and seek out newer, cooler friends to hang out with. Your childhood friend and you may share a special bond, forged in the emotional crucible of adolescence, that cannot possibly be duplicated during the course of adulthood. But is that as cool as hitting the go-kart track with Tim McGraw? *Pfft*. Hardly.

You can't afford to hang out with any bad influences. If your friend gets busted selling rocks on the corner to make ends meet, fans and the media will immediately project that behavior onto you, and assume that you have the potential to commit similar horrifying acts. That could, in turn, jeopardize your deal with Vitamin Water. Would your old chum want that to happen? Of course not. That's why you have to drop him like a fucking stone. You can't help him. That takes time and effort, time and effort your coaches will want you to put into improving your defensive footwork.

How do you handle the breakup? Easy. All you need is his number and a Dictaphone. Give him a call. Be sure to turn the Dictaphone on before you do so!

**Your BFF:** Hello?

**You:** Hey, it's me.

**Your BFF:** What's up?

**You:** Listen, we need to talk. Remember how you shot that livery cab driver to death last week?

**Your BFF:** Oh, yeah. That was funny.

**You:** Yeah. Listen, I was thinking that, in retrospect, that wasn't a very cool thing to do. Like, maybe you should go apologize.

**Your BFF:** What are you saying? You saying I should fucking snitch on myself?

**You:** Does confessing count as snitching? I was unaware of that.

**Your BFF:** Not happening. That guy deserved it. Livery cab drivers are *assholes*. Everyone knows that.

**You:** Look, I'm gonna come clean. I just don't think we should be friends anymore.

**Your Former BFF:** What are you talking about?

**You:** I just . . . I just can't have you setting such a bad example. It's hurting my image, and I just don't think being around you is a good thing for me. I think we're just in different places, you know? We've had some laughs, but I think it's time you grew up and took some responsibility for your actions. I'll always love you like a brother, but you know . . . I think I just have to move on.

*(two minutes of silence)*

**Your Former BFF:** I'M GONNA FUCKING KILL YOU.
I'M GONNA GRAB A RUSTY BREAD
KNIFE, COME OVER TO YOUR HOUSE,
AND GUT YOU LIKE A WILD BOAR.
AND WHEN I'M DONE DOING THAT,
I'M GONNA KILL YOUR FAMILY, AND
YOUR FRIENDS, AND ALL YOUR PETS,
EVEN THAT PUNKASS COCKATOO YOU
GOT. WHO THE FUCK ARE YOU TO
ABANDON ME, BITCH? THINK I DON'T
KNOW A THING OR TWO ABOUT YOUR
PAST THAT THE COPS MIGHT LIKE
TO—
*(Hang up now! Hang up now!)*

Did you get all that? Excellent. The FBI will handle the rest of this messy breakup for you. You won't have to worry about your old friend for at least eight years. Out of sight. Out of mind. Chances are, you'll forget about him entirely. Until he shows up in your hedge one day to brutally avenge himself.

# DID YOU KNOW?

The most infamous bad influence in the history of professional sports was former Yankee manager Billy Martin. Martin alone was responsible for more than 782 cases of relapsed alcoholism, 189 drunk-driving deaths, 57 group stabbings, and 20 farts in church.

# HEAR IT FROM AN ATHLETE!

## I am not a role model, because I am too fat to be a role model

### by Charles Barkley

I am not a role model.

Now that you're famous, lots of people will tell you you're a role model whether you like it or not, but that is some heavy bullshit. People that say you're a role model are people who are too damn lazy to raise their own kids. It's a free country, and if you want to be someone who no one in their right mind would consider a good example for children to follow, that's your right. That's what I did. I'm no role model. Shit, I'm too fat to be a role model.

Imagine if some kid decided to follow my dietary habits. Jesus, they'd need daily insulin shots by age four if they saw the shit I stuff in my enormous piehole. Every morning I eat a pound of bacon and tuck six extra slices into my back pocket for snacking on the go. I don't think I've eaten anything with any sort of nutritional value since age six, and that's because my gramma slipped a leaf of romaine into my cheese-burger without me looking. Sometimes I drink Wesson right out of the bottle. When I eat apple pie, I don't even eat the apples. I just eat the crust and the sticky, cinnamony syrup surrounding the apples. I don't have no time in my life for apples. I'm rich. If I have a heart attack, I can just pay some surgeon to unclog my shit. So don't tell me I need apples. I'm not a role model, and I don't like fruit. Fuck fruit.

And there are so many other reasons that I'm a poor role model. For example, my gambling habits. When I hit the roulette table, I never bet

(*continued on next page*)

on red or black or anything sensible like that. That's for poor assholes. I bet $5,000 on #32. Every single time. I don't think I've hit it even once. But I don't give a shit, because I am not a role model. Role models are people who care about math. I went to Auburn. You think I know math from the hole in my ass?

Good kids should, ideally, end up nothing like me. They should be thin and frugal, and they should try and form coherent thoughts before attempting to speak. I don't do any of that shit. I just say the first thing on my mind, no matter how crazy. It's part of my charm. Did you know they made Augusta National longer because they're racist against Tiger Woods? Sure, lengthening the course arguably favors Woods more than any other golfer, but screw that. That shit was *racist*.

Say, are you gonna finish that burrito? Man, don't hog that thing like some kind of goddamn Republican. Give Chuckie a nibble, man.

*(eats the rest of your burrito)*

Of course, I can get away with all this, because I clearly stated up front that I am not a role model. I suggest you do the same thing as well. Not only does it provide you with a mantra to justify all sorts of ignorant behav-

## "I said I'm not a fucking role model!" Raising your kids.

Many athletes live with two or three of their closest children. As a father, I can tell you that children are a lot of hard work. But they're worth it, especially if you aren't the one doing all that hard work. Your "job" requires far less effort and mental strain than what goes into staying at home to raise a child. But you can't let your wife know that. You have to get her to believe that all the time you spend clowning around with your teammates, attending team banquets, and playing games in front of an

ior, it also appeals to the womenfolk. Ladies don't like a guy who plays by the rules. That's why they go out with me, even if I have a size 62-inch waist. That just adds to the intrigue. Where's my penis? You'll just have to find out for yourself, honey.

Not being a role model also freed me up to steal Kenny Smith's chair from the TNT set. Fuck you, Kenny. You ain't getting your Aeron back. I need the support. Quick, someone find me a production assistant who's willing to be my footrest. I had to walk here from the elevator, and my dogs are fucking sore.

Remember: you are not paid to be a role model, just like I wasn't paid to be a role model. You're paid to go out and wreak havoc. I'm sure being a good role model has some sort of intangible reward. I'm sure it's a nice feeling to get kids across America to dress, act, talk, and make love just like you. But that doesn't mean you have to do it. You don't have to do shit. I don't.

Just because I dunk a basketball doesn't mean I should raise anyone's kids. And that's a good thing. Because those kids would get fat as shit.

adoring crowd really takes its toll. If she finds out that your job is insanely fun, which she already suspects, you're fucked.

To keep your wife satisfied, you only need to appear to be a great parent, rather than actually be one. Here are some tips for doing so.

**SIGN WITH A TEAM IN YOUR HOMETOWN.** Your family may live in a different city than the one you play for. While this gives you six months away every year to live like a free man, you will pay for it in the long run. Once you return home for the off-season, you'll be forced to attend any number of play dates and pediatrician appointments to make up for the time you lost. The horror! Why not, instead, follow the example of Roger Clemens, who once signed with the Astros as a free agent to be "closer" to his family, then spent all of his time back home playing golf and going "fishing" with his then longtime companion, Andy Pettitte? By simply being in the same area code you're showing more pretend devotion to your family than most athletes. And your wife will adore you for it.

**TAKE YOUR CHILDREN TO PHOTO SHOOTS.** Your wife will love you for being a good father. But, if that's not possible, she'll be more than happy to settle for you *looking* like a good father. It helps give her bragging rights over all the other wives in the neighborhood. So do whatever limited parenting you do out in public. Be sure to mention how much you love your kids in all interviews. Have Walter Iooss shoot you for *SI* at your home, in the pool, holding your child way up in the air as you both laugh gaily. That's a money parenting shot, one Phil Mickelson uses all the time.

**TAKE YOUR CHILDREN TO PRACTICES AND GAMES.** Let's be honest: you're two steps ahead of any other dad out there simply because of who you are. Do any of the other dads at your kid's school play for the Giants? Fuck and no. So use it to your advantage. Take your kid to practice and introduce him to all the other famous guys you play with. He'll be the happiest, most insufferable kid in town within a week. More important, those few minutes he spends with you at the ballpark every so often will earn you his fervent worship no matter what else you do. Your kid will think you're a god. He'll want to be you, until he hits puberty and realizes he got too many of your wife's useless genes. Then he'll spend the rest of his life trying to escape your enormous shadow, cursing you to his grave. That's A+ daddying, right there.

**HIRE A NANNY.** Hiring a nanny gives both you and your wife enough time away from your children to properly enjoy them.

**TREAT YOUR FAMILY LIKE YOU TREAT THE MEDIA.** Your family has no idea what it's like to be out on that field. Be sure to remind them of that. Let them know that there is no possible way they can understand the pressures and physical wear and tear of standing in center field for three hours. After any game, walk into your home bearing the weight of the world on your shoulders. Rub your knee and grimace. Declare to them, "I had no idea the Raptors would be so *physical!*" Then collapse, exhausted, on your recliner. Relax. Crack open a beer. Pat your kid on the head and tell him to have all the ice cream he wants. You, good sir, are an all-star parent. To your legitimate children.

### Clippable Helpful Trick the Pros Use!

*The best way to remember the names of your illegitimate children is by getting a tattoo.*

## Chapter 8

# Favored Children of the Antichrist
## The Media

**The unnecessary evil: everything you wanted to know about the media, but were too much of a pussy to ask.**

I have two hard-and-fast rules in life. The first is to never eat while watching pornography. I don't think that requires any explanation. The second is to avoid the media at all costs. Given that the media has little interest in a thirty-two-year-old father of one with an ample bosom and no discernible talent, the latter has not been a difficult rule to adhere to. For you, Mr. All-Star, it's another matter entirely. The media is like chlamydia—the longer you ignore it, the more irritating it becomes. But fear not. This handy FAQ will answer everything you need to know about the Fourth Estate.

**Q:** What is the media?
**A:** The media consists of beat writers, columnists, investigative reporters, TV reporters, TV anchors, studio hosts, play-by-play announc-

ers, game analysts, media analysts, stat analysts, analyst analysts, talking heads, authors, talking animatronic baseballs, talk radio show hosts, talk radio sound effects operators, Internet writers, message board posters, bloggers, podcasters, animated cell phone "hosts," photographers, producers, freelance journalists, gossip columnists, sideline reporters, team fan fiction writers, blimp operators, and weathergirls with big tits. Essentially, the media is everyone who is not you.

**Q:** **What is their purpose?**

**A:** As I said before, the purpose of sports is to distract fans from having to attend to matters in the real world. Well, the media serves to extend that distraction into perpetuity, and at a hefty profit. Fans will consume any sort of sports media, regardless of quality. This makes sense when you think about it. Would you rather worry about your growing tax debt, or delay that worry by enduring an episode of *Around the Horn*? I don't see any better alternative out there. Do you?

With twenty-four-hour sports networks and new blogs springing up every minute, there is now enough sports media available to consume the entirety of one's life. In fact, that's the goal of the media: to turn fans into constant media users by infiltrating every orifice of modern communication and trapping them inside a *Matrix*-like web of influence. I should know. Between watching games, watching pregame shows, watching postgame shows, reading columnists I do not enjoy, and writing a blog of my own, I see my daughter for only five minutes out of every month. She's such a little lady now!

**Q:** **Is it true that the Jews run the media?**

**A:** No. The Jews run *Hollywood.* Between making movies and being responsible for starting all the wars in world history, their plate is pretty full.

**Q:** **Why does my league mandate that I be available to the media for twenty minutes after the game?**

**A:**  Because no one in his right mind would talk to the media *voluntarily*. It's a painful way to spend your time. Almost as bad as having to sit through a Tyler Perry film. The only way anyone would be caught dead in a room with those heartless vultures is by contractual force.

Part of your league's broadcast deal with any network like ESPN includes mandatory interviews with players and coaches for this very reason. Why? Well, ESPN can't be showing *sports* all the time. That would be weird. They need to mix it up, and they can only analyze a game so much. It's more fun to force you, the athlete, into an uncomfortable public speaking situation where you will inevitably fuck up. That way, your comments can be taped, cut, replayed, and scrutinized for hours on end. In many ways, it's much more enjoyable than watching you play. On the field, you are perfect, and that's boring. Watching you, the flawless athlete, botch a simple press conference question makes everyone around you feel better about themselves, especially all the mouth-breathers asking the questions.

**Q:**  **There are so many lights on me in these press conferences. Is this what dying in an operating room is like?**

**A:**  Yes.

**Q:**  **I have an opinion on something. Should I offer it?**

**A:**  No! Offer nothing of yourself. These are reporters we're talking about. They got into this business because they loved sports, only to discover that turning something you love into a job corrupts and destroys everything you once loved about it. If they can't be happy doing their jobs, neither can you. They're just *dying* to fuck you over. Even the most ordinary-sounding quote can be twisted and distorted into something controversial. How? Through the power of *ellipses*. Allow me to demonstrate. Let's say a reporter asks you how you're feeling after a tough loss, and you say, "You know, it hurts. We just didn't play well tonight. It's easy enough to point fingers and say, 'It's Jay's fault,' or, 'Mikey didn't do this,' but we have to get through this as a team. We'll start winning if we get it together and keep working to achieve a common goal."

That's what you said. But here is how, through the power of ellipses, you might be quoted: "It's Jay's fault . . . Mikey didn't . . . get it together."

What's that? That's not what you said? You were deliberately misquoted? Tough shit. No one cares. That excuse has been used too often to be effective. As far as the general public knows, you are now officially a malcontent who brazenly accuses fellow teammates of shitting the bed. That little goddamn ellipsis wields all the power of a *MAD* magazine fold-in.

**Q:** **Why would a reporter distort my words? Isn't that unethical?**

**A:** Probably. But a good reporter is also a judicious editor. Your quote was boring. But through the magic of editing, it is now scintillating! Ellipses remove context and add flavor. I'm . . . gay . . . for them!

**Q:** **So, what should I do?**

**A:** Follow your teammates' lead and offer up nothing but trite clichés that are virtually tamperproof. Failing that, mumble. It's worth being branded as "surly."

**Q:** **Is Jim Gray really 3'2"?**

**A:** Yes.

**Q:** **Do most sportswriters believe in evolution?**

**A:** No.

**Q:** **Do they enjoy masturbating to videos of dogs being put down?**

**A:** Yes.

**Q:** **Are any of them secretly members of the Aryan Brotherhood?**

**A:** Yes. To be sure your local columnist or golf broadcaster isn't a member, simply lift up his comb-over and look for a shamrock tattoo with the number 666 on it. If you see one, don't fuck with him. He's hardcore.

## The dregs of humanity: your guide to the average sports columnist.

All major newspapers and sports Web sites employ beat writers that do the yeoman's work of attending press conferences, covering games on a day-to-day basis, and interviewing you in the locker room while your cock is still hanging out. These are the only people in sports media who serve any useful purpose. They are tireless, dedicated professionals who lay the journalistic foundation for the rest of the sports media industry by following teams back and forth across the country and reporting the basic facts about you and your team. After paying dues for decades, many of them go on to become excellent investigative reporters and feature writers.

And all of them are total suckers.

The real money is in being a columnist. Sports columnists are the ones who get paid hundreds of thousands of dollars every year to type up the same opinions you can get from caller 42 on *The Jim Rome Show*. Many, like Ron Borges, will even lift them verbatim. It's a nice tribute to the common man. None of the opinions your hometown columnist offers will be the least bit insightful or original (just like the content of this book!). He may even contradict himself within the same column. Why does he get paid so much to be so inane? Simple: columnists are hired by editors to boost the overall self-esteem of the general sporting public. Most fans read the work of an idiot like Jay Mariotti and conclude, "Christ, I'm smarter than this asshole." And they're right. That helps make them feel more confident and better informed.

Unfamiliar with the distinguishing characteristics that make these gents such miserable human beings to be around? Not to worry. I've listed them here for you.

**Height:** 5'4"

**Weight:** Either 100 pounds or 400 pounds. There is no in-between.

**Salary:** Six figures at a newspaper. Working at a newspaper is a union job, and newspaper columnists are the only people on Earth who earn more to do nothing than your local Teamsters.

**Favorite Food:** Pasta primavera that's been sitting in a hotel pan for four hours or more, Caesar salad made entirely with Caesar dressing and croutons, muffins, brownies, blondies, bacon paste

# Men with Balls

**Preferred Stance:** Inside press box, hunched over laptop, sweating, occasionally snickering to self

**Wardrobe:** Pleated Haggar pants, American Eagle Outfitters denim dress shirt

**Favorite Brand of Cigarettes for Smoking Three Packs a Day:** Pall Mall

**Teeth Color:** Grayish mustard

**Skin:** Thinner than a pubic hair

**Hair:** None

**Musk:** Turkish bath, with just a hint of Beefeater

**Preferred Name While Cross-dressing:** Sheila

**Turn-ons:** Children, sound of own voice, Sanka, fresh tray of eggs Benedict at Quality Inn breakfast spread, old Smith-Corona typewriters, free promotional golf shirts, radio show call-ins, mute hookers, a Xanax prescription refill, talking with others about back pain

**Turnoffs:** Sports, you performing well, criticism, effort, the sinking feeling that the rise of self-publishing electronic media will lead to his inevitable and just demise

**Marital Status:** Thrice divorced

**Children:** Two, whom he never sees

# Deeply Penetrating the Numbers

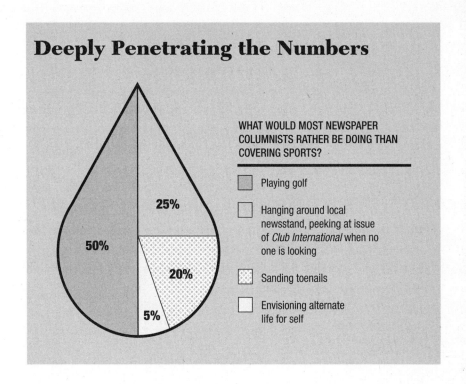

WHAT WOULD MOST NEWSPAPER
COLUMNISTS RATHER BE DOING THAN
COVERING SPORTS?

- Playing golf
- Hanging around local newsstand, peeking at issue of *Club International* when no one is looking
- Sanding toenails
- Envisioning alternate life for self

50%  25%  20%  5%

**How to Get Him to Like You:** Don't bother trying to curry favor with your hometown columnist. His job is to bitch about you no matter what you do. If you don't talk to him, he'll crucify you for being media-unfriendly, and actually assume readers will care about such a characteristic. If you give him a decent quote to work with, he'll thank you, and then crucify you for speaking your mind. You can't win, nor should you even try. Turn the page to see what I mean.

**Credo:** "No cheering in the press box." Peter King once said he never roots for a team, but that he roots for a story. This is a hard-and-fast belief among all sportswriters. They don't care about your game. They care

# HEAR IT FROM A COLUMNIST!

## I'm the star here, asshole
by Mike Lupica, *New York Daily News* columnist

Hey, you.

Yeah, you.

Let me explain something to you before you walk out onto that field for the first time, okay? I'm gonna tell you a little something about how this whole industry works. And take it from me, because I've been around here a whole lot longer than you have. So I think I have a pretty goddamn good idea of what I'm talking about.

I'm the star here, asshole.

You hear me?

I AM THE STAR HERE.

I know you think you're a big deal now that you're a pro. I know you think the universe revolves around you. Well, I have news for you. Let me just cut you down to size now and save you the time. The fact is that I can walk into any neighborhood in Santo Domingo and find another asshole who's just like you, okay? You are just one more asshole in the long line of players parading in and out of this city.

You're not Lupica, that's for goddamn sure.

*(pokes you in the chest)*

*You* merely play sports. But I make sports into art. I am a composer. I am a recorder of history. I tickle the imagination. When people centuries from now want to find something that captures the quintessence of the times in which we currently live, they're not gonna watch some highlight of you rounding the bases like some jackass. They're gonna get it from

Lupica. I *create,* okay? I am a creator. I am *the* creator. So I don't want to see you trying to upstage me with some bullshit home run pose. And I don't want to hear you mouthing off some uninformed opinion to the rest of these slobbering idiots in the press, like you actually know something. You do the hitting, and I'll do the writing. You got me? *Know your role.*

Oh, you wanna challenge me? Yeah, you don't wanna do that. Cross me and I'll write a piece so scathing you'll need to rub Vaseline on your ass for a month. I'm the kind of guy that reads crossword puzzle answer keys and then writes his *own* clues, so you don't want to try and match wits with me. The Yankees displeased me once. *Once.* You know what happened when they did? They got the full frontal force of Lupica crammed right down their throats. Look at this dagger, which I actually wrote on June 26th, 2007.

"Bronx Bombers? The Bronx Bomb is more like it."

BOOM! See how I modified "Bombers" to "Bomb" to reverse the connotation? Holy shit, am I good. I'm just gonna sit back and read it to myself one more time.

*(snickers)*

God, I kill.

You wanna screw with that, jerkoff? If you think that's bad, wait until I excoriate you on national television. One second listening to my voice and your scrotum will tighten like a beggar's purse. And I'll keep lecturing you until the myelin sheaths have been completely stripped from your nerves. It's my gift, and you don't want a taste of it.

*(peers over glasses at you)*

I'm sorry to break this to you, buddy, but the fans aren't here to see you. That's the hard truth. They're here to see you in order to prepare themselves for the majesty that will spring forth from my keyboard the next day. I'm the show here, asshole. You're just the fuel driving the engine.

(*continued on next page*)

Athletes come and go. You're here now, but soon you'll move on. Or you'll retire. You'll have no lasting impact on this city. But I will. I am a goddamn institution. You are *nothing*. You're less than nothing. You're an accessory. A trinket.

What's that? *I'm* the asshole? What, you think I give a shit what some two-bit Neanderthal like you thinks? There's only one opinion that matters here, kid: Lupica's. I've spent years building up an immunity to any sort of criticism. You're not the first person who wanted to push me down a flight of concrete stairs, and you certainly won't be the last.

Get it straight now, and maybe I'll spare you my legendary wrath. But if you want to try and be Mr. Big Shot, don't say I didn't warn you. I'll always be more important than the event I cover. You're superfluous to the whole enterprise.

So don't get too full of yourself.

That's my job.

about using your game as a way to indirectly talk about themselves. It's a bold, innovative way of being completely useless, and it helps explain why Peter King so often writes about playing with his dog and going to the proctologist.

## The sports network for people who don't like sports: ESPN.

If you're unfamiliar with the history of ESPN, simply tune in to *Sports-Center* tonight. They'll almost certainly be celebrating an ESPN milestone of some sort. You'll see old footage of Chris Berman that only Chris Berman enjoys watching. Then you'll see footage of that crazy Stanford-

Cal band play. Is it just as exciting the 56,872nd time you've watched it? Sure is!

In the old days, ESPN was an upstart company dedicated to serving sports fans with round-the-clock sports coverage and a *SportsCenter* anchored by Dan Patrick and Keith Olbermann that featured actual highlights of that day's games. But times have changed, and so has ESPN. As you are probably aware, ESPN is now a gigantic, soul-sucking collective that stays alive only by feeding itself its own shit. They currently have partial to total broadcasting control over the three major sports leagues in America. But that's only the beginning. By the end of this century, ESPN management hopes to control the forty-eight contiguous states, along with parts of Southeast Asia and the Bering Strait.

The company has already begun its own human-clone farm to provide for its massive energy needs. The cloned fetuses are harvested into large cryogenic chambers and kept alive but unconscious. Large tubes are then inserted directly into the fetuses' eye sockets, pumping vital plasma into the company's bionic central nervous system. With any luck, ESPN will get most unsuspecting sports fans to become part of their gigantic human plantation project by 2067. At least, that's the current timetable.

What's this mean for you, the athlete? It means that getting on *Sports-Center* is harder than ever. Being in a *SportsCenter* highlight used to be a rite of passage for young pro athletes. It was a sign that you had finally made the big-time, and that a lucrative deal with Taco Bell or any of the Yum! Brands restaurant franchises awaited you. Those highlights have grown ever more scarce on the show as of late. Highlights only appeal to sports fans, and ESPN could give two shits about them. What ESPN craves is . . . branding! Branded sets! Branded segments! Branded events! Branded brands! Ever heard of ESPN presents the ESPN World Series brought to you by the Ford Motor Company sponsored by GlaxoSmith-

Kline in association with ESPN? It's coming soon, and everyone at ESPN agrees by coercion: you'll love it!

After all that branding, the only highlights you now see on *Sports-Center* are highlights of *other* highlights. You might catch the last three nanoseconds of a dunk, or a really big football hit that's been taken completely out of context from the game in which it took place. Otherwise, the show simply doesn't have time. I asked a senior producer at ESPN, who will soon be found dead, to take me through a typical hour of the show. Here was the template he gave me before asking me to tell his children he loved them:

11:00 p.m. — Introduction of *SportsCenter* introduction

11:02 p.m. — Highlights of what you can expect during the show, including one story that looks interesting and will occupy five seconds at the end of the broadcast

11:03 p.m. — Cut to commercial

11:05 p.m. — The real *SportsCenter* title sequence, featuring a giant *SC* logo striding atop a giant graphic phallus, with all kinds of crazy rings and shit shooting over it

11:06 p.m. — Voice-over guy with no gravitas says, "This is *SportsCenter*." You are blinded by greatness.

11:08 p.m. — Cut to commercial

11:10 p.m. — Ten-minute Stuart Scott slam poem that only serves to reinforce his middle-class upbringing

11:20 p.m. — Cut to commercial

11:22 p.m. — "Coors Light Cold Hard Facts," in which analysts Mark Schlereth and Merril Hoge (combined number of concussions: 248) give you their hardcore, producer-coached opinions

11:24 p.m. — Thirty-second teaser for what's ahead on the second half of *SportsCenter*

11:25 p.m. — Cut to commercial

11:27 p.m. — Linda Cohn broadcasts from a remote location in Rhode Island to tell you what a fun week it's been watching the X Games, and that these guys *are* athletes

11:29 p.m. — Top Five College Football Plays of the ESPN Era!

11:32 p.m. — Cut to commercial

11:34 p.m. — Five-minute recap of *Pardon the Interruption*

11:39 p.m. — Cut to commercial

11:40 p.m. — Cut to ESPN commercial break within commercial break. Airing next week: the ESPN original movie *Game of Shadows*, starring Mario Van Peebles!

11:42 p.m. — "What2Watch4" segment takes you through all your programming choices on the ESPN family of networks for the following day, without pesky prepositions!

11:44 p.m. — "Budweiser Hot Seat!" This segment gives the anchors a chance to really put the screws to an athlete or coach. Tonight's guest is Mario Van Peebles.

11:46 p.m. — "Fact or Fiction" segment! This differs from "Cold Hard Facts" because it allows retards like John Kruk to be unnecessarily strident about things that they think are true *or* false.

11:48 p.m. — Cut to commercial

11:50 p.m. — Chris Berman appears. Introduces the other four people in the studio, using the same jokes he's used for the last *twenty-nine fucking years.* Everyone laughs. Throws it back to Stuart.

11:52 p.m. — Cut to Ed Werder outside the Cowboys practice facility, waiting for something to happen

11:54 p.m. — Cut to commercial

11:56 p.m. — "*SportsCenter* Xpress" takes you through all the day's games in two minutes or less! It's highlights for people on the go! Wasn't that thoughtful of them?

11:58 p.m. — "Did You Know?" And you did.

12:00 a.m. — We start all over again!

## DID YOU KNOW? BONUS!

Due to corporate obligations, future installments of *SportsCenter*'s "Did You Know?" segment will focus exclusively on just what gives Budweiser such a crisp, clean taste.

I tell you, it's the tightest show on sports. You have to work extra hard to get your break on that show. A plain old dunk, home run, or touchdown won't do. You're gonna have to be creative. I suggest drop-kicking an opponent, breaking a hallowed record through suspect means, or spitting on someone. That's the kind of stuff advertisers really gravitate toward these days, and it's your only hope.

There is one saving grace of ESPN, however. Because ESPN is in bed with the principals of every major sport, it behooves them to give you softer treatment than an Upper East Side mother gives her offspring. Did you get arrested once? What arrest? Stuart Scott doesn't remember any arrest! That must have been some crazy dream you had!

## It's like sodomy for your ears! Your guide to the average talk radio host.

Radio, the medium for people too poor to afford an iPod, has been taken over by the sports talk format in recent years. Why? Consider that the average American spends roughly two hours a day sitting in traffic. It's tough sitting there in your car, all alone, with no one to talk to. Sometimes, I think about death. Not cool. That's why I turn on the radio. You need something to break the silence and protect you from having to deal with your own thoughts. Talk radio shows save you from isolation by forcing you to listen to a former high school physical education teacher give a rambling, incoherent soliloquy about the state of modern sports. It's not very entertaining, but considering that music stations play warmed-over donkey shit like Nickelback now, there's no real alternative.

Talk shows thrive on vitriol. These are three-hour-long shows hosted by people like Colin Cowherd, who has all the charisma of a dying ferret. There's a lot of dead air to fill. And apart from making. Very long. Dramatic pauses. In order. To fill. The space, the best way to make those hours fly by is to verbally tear you, the athlete, limb from limb. It's hard for people to be passionate about something they love. It's much easier for them to be passionate about something they hate. And that something is you. Take a look at this sample transcript:

# Men with Balls

*(Loud guitar stock music comes on)*

**OVERLY MACHO VOICE-OVER:**

You are in . . . the House of Pain!

The House of Pain?

THE HOUSE OF PAIN!

With Steve "the Madman" Franklin!!!!

He's talkin' sports! Goin' at it HARD!

Ready to bring the HEAT!!!!!!!

And now, from the AutoZone studios at Fox
Sports Radio, it's THE MAAAAAAADMAN!

**MADMAN:**

What's up. It's Tuesday. It's the Madman. You
know the drill. I want you guys to come hard
with your opinions. That's how we operate
here. Go hard, or go home. That's our motto.
Before we get raw, I just want to thank
Einstein Brothers Bagels for bringing in
today's breakfast. Tim, you like the bagels?

**PRODUCER STATIONED BEHIND THE GLASS
WHO SECRETLY HATES THE HOST:**

Absolutely.

**MADMAN:**

Bet you had the poppy seed one, right?
You're such a homo, Tim.

**PRODUCER STATIONED BEHIND THE GLASS
WHO SECRETLY HATES THE HOST:**
*(joking but not joking)* Bite me.

**MADMAN:**

Ha! I love it. I'm gonna get to the phone
lines in a sec, but first, I want to talk
about this *(your name)* situation. Okay? This
guy . . . *(long pause)* I don't even know what
to say. I mean . . . *(long pause)* how do you go
from hitting .320 in August to hitting .190
in September? *(long pause)* Can you explain
that to me? *(long pause)* Anyone? *(long pause)*
I mean, it is just inconceivable to me. *(long
pause)* To go from hitting .320 in
August . . . *(long pause)* to hitting .190 in
September. *(long pause)* That's a full 130
points less. *(long pause)* That's 13 percent.
*(long pause)* That's a big drop. *(long pause,
takes a sip of coffee)* That's in just one
month. And this guy's perfectly healthy! And
he's making $5 million a year! *(long pause)* I
don't make $5 million a year. Do you make $5
million a year, Tim?

**PRODUCER STATIONED BEHIND THE GLASS
WHO SECRETLY HATES THE HOST:**
Nope.

---

# Men with Balls

**MADMAN:**

Yeah, I know Tim *definitely* doesn't make that much. You know what this is? This is symptomatic of today's professional athlete. We guarantee these guys millions of dollars up front, and they're playing like they've already earned it. And then they just start slacking!

**JEFF SPICOLI SOUND BITE:**

"Aloha, Mr. Hand!"

**MADMAN:**

Ha! Nice pull, Tim! Anyway, want to get your thoughts on this. Call us or text us at 640 on your T-Mobile phone. Going to Jeff. Jeff, what do you think of this jackass? Bring it hard! Don't spare this guy!

**JEFF:**

*(static)*

**MADMAN:**

Okay, Jeff, I need you to turn down your radio to talk to me. People, I tell you this every day. Let's go to Jenny. Ooooh, a lady! Jenny, what do you got?

# Favored Children of the Antichrist

### JENNY:

I think we should definitely trade him, but
for *youth*. We need more youth on the team,
Madman!

### MADMAN:

That's a great point. A *great* point. This
guy's thirty, okay? He's not getting any
younger. Next comes thirty-one, then thirty-
two. That's gettin' up there. Let me ask you,
Jenny: how much do you weigh?

### JENNY:

How much do I weigh?

### MADMAN:

Yeah.

### JENNY:

135?

### MADMAN:

Nah, no way! You definitely sound like you're
two bills. At least. Anyway, great call.
Let's go to Dave. Dave!

### DAVE:

Yeah, I just want to say that player slumps
are fairly common and that part of the beauty

of watching sports is to see if these guys can bounce bac—

**MADMAN:**

*(cuts him off)* I'm sorry, Dave. I'm getting the signal from Timmy that we have to cut to break.

**PRODUCER STATIONED BEHIND THE GLASS
WHO SECRETLY HATES THE HOST:**

I never said that.

**MADMAN:**

Well, it looked like it to me! Great, now we lost him. Besides, I don't think Dave was really listening to my original point. If he had, he would have picked up on what I was saying. Gotta get better phone lines in here, Tim. Just terrible equipment. We're operating in the eighteenth century here, people.

**PRODUCER STATIONED BEHIND THE GLASS
WHO SECRETLY HATES THE HOST:**

I hate you.

I suggest keeping your radio off at all times. If you own one. Most rich people don't bother.

## More bottom-feeders: those fucking blog nerds.

Blogs are the newest menace to the professional athlete. There's a new sports blogger created every .7 seconds, and these people don't start a blog just to write you love sonnets.

We are at a terrible moment in history, when anyone can write anything they want and then share what they write with others. This was not what the Founding Fathers had in mind when they created freedom of the press. Back then, the press consisted of four people, all of them drunks, who could be easily controlled. There was one newspaper, and it was printed on birch bark. And since Ben Franklin hadn't invented reading glasses yet, none of the six people who had subscriptions could read it. How could they have envisioned a day where any asshole—without a journalism degree!—could print anything? It's a goddamn tragedy.

The worst thing about blogs is that people actually read them. You wouldn't think there's an audience out there for some lady chronicling the daily shitting habits of her cat, but you'd be wrong. That blog gets more than 4 million hits a week. Since everyone hates the mainstream media, blogs have become a popular reading alternative. Why? Because if you can't trust a mainstream outlet for your news, why not go all the way in the other direction and get your news from people who have even *less* credibility? It makes for juicier reading, that's for damn sure.

This is why blogs are so dangerous for you, the athlete. Sure, no one believes anything they read on a sports blog. But they *want* to believe it, and wanting to believe it is just as bad, if not worse. Now anyone can publish any story they want about you, without giving you a chance to refute the details. And people will associate that story with you forever, regardless of its veracity. What kind of Internet rumors about major sports personalities are out there? Get a load of some of these. Now, at the request of Little, Brown & Co.'s lawyers, I had to cross out all of the names listed below. Fucking lawyers. But you get the idea. Of course, none of these rumors are true. But man, you can really picture this shit once it's in writing.

- One time, this kid went up to big leaguer ▮▮▮▮▮▮▮▮ and asked for an autograph, and ▮▮▮▮▮▮▮▮ just whipped out his dick and slapped the kid across the face with it. Then ▮▮▮▮▮▮ ▮▮▮▮▮ laughed and said, "I just gave you a lifetime of memories, kid."
- One of NFL great ▮▮▮▮▮▮▮▮▮'s baby mommas went up to him one day demanding he pay child support. ▮▮▮▮▮▮▮▮ laughed at her and said, "Girl, I gave you a child! Isn't that enough of a gift? When you buy someone a car, they don't expect you to pay for the gas!"
- Not only did ▮▮▮▮▮▮▮▮ do steroids, he also used an aluminum bat wrapped in faux-wood linoleum.
- ▮▮▮▮▮▮▮▮ will report to the FOX TV studio three hours in advance to practice smug glances.
- ▮▮▮▮▮▮▮▮ cheats on his wife with an assortment of strippers and leather-clad biker chicks, and when he makes love he insists on wearing a Hawaiian shirt.
- *Sports Illustrated* writer ▮▮▮▮▮▮▮▮ killed a man in 1936.
- Former all-pro QB ▮▮▮▮▮▮▮▮ never formally attended school at any level, and only learned to read by looking at the backs of cereal boxes.

Are you feeling simultaneously disgusted and titillated right now? I am. Even worse, bloggers will sometimes post candid pictures of you. And not just any pictures, but pictures of you fucking *hammered*. And since we're a nation that consumes more alcohol than any other, while simultaneously being complete tightasses about it, that could really hurt your image.

So what can you do against this kind of slander? Well, remember what I said about racism and prejudice being your friend? Time to call that friend up and do a little stereotyping of your own.

The best way to defuse any blog criticism is to perpetuate the stereotype that bloggers are nothing more than fat, slovenly, sci-fi-loving masturbators with shitty lives and axes to grind. Take me for instance. I'm a blogger, and I look exactly like Tackleberry from *Police Academy*. And I just *adore* masturbating. Think fans aren't ready to hate my guts at the drop of a hat? People have already turned on the old media. They can't wait to turn on the new.

## CLIPPABLE MOTIVATIONAL SLOGAN!

*EVEN IF YOU AGREE WITH SOMEONE, IT IS IMPORTANT TO CONTINUE TO SHOUT AT THEM AS IF YOU ARE ARGUING. THAT WAY, YOU CAN ALWAYS MAINTAIN THE UPPER HAND.*

— STEPHEN A. SMITH

## Chapter 9

# "What Do You Mean, She Wants to Press Charges?"

## Trouble

### Oh, fuck! You've been arrested!
### A short guide to illegal behavior.

Being a pro athlete means living under a microscope. And not just one of those pissy little high school microscopes. I'm talking one of the big, backed-with-federal-funding atomic fuckers they have over at the National Institutes of Health. The ones that can show you the miniature, superintelligent reptile civilization hidden inside your thumbnail. People love to watch athletes, but they love *judging* them even more. So, when you get into trouble, you should expect a Category 5 shitstorm that will test the very limits of your faith in mankind. Don't expect to get away with anything. Unless you're white, in which case you get a two-crime grace period.

One of the reasons athletes always seem to find themselves in trouble is that they don't take the time to learn what is legal and what is not.

After all, having sex with a smoking hot fifteen-year-old certainly *feels* like the right thing to do. But the law (again, outside of Louisiana) tells us that this is not the case. So don't bother trying to follow your own moral compass. Because it's pointing you straight to hell, my friend. The only magnetic pole that thing is attracted to is the one swinging between your legs.

So what kind of behavior is illegal, and why does society consider it a crime?

# DWI

**What It Is:** Driving while intoxicated. This is also known as DUI, or driving under the influence, which expands the definition of the crime to include driving under the influence of alcohol, illegal drugs, prescription drugs, or Aphex Twin. Most states outlaw driving with a blood-alcohol level of .01 or higher, which translates to roughly one drink per hour. If you're an alcoholic like me, you know just how unfair that is. One drink per hour barely changes the mood in the room.

**Why It Is Wrong:** Because being intoxicated impairs your vision and reaction time, and makes you more likely to hurt other motorists. That is, unless you're me. After ten beers, I am Jason fucking Bourne in a Honda. I am dialed in and can hit corners going ninety with the utmost precision. Nothing's getting in my way. I am goddamn *bulletproof*. If you get busted for driving drunk, it just means that you aren't good enough at it. Real pros don't get caught by the fuzz. They have all police blockade locations committed to memory, as I do. Keep at it and eventually you'll get the hang of it. Oh, and don't bother hyperventilating to try to beat the Breathalyzer. That's an urban legend. Trust me.

fucked

safe

**Bad Publicity Factor (1–10):** 2. The good news about getting busted for DWI is that, since it is such a common offense, people barely bat an eyelash. In fact, the more often athletes get busted for DWI, the less attention it gets. So, in a way, you're doing your fellow athletes a favor. So keep at it, my friend. You're drunkenly, recklessly bulldozing a clear path for those of us who like a roadie or six before heading in to work every morning.

**Famous Perpetrators:** Tony LaRussa, Mike Tyson, J.J. Redick, Michael Phelps

# Domestic Violence

**What It Is:** Wife-beating. This can range from a light slap to a full-on thrashing. Either way, when your ladyfriend dials 911, expect the fury of all womankind to rain down upon you. Hope you enjoy a lifetime of ultimately futile apologizing. You're in for a real treat.

**Why It Is Wrong:** Because it's wrong to hit a woman, okay? Women are soft and pretty. And sometimes, their hair smells like the juice from a maraschino cherry jar. Oh, how I wish I had one to hold in my arms right now! How could you harm such a weak, defenseless little animal? You monster! Pick on someone your own size, prick! Hitting a woman is nothing more than the act of a coward. Unless the woman in question is Nancy Grace, in which case I'd like to shake your hand.

Besides, violence solves nothing. The best way to solve problems with your woman is to sit down and talk. And talk. And talk some more. And to revisit the same argument over and over again, and to force yourself to confront unpleasant facts about yourself you didn't really want or need to address. That's the best way to build a long, lasting relationship. Provided that's what you're looking for. That was what you wanted, right?

fucked

**Bad Publicity Factor (1–10):** 8. People only like wife-beating when they're watching mob films. You pretty much deserve the scorn here. No one likes a wife-beater, unless that wife-beater is Ike Turner. The man was charming even when he was giving you a shiner.

**Famous Perpetrators:** Jason Richardson, Ron Artest, Dave Duerson, Wil Cordero

safe

# Assault and Battery

**What It Is:** Laying the smack down on a motherfucker

**Why It Is Wrong:** Every now and again a belligerent provocateur (usually wearing a Lacoste shirt) will try to goad you into a fight. Why does this happen to you, the pro athlete? Because you are the ultimate man. You are big, strong, and rich. Everyone loves you. The common man, such as myself, simply cannot compare. I bet you think your shit don't stink, don't 'cha? Well, fuck that. I'm not afraid of you, *bitch*. Let's see what you're really made of, tiger!

As you can see, you inspire great feelings of jealous rage among average Joes. Provoking you is a manifestation of their own insecurity. If you beat the ever-loving shit out of some aggressive idiot (which is what would happen if you fought him), you're only sending him further down his spiral of self-loathing.

Which is fine. Except that this is illegal for some reason.

fucked

Bad Publicity Factor (1–10): 1. Fighting doesn't make you look tough. Unless you win. Everybody loves an asskicker.

Famous Perpetrators: Lawrence Phillips, Ruben Patterson, Mike Tyson

safe

# Illegal Firearm Possession

**What It Is:** Owning or concealing a gun without a proper permit

**Why It Is Wrong:** Guns are legal in America. Anyone can own them. Even the mentally ill. But you can't just go and buy a gun. You first have to fill out a form. That way, everyone will know you're fit to own one.

Many athletes are gun owners. It's a matter of personal security. If you're confronted with an assailant, it's far easier to shoot the assailant dead than to run away from him using your God-given speed. You could pull a hammy doing that.

fucked

**Bad Publicity Factor (1–10):** 5. Getting booked on gun charges says to people that you are a dangerous individual liable to go off at any second. Frankly, it's a bit of a turn-on.

**Famous Perpetrators:** Maurice Clarett, Tank Johnson, Mike Tyson

safe

# Rape/Sexual Assault

**What It Is:** Rape, also known as pop-in sex, or gotcha! sex, is defined as nonconsensual sex. This is a bit of a misnomer. It's actually half-consensual sex. Obviously, *you* consented to have sex. The woman? Not so much.

**Why It Is Wrong:** You mean, apart from it being the most heinous crime in humankind? Well, there's also the fact that it's not terribly sexy. It's also quite a difficult crime to perform on a technical scale. Most guys have a hard enough time getting in there when the woman is *willing*. I can't imagine how hard it would be without her cooperation.

There's also the fact that raping a woman scars her for life, forcing her to make the terrible decision to either remain silent and ashamed about her attack, or to press charges against you, only to have her name and reputation trashed by your high-priced legal team, which is tantamount to being raped over and over again. Oh, and there's the fact that, should she choose the latter, she'll go through the terrible ordeal of a trial that will discourage future victims from coming forward and encourage future perpetrators to continue their treachery.

Other than that, I can't think of much else wrong with it.

fucked

**Bad Publicity Factor (1–10):** 10. Nobody likes rape. Except for indie filmmakers, who can't seem to get enough of it. Rape a woman, and you can expect an angry mob to follow you throughout the rest of your time here on Earth. Be sure to look for me. I'll be the one with the battle-ax. You fuck.

safe

**Famous Perpetrators:** Mike Tyson, Mike Tyson, Mike Tyson

---

203

# Murder/Manslaughter

**What It Is:** Making another person dead

**Why It Is Wrong:** Look, everyone has four or five people they'd love to take out. My list is actually quite extensive, with Jimmy Fallon and Paris Hilton being the most notable names in the top 250. My wife would strangle Ann Curry with piano wire if it were legal. But you can't do it. It's the sixth commandment, which actually seems a little low on God's priority list. But whatever. Don't kill anyone. Aside from taking away someone's life, the ensuing Dostoyevskian inner struggle you experience will make you a real drag to be around.

fucked

safe

**Bad Publicity Factor (1–10):** 10. But you will get random marriage proposals while you're in the pokey. I suggest marrying the first one to send a decent photo. What's the downside?

**Famous Perpetrators:** Mike Tyson (scheduled for 2010)

There's your guide. Apart from drug possession, which I will discuss later on, this pretty much covers it. You have no excuse to go committing crimes now. Unless you can't read, in which case you can plead ignorance.

## Oh, fuck! You said something dumb!

Think a clean police record can save you from being trapped at the bottom of the media port-a-potty? Wrong. All it takes is one mildly controversial viewpoint on a slow news day (usually a Tuesday), and you may as

# DID YOU KNOW?

The worst criminal in the history of professional sports was Earl "Stabby" Jameson, an outfielder for the Red Sox back in 1911. Stabby stabbed more than 700 prostitutes that year alone, but journalistic etiquette at the time dictated that a player's off-the-field exploits were strictly out-of-bounds.

well write the word *CHUM* in red marker on your head. Most athletes are smart enough to keep their opinions to themselves. It's a lesson actors never seem to learn. But there have been a few athletes who have expressed a poorly articulated opinion and then paid dearly for it, usually with a small fine and/or a team-mandated forty-five-minute sensitivity-training seminar. Yikes. You don't want any piece of that. Read now their tales of woe, and be forewarned!

# Case Study #1: John Rocker

**The Quote:** "Imagine having to take the [Number] 7 train to the ballpark . . . next to some kid with purple hair next to some queer with AIDS right next to some dude who just got out of jail for the fourth time right next to some 20-year-old mom with four kids. It's depressing." (from *Sports Illustrated*)

**The Judgment:** Racist! You can't insult every ethnic group like that and expect to get away with it. Who do you think runs the media? That's right: purple-haired kids and queers with AIDS. There are still millions of minorities and gays who are routinely oppressed in our country on a daily basis. And when you piss those people off, they *stay* pissed off. They need an outlet for their frustration, and that would be you. If you insult them, they'll push for a suspension, a public apology, or anything else that constitutes an ultimately Pyrrhic victory. It's all they have to hold on to. And to think, all Rocker had to do was say, "It's amazing!" at the end of his diatribe instead of, "It's depressing," and he would have been cast in *Rent* a week later. Moron.

# Case Study #2: Kevin Garnett

**The Quote:** "It's game seven, man. That's it. It's for all the marbles. Sitting in the house, I'm loadin' up the pump. I'm loadin' up the Uzi. I got a couple M-16s, a couple nines. I got a couple joints with some silencers on them. I'm just loading clips, a couple grenades. I got a missile launcher with a couple of missiles. I'm ready for war."

**The Judgment:** Insensitive! Not to our soldiers overseas, of course. No one pays attention to them anymore. No, Garnett was guilty of being insensitive to the sport of professional football. Everyone knows that football has the market cornered on war metaphors. Those guys are the real heroes. In the NBA, you get whistled for a foul just for *thinking* about committing a foul. You call that pretend war? I call it bullshit.

# Case Study #3: Derek Bell

**The Quote:** "I ain't going out there to hurt myself in spring training battling for a job. If it is [open competition], then I'm going into Operation Shutdown."

**The Judgment:** Lazy! You can't half-ass your job simply because you aren't happy with your current situation at work. Only fans get to do that. In fact, that's how they were able to sneak out to the ballpark to watch you play.

# Case Study #4: Keith Hernandez

**The Quote:** "I won't say that women belong in the kitchen, but they don't belong in the dugout."

**The Judgment:** Sexist! You aren't supposed to give voice to the blatant sexism inherent in your sport. You're supposed to let it fester just below the surface, where it remains glaringly obvious to everyone without ever having to be addressed. Let women bring up the subject of sexism in sports. That way, all the male fans and writers can make fun of them for getting their panties in a bunch. Also, note that Hernandez brought up the stereotype of women belonging in the kitchen, but didn't formally endorse it. My friend, just mentioning the stereotype will piss everyone off anyway. You may as well go all the way with it. Say women belong in the kitchen, wearing nothing but an apron, ready to please your appetite both for a sandwich and intercourse simultaneously. At least you'll be able to say you were truthful.

# Case Study #5:
# Jason "White Chocolate" Williams

**The Quote:** (to an Asian fan during a game) "I will shoot all you Asian motherfuckers. . . . Do you remember the Vietnam War? I'll kill y'all just like that."

**The Judgment:** Antagonistic! Don't antagonize fans. Stadium personnel already have an obnoxious PA announcer and the entire Technotronic catalog on hand to do that job for you. Besides, those Asian motherfuckers are quite well trained in shooting people themselves. Do you remember the Vietnam War? They'll kill y'all just like that.

# Case Study #6: Latrell Sprewell

**The Quote:** (wanting a new deal while then making $14 million a year) "Why would I want to help [the Timberwolves] win a title? They're not doing anything for me. I'm at risk. I have a lot of risk here. I got my family to feed."

**The Judgment:** Insulting! You can feed a family for far less than $14 million a year, unless that family is Prince Fielder's. This quote is also incomplete, because what Sprewell really said was, "I got my family to feed . . . to my pack of voracious pit bulls." Don't publicly complain about your salary. Fans already despise you for who you are. It's what they live for. There's no need to give them extra kindling for their burning pyre of hatred.

# Case Study #7: Garrison Hearst

**The Quote:** "Aww, hell no! I don't want any faggots on my team. I know this might not be what people want to hear, but that's a punk. I don't want any faggots in this locker room."

**The Judgment:** Homophobic! Look, we already know that gays are not welcome in professional sports. The longer you keep that fact quiet, the longer your league can continue to do nothing about it. It's just like sexism. Don't spoil the rampant homophobia for everyone else. Dick. Bashing gays, especially when using a word as insensitive as *faggot*, will earn you fines, and suspensions, and keep reporters and GLAAD protesters badgering you for months on end. Now *you're* the one being buttfucked. Not so much fun now, is it, Mr. Macho?

# Case Study #8: Elijah Dukes

**The Quote:** (to his wife, via voice mail) "You dead, dawg. I ain't even bullshittin'."

**The Judgment:** Stupid voice mail! Elijah Dukes obviously failed to understand that voice mail exists to replay exactly what you said, often multiple times if necessary. If you're going to threaten someone, for God's sake, don't do it over voice mail. For one thing, it's impersonal. For another, it's just about the dumbest thing I've ever heard of. Seriously, Elijah Dukes might just be the dumbest man on the face of the Earth. I ain't even bullshittin'.

# Case Study #9: Mike Tyson

**The Quote:** "My style is impetuous. My defense is impregnable, and I'm just ferocious. I want your heart. I want to eat [Lennox Lewis's] children. Praise be to Allah!"

**The Judgment:** Insane! Eating children is only acceptable to the Lau'ii tribes of Papua/New Guinea. The rest of the world will not stand for it. Besides, children are resourceful. One minute, you're getting ready to enjoy a little Hansel and Gretel Stroganoff, the next minute Hansel's big poppa is throwing your ass in the oven. Not fun.

# Case Study #10: Carl Everett

**The Quote:** "God created the sun, the stars, the heavens, and the earth, and then made Adam and Eve. The Bible never says anything about dinosaurs. You can't say there were dinosaurs when you never saw them. Someone actually saw Adam and Eve. No one ever saw a Tyrannosaurus rex."

**The Judgment:** Retarded! Seriously, what a fucking dumbass. Step aside, Elijah Dukes. I've found me a bigger idiot.

Saying the wrong thing isn't an automatic career killer. Many athletes have bounced back from the ill-timed faux pas. If you apologize publicly for your comments, keep your big piehole shut, and get back to playing ball, you should find yourself back in everyone's good graces in no time.

---

### Clippable Motivational Slogan!

*Young athletes today lack the cognitive ingenuity and verbal adroitness necessary to be able to pontificate in front of a microphone with any semblance of sagaciousness. HOLY SHIT! LOOK AT THAT LITTLE MONKEY RUN DOWN THE FIELD!*

— HOWARD COSELL

---

After all, we are a country that loves to give people second chances, largely because it gives *us* a second chance to tear you fuckers down again.

## Oh, fuck! Reporters! Your guide to the media news cycle.

If you did something wrong, you aren't immediately going to know it. No, the media enjoys building stories to a long and excruciating crescendo, as a way of punishing both you and the viewer. A quick timeline for you.

**DAY 1.** This is the day you did something stupid. Because you were stupid enough to do whatever stupid thing it is that you did, chances are you are also too stupid to know that what you did was stupid. Sound complicated? This is because you are stupid. You will spend your day skipping around in a blissful state of ignorance. I suggest going outside and tossing an Aerobie around. It's like a Frisbee, only gayer!

**DAY 2.** Still no sign of trouble. You hang out, read *TV Guide,* and take a nice steam bath. Everything seems to be okay! Cherish this day, because you're about to get totally reamed.

**DAY 3.** Your remark/crime/illegal canine mixed martial arts federation is noted deep inside a small local paper with a relatively limited circulation, like the *Newark Star-Ledger*. You worry for a moment about your transgression going public. But hey, it's a small paper. Maybe, just maybe, this whole thing will blow over. After all, few people will notice this item. The problem is that the ones who do will say to themselves, "Holy shit! He [raped a puppy/insulted the ambassador to Cambodia/beat a tranny]? What an idiot!" And they will all be journalists.

**DAY 4.** Your little story is listed in the headlines section of ESPN.com. Uh-oh.

**DAY 5.** That little ESPN.com story is now a headline on all major AP sports newswires and sports Web sites. The blogs have now picked it up and immediately make the first round of obvious jokes about your incident. Things like, "Well, he *does* play for the Bengals." I suggest booking a ticket to Curacao immediately.

**DAY 6.** Don Yaeger talks to your mother on the phone for an hour before she realizes that he is (a) a reporter, (b) interviewing her for an extended piece about your mistake, and (c) not you.

**DAY 7.** Yaeger's scathing blow-by-blow account of your fuck-up is posted on SI.com. It's one of those five-thousand-word pieces that no one reads. But the AP will do a news story *about* that news story, gathering together all the most damning quotes from the piece ("That boy was crazy with that shovel!") in one concise, easy-to-read item. And that will be enough to drive your story into Stage 2 of media overkill. This is when the media takes your story and uses it as a platform to discuss larger social issues. Were you caught with a gun? Then the media will discuss gun control. Arrested on a domestic violence charge? Then the media will discuss society's endless coddling of athletes. And, no matter what you did, you can expect people to pull the race card and to be outraged that the story has been blown out of proportion (if you're black) or not blown out of proportion enough (if you're white). Either way, you are now fucking miserable.

**DAY 8.** The media camps outside your home, your team's practice facility, your parents' house, the courthouse, and your urologist's office. Remember: if you give them a quote, you're only adding extra life to the story. So run! Run for your car as fast as you can! You should be able to easily outrun any member of the media.

**DAY 9.** Your arraignment. You plead no contest. Always plead no contest. It's what every athlete does. What does no contest mean? No clue.

**DAY 10.** You issue a press release that serves as both a half-assed apology and a denial. Be sure to mention God in there somewhere. Christians are real suckers for forgiveness when they think you're one of them. You shut yourself in your home, turning off all the lights and duct-taping the blinds shut, vowing never to come out again.

**DAY 11.** Another player just choked a stripper! The media retreats and goes off to pick a fresh rotting carcass.

# HEAR IT FROM AN ATHLETE!

## Obstructing justice in a murder case is especially hard on the person who obstructed justice in a murder case

by Ray Lewis

You come into this league, you're gonna be dealing with some haters. Oh, you can't see them now. They ain't found you yet, like they found me. But they're out there. These haters . . . these hateraters . . . these agents of hateration . . . these hatemongeraters . . . they're lying in wait for you. I know. Because they came after me. And you know why? All because I was at the scene when two men were stabbed to death, then fled in a limo rather than call for help, then obstructed justice, then turned rat on my two friends who were there with me.

All because of that.

These haters don't understand *my* pain. They don't believe in God, like I do. They don't believe in salvation, like I do. These haters in the media, and on the Internet, and in the stands, and in the Federal Bureau of Investigation, and in the way-back of my conscience, they're not interested in learning the deeper truth.

They don't understand that obstructing justice in a murder case is especially hard on the person who obstructed justice in a murder case.

Yeah, those guys that got stabbed probably aren't too happy about being dead. But what about me? What about what *I* went through? My God. There were nights . . . I couldn't sleep. No joke. All I could think was, *Is this gonna be the end of my career? Am I gonna have to forfeit the prorated portion of my signing bonus? What will become of Ray Lewis and his lucrative endorsement deal with Converse?* Did Richard Lollar and Jacinth Baker ever have to worry about that? HELL 2 DA NAW! No, they probably went straight up to heaven and are just sittin' pretty now. Okay? They didn't have to deal with all this media-circus bullshit. They didn't have to go look their teammates in the eye and say, "Brother, I let you down." They didn't have to receive a huge contract extension a year later. They didn't have to do any of that. Ray Lewis did. They got off clean. Me? I had to spend two whole days repenting for what I did. What did those two guys know about personal anguish? Nothing. They ain't lived through what Ray Lewis has had to live through. Probably because they are dead now.

This is what you're gonna have to deal with now that you're a professional. This is what the media does. They build you up into a bigass hero. Then, when you obstruct justice after two people are stabbed, they knock your ass down. Like those reporters don't have anything to hide. No skeletons in their limos. Well, they're liars. Hippopotamuses.

See, these people don't have God inside them. They judge me, without seeing the whole story. They don't see Ray Lewis, the Super Bowl MVP. They don't see Ray Lewis preaching at church every third Sunday of the month. They don't see all that I've done to atone for my sins, and then some. No, all they do is keep their minds closed and judge me based on one mistake I made. Well, two mistakes.

(*rises up*)

BUT I AM NOT ABOUT TO STAND FOR THAT HATE, MY FRIEND! I AM NOT GOING TO LET THOSE HATERS GET TO MY SOUL, ASSUMING THAT I HAVE ONE! NO, I AIN'T! I AM NOT GOING TO LET THEM CHANGE WHO RAY LEWIS IS, EVEN IF THAT COULD POTENTIALLY BE FOR THE BETTER! I AM NOT GOING TO LET THE FAMILIES OF THE VICTIMS CONTACT ME EXCEPT THROUGH MY LAWYER! CAN YOU FEEL ME NOW, MY BROTHER? CAN YOU FEEL THE REDEMPTION? PREACHER RAY IS

(*continued on next page*)

> PUTTING ON A SHOW FOR YOU! PREACHER RAY IS SHOWING YOU
> THE TRUE PATH TO SALVATION! IT IS NOT THROUGH HATE! IT IS
> THROUGH LOVING YOURSELF, AND NEVER FINDING ANY FAULT
> WITH YOURSELF! HALLELUJAH!
>
> How you feel now? You feeling me? Now, I've learned how to block all
> that shit out. I don't read the papers anymore. I don't listen to the radio
> or to fans or to my own inner monologue. I don't have room for haters in
> my life. I am all about the positive, the now, the future. I just keep my
> nose to the grindstone and keep on goin' with God.
>
> And by God, of course, I mean me, Ray Lewis.

**DAY 12.** Almost all the media have abandoned the story and dissipated from your home. A few tenacious ones remain, but they can be easily frightened by a hungry Rottweiler.

**DAY 13.** You step out of your home and witness sunlight for the first time in seventy-two hours. You breathe in the fresh oxygen. Ahhhhhh! Finally, your ordeal is over.

**DAY 14.** FUCK! SOMEONE HAS VIDEO!

**DAY 15.** Repeat the past two weeks. Search for a sturdy rafter in your basement.

# Oh, fuck! You took performance-enhancing drugs!

You already know performance-enhancing drugs have the potential to petrify your testicles. But here are ten other things you may not know about them.

**1. THE PRESSURE TO TAKE THEM CAN BE ENORMOUS.** There is great pressure in professional sports to take illicit substances that can help you become faster, stronger, and douchier. After all, the league minimum salary in most sports is only in the hundreds of thousands of dollars. That's not enough money to live an unnecessarily opulent and shallow lifestyle. You're going to feel an awful lot of peer pressure when Gary Sheffield comes strolling through that clubhouse wearing an actual-size gold medallion of his own head. Steroids could mean the difference between just scraping by and living in a house with its own rotunda. Is that worth possible side effects such as infertility, severe rectal acne, and making the sport of baseball more interesting? For many, the answer is yes.

**2. USING THEM IS TANTAMOUNT TO CHEATING.** Taking a substance that makes you stronger or helps you improve your recovery time is nothing more than cheating. Unless that substance is creatine, which, despite never having been studied on a long-term basis, is okey-dokey. Why? Because it only helps you a small amount, whereas steroids and human growth hormone are exponentially more effective. You see, you can improve yourself, you just can't improve yourself *too much*. You're already a really fucking good athlete, okay? You don't have to rub everyone's face in it. That really pisses people off.

**3. YOU ARE RESPONSIBLE FOR KNOWING EXACTLY WHAT YOU ARE PUTTING INTO YOUR BODY.** If you want to stay clean, you must be vigilant. No excuses. You are a pro athlete now, so everyone will expect you to be an expert in advanced body physiology. So get cracking. Go to Section XII, Subset A, Section 12, Article 8 of your league's collective bargaining agreement and look up which substances are banned. Then cross-reference that list with the ingredient labels of each and every product you buy. Of course, some of these substances may be legal in trace amounts, so you'll have to check the percentage of a certain ingredient, then write out a proportional equation to figure out the exact metric amount contained in a single pill, and then double-check the CBA to make sure it is equal to or below that value.

The media says this is an easy thing to do, so I don't want to hear you complaining about it.

**4. NOT ALL PERFORMANCE-ENHANCING SUBSTANCES ARE BANNED.** There are many performance-enhancing supplements that are perfectly legal to take and taste like complete and utter shit. Products such as Weight Gain 5000, or Joe Weider's Super Whey Fuel, or anything else at GNC that will make your sweat smell like pet food. These are all substances that give you some of the benefits of cheating without *technically* cheating. The key is knowing the difference between a drug and a supplement. You see, a **drug** is an ingestible chemical compound that is regulated by the Food and Drug Administration. A **supplement** is an ingestible chemical compound that is *not* regulated by the Food and Drug Administration. You see how that makes sense? Good.

**5. YOU CAN TOTALLY GET SOME AT ANY GOLD'S GYM.** Let's say you decide to cave in to the pressure and take performance-enhancing drugs. The first thing you need to know is where to get them. And let me tell you, Gold's Gym is *the* place to go for steroids and/or closeted gay sex partners. Just stroll on in, head to the free-weight room, and look for the forty-five-year-old Italian guy who looks like a personal trainer but is actually just a customer harassing other customers about remembering to work the negative. He'll be the one doing shoulder shrugs in jeans, a tank top, and Lugz boots. Ask him to spot for you. Compare workout routines. Grunt together. In no time, you'll have yourself a shady friend who will latch on to you like a goddamn lamprey. After a week of hanging out together, tell him, "You know, Todd, I'm really hitting a plateau on my dead lifts."

Say no more. Within seconds, words like *Clomid, Clenbuterol,* and *buffalo mating stimulant* will pour out of his mouth. He'll procure every known steroid for you to sample, direct from the nearest Mexican apothecary. He'll show you how to use them. You can inject them, swallow them, rub them in, smoke them, insert them as suppositories, drop them on your tongue, spray them in your nose, or bake them into cranberry muffins. Your new gym friend will show you the best way to do it, and then do it with you! Then, you two will wrestle naked in the steam room for an hour. Within days, you'll find yourself more powerful, more energetic, and more prone to slamming your loved ones against the wall at the drop of a hat. Welcome to your new body, my friend. Soon, the aggressiveness you try so hard to rein in off the field will consume you entirely. You'll be like a superhero, with bonus raping ability.

**6. IF YOU'RE GOING TO TAKE A PERFORMANCE-ENHANCING SUBSTANCE, TAKE HUMAN GROWTH HORMONE.** There is no reliable test for it yet. So binge away. Oh, sure, people will say there's "anecdotal evidence" of you cheating. And yeah, there are a few horrifying physical side effects, such as cranial doubling. But who gives a shit if it bags you an extra $100 mil? So you have an abnormally large head now. Big fucking deal. Buy an Escalade with a sunroof. Problem solved.

**7. IF YOU TAKE THEM, YOU ARE IN GOOD COMPANY.** Using steroids doesn't have to be your dirty little secret. Find a teammate or a group of fellow players and make it a dirty *big* secret. It's much more fun to engage in illicit behavior in groups. At least, that's what I've found. The number of professional athletes who have allegedly used PEDs is huge, and only growing: Barry Bonds, Mark McGwire, Roger Clemens, Rafael Palmeiro, Floyd Landis, Mike Webster, Lyle Alzado, Darrell Russell, Sammy Sosa, Ben Johnson, Marion Jones, Tim Montgomery, Ken Caminiti, Jose Canseco, and pretty much the entire roster of the WWE. Sure, many of these people are dead, or disgraced. But, should the same fate befall you, you'll at least have someone to commiserate with.

**8. YOU *WILL* BE TESTED FOR THEM.** Random drug testing is a staple of every major league's collective bargaining agreement. Unless you play baseball, in which case your test will take place on March 3 at 3:00 p.m. sharp every year. Don't forget!

Here's how the testing will go down. You will receive a call from league officials to report to team headquarters. A league official will then meet you in the foyer and escort you to the bathroom. Then, he will escort you to the handicapped stall for privacy. Then, he will make you strip naked, checking underneath your scrotum for any smuggled bags of clean urine. Then, he will tug on your penis to make sure it is not a prosthetic. Then, he will have you urinate into a brandy snifter. He will then swirl the urine three times, take in the bouquet, and give it a taste. Depending upon whether or not he disapproves of it, he may then elect to spit the urine out. That's his decision. He will then have you fill the specimen cup. This cup is then sent to a lab in Alabama, where the urine is placed in a vial and spun around real fast in one of those bitchin' centrifuge things. Then, a lab technician will test the urine. If it comes up positive . . . *BOOM!* One-month suspension. You'd think the process was punishment enough.

**9. TESTING CAN BE BEATEN.** You may also think this process is foolproof, but it is not. Are you urinating your own urine? You asshat. Only amateurs do that. Check online for random strangers who will happily sell you pouches of clean, injectable urine for testing purposes, or just for partying. You can also procure powdered urine, which looks and tastes exactly like Crystal Light. Or you can choose to "cycle" your steroid use in order to test clean during the months of the year you know testing is taking place. It's based on the same principle as timing ovulation, which may also come in handy for you down the road, since using steroids will cause you to grow vestigial female reproductive organs.

**10. IF YOU TEST POSITIVE, NEVER ADMIT IT.** Always blame a tainted supplement. Or blame a Snickers Marathon bar. No one knows what's in those fucking things. Or blame Miguel Tejada. No one ever buys these defenses, but that's beside the point. Blaming a scapegoat keeps you from having to *admit* that you did steroids, and that's all that matters. But you have to stick to your story. Reporters will urge you to come clean, telling you it can only improve your image. Don't believe them! It's the notorious Schaap trap! They'll fuck you blind! Stay strong, my friend! The longer you continue to deny it, the less interested people become in whether or not you confess.

There's also the added bonus that the longer you lie, the more apt you are to begin believing the lie. And once you've phased out the reality of your circumstances altogether, it's like it never happened. Your slate is clean!

# Deeply Penetrating the Numbers

The percentage of athletes using steroids has long been the source of great speculation. But now, I have acquired the official percentages by sport. Here they are:

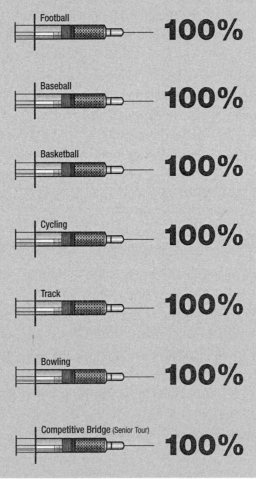

Football — 100%

Baseball — 100%

Basketball — 100%

Cycling — 100%

Track — 100%

Bowling — 100%

Competitive Bridge (Senior Tour) — 100%

Also, if you test positive for drugs, always appeal the ruling. Urine can be mishandled, spilled, or even switched with other urine. Scientists are legendary for their clumsiness, so take advantage.

## Oh, fuck! You got hooked on illegal drugs!

In addition to being tested for performance-enhancing drugs, you'll also be tested for illegal recreational drugs such as cocaine, ecstasy, and that saucy little temptress known as marijuana. A positive test for illegal drugs will merit a suspension without pay. This despite the fact that they have no performance-enhancing qualities, except in professional table tennis, where cocaine can make you *unstoppable*.

But let's skip the practical reasons to avoid drugs for a moment and focus on the moral reasons. Doing illegal drugs isn't just a crime, it's a sin. You can only take legal, prescription drugs engineered by multi-billion-dollar corporations that operate with little to no congressional oversight. That's the ethical way to take drugs. Otherwise, abusing illegal drugs is wrong.

That is, unless you're doing them correctly. If you do drugs the right way, holy shit. I mean, seriously, *holy fucking shit*. You will become an ethereal spirit transcending multiple planes of existence. Every neuron in your body will pulse with red-hot, orgasmic joy. Every step you take will feel like a growing leap toward the stratosphere, and suddenly all that is good in life will collide into one gigantic white dwarf of ecstasy. You will feel as if your heart has burst from your chest and risen to the heavens. I tell you, people who say getting high isn't worth it have never been high. It's *amazing*.

Now, this all comes at a price. Illegal drugs are addictive and can ruin your career. Is it worth alienating your friends and losing your job just so you can do drugs? Probably not, unless the shit you get is really potent.

Let's go through each drug one by one and see the bodies left in their wake.

# Marijuana

**The Victims:** Ricky Williams, Nate Newton, Isaiah Rider, probably a bunch of dipshit snowboarders

**The Danger:** Marijuana is cheap, plentiful, all-natural, has very few known side effects, is not chemically addictive, and even has some healing properties. *That's* what makes it so dangerous. Pot's inherent harmlessness is what draws so many athletes to it, and that can be very harmful. It's understandable why so many jocks love the chronic. You train all day long, then spend all night busting your ass in front of a crowd of forty thousand people throwing ice at you. You can hardly be blamed for heading home, sparking up, and then just chilling the fuck out with some strongass ganja that makes everything look like it's in Claymation. But beware! You may grow to enjoy chilling the fuck out so much that you decide you don't really feel like doing much else. Ask Ricky Williams. That guy loves pot almost as much as I love reading *Sally Forth* every morning.

Pot also makes you fat. I can tell you my physique is the direct result of numerous evenings smoking up and then eating Coffee-mate straight out of the canister. Pot can also make you gay. No joke. One time, in college, I smoked up and thought, *You know, under the right circumstances, I'd consider nailing a dude.* That freaked me out for, like, a week.

Worst of all, smoking pot makes you, almost instantly, a staunch defender of pot. One toke, and you'll soon find yourself calling the DEA "fascist pigs," organizing progressive rock festivals with Tom Morello, and taking up the inevitably futile cause of legalizing pot in America. If there's a bigger waste of time than smoking pot, it's fighting for your right to smoke it. That's the one side effect of weed no one talks about: it can make you the world's laziest tightass.

# Cocaine

**The Victims:** Steve Howe, Shawn Kemp, Len Bias, Dwight Gooden

**The Danger:** Cocaine can cause heart attacks, overdoses, brain damage, and, worst of all, sniffles. George Carlin once said that cocaine makes you feel like having more cocaine. But he never said why. Well, I'll tell you why. If you happen to be someone who is insecure and unhappy, there's no quicker way to speed right through life than snorting rails off a toilet seat every morning. You'll be fifty years old in no time flat, and that much closer to the end.

Cocaine's allure also lies in the fact that it's a huge party drug. It makes women extremely libidinous. I mean, look at Lindsay Lohan. That girl's had more men inside her than FedExField. Once a woman does cocaine, she loses all her inhibitions and becomes singularly obsessed with finding a cheap sexual thrill. That's why I suggest not doing cocaine yourself, but rather keeping it on your person at all times to give away to the honeys.

# Ecstasy

**The Victims:** None that I know of, but if you see another player extending his touchdown dance past the nine-hour, fifty-five-minute mark, he's probably on it.

**The Danger:** Ecstasy can cause severe dehydration and accelerate your heart rate. But, more important, it will turn you into a real dipshit. One hit, and you'll find yourself making weekend trips to Ibiza, listening to Sasha & John Digweed albums that were passé even before the turn of the century, sucking on glow sticks, and walking up to other men and saying, "Oooh! Can I touch your hair? I feel so incredible!" *Guhhhhh.* Leave ecstasy to the Eurotrash. Real Americans do drugs that come from Latin American rebel war zones partially funded by the U.S. government.

Besides, ecstasy is too easy to take. If you want to get high, it shouldn't be as simple as taking a pill with a lightning bolt on it. You should have to bust your ass trying to smoke, shoot, or snort that shit. An *earned* high is way more rewarding.

# Heroin

**The Victims:** None that I know of, but if you can shoot heroin and then go out and play quarterback an hour later, then you must be some kind of superhero or something.

**The Danger:** Are you kidding? Did you not see *Trainspotting*? You see babies crawling on ceilings, man. That's fucked.

# Meth

**The Victims:** Todd Marinovich

**The Danger:** Preferred drug of choice for thirteen-year-old Nebraskan white trash, meth is the rare drug that causes you to lose your teeth *and* develop open sores all over your body. The appeal of that is undeniable. And, for the many young people in Middle America who get hooked, it totally beats hanging out outside the Old Navy again. Still, I'd suggest avoiding it. Any of the above drugs gives you a way better high, and are far more fashionable.

# Crack

**The Victims:** Lawrence Taylor, Darryl Strawberry, Dexter Manley

**The Danger:** See the following page.

# HEAR IT FROM A CRACKHEAD!

## Help! There are centipedes all over me!
### by Darnell Taylor, Crackhead

Help me!

Help me!

My God, you have to help me! There are centipedes all over me!

Can't you *see* them? How can you not see them? My God, they're all over my body! I feel them burrowing into my skin! My lips are turning white! My fingertips are cracked! Ahhhhhh! Help me!

NO ONE IS COMING TO HELP YOU, YOUNG DARNELL.

Oh, no! The Centipede Queen has found me! Quick! Find something to beat her away with! A magazine! A PR-24! Anything!

THERE IS NO HELP FOR YOU NOW, YOUNG DARNELL. WE HAVE DUG DEEP AND MADE A NICE HOME FOR OURSELVES HERE. YOUR CAVELIKE NOSTRILS WILL MAKE A FINE MATING HABITAT, IN-DEED.

You'll never take me alive, Queen! NEVER! Please, help me! Can't you see that they're real? Don't abandon me in my darkest hour! You and you alone can help me find the precious White Stones of Jersey City! Wait in the back alley behind the Gristedes, and a man named Fabrice will appear. He is a purveyor of valuable crystals contained in very small Ziploc bags, and he'll be able to save me! Please! Do it with all haste!

IT IS TOO LATE, YOUNG DARNELL. TIME TO SAY GOOD-BYE.

No, no, NOOOO!

## Chapter 10

# It's About Goddamn Time

## Money

### Mother. Fucking. Paid.

You know, I've spent a majority of this book coaching you on avoiding certain kinds of behavior and outlining troublesome scenarios that may occur as a result of your newfound fame and fortune. And frankly, I've been a bit of a buzz kill. I apologize. I'm a douche. I certainly don't mean to paint your new life as a pro athlete as something horrible. Quite the contrary: as a modern pro athlete, you're entitled to an income and perks that would make Curt Flood shit a brick. So it's time to sit back and enjoy it. What kind of luxurious life awaits you? Consider the game of MASH I designed just for you, on the following page.

Have a friend draw little ticks in the center box until you say stop. Count the number of ticks in the box, and that is your magic number. Count through each option consecutively until the magic number is reached. Then cross off the option that you land on. Do this until there is only one option left on each side. As you can see, you will be left with

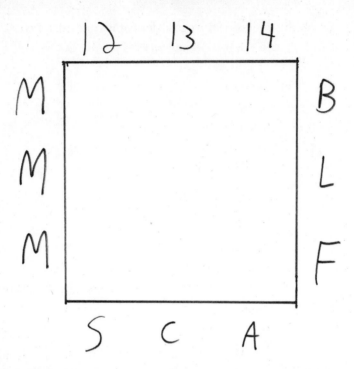

either a Mansion, a Mansion, or a Mansion; a stripper, a cheerleader, or an actress; a Ferrari, a Lamborghini, or a Bugatti; and anywhere between twelve and fourteen children. Sound good to you? Fuck and yes.

The best part of having lots of money is that it allows you to buy things that let other people know that you have lots of money: mansions, limos, speedboats, white tigers, etc. Items like these aren't merely status symbols. That's a shallow way of thinking. No, these material goods are *victory* symbols. You excelled at sports long enough to earn a $40 million guaranteed contract. In the game of life, you just won! You have fuck-you money now! Game over, baby! Everything you buy with that money is a tribute to your triumph over having to spend the rest of your life working like a sucker, like everyone else has to. Every fancy house you buy is a stop on the endless victory parade that is your existence. It's not superficial. It's a celebration. And anyone who thinks otherwise is, pardon my French, a fucking tightass.

So let's shop! I'm taking off the hat of Life Coach for this chapter and putting on the hat of Personal Stylist. It's made of pink satin and has gorgeous yellow feathers sticking out of it. Follow me, girl!

## If it doesn't have a home theater, you're a pussy. Choosing a house.

Allow me to take you through your new 30,000-square-foot dream house. Many pros make the mistake of tying up all their money in new estates and then personalizing them to the point of having little to no resale value. I don't want that to happen to you. I have listed below twenty-six state-of-the-art amenities for your new home. I suggest including only twenty of them. It prevents your new home from becoming a financial albatross, one that only Billy Joel would be stupid enough to buy.

Welcome home, my friend. This is your own private Xanadu. Don't forget to wipe your feet before coming in!

I'm just kidding. It's your house. You don't have to wipe jack shit.

**ATRIUM.** Every mansion needs a gigantic atrium, or foyer. An atrium lets guests know that your house is, in addition to being big on the outside, big on the inside. Be sure to get marble floors installed, or do a tile mosaic of your jersey number. If you're single, or estranged from your wife, I also suggest having random women in bikinis and high heels milling about. You also may want to place a house directory in your lobby, so you know where to go if you really gotta pee.

**GLASS ELEVATOR.** Ever been to a mall? Glass elevators rule.

Sturdy wrought-iron gates help protect you from potential groundlings!

**DUAL ESCALATORS.** A refreshing alternative to the glass elevator for those who want to get a little exercise. Also fun for children to play on.

**PROFESSIONAL CHEF KITCHEN.** Complete with butcher block, All-Clad pots and pans, Viking oven and range, Sub-Zero fridge, and more. Now, you too can be a yuppie asshole who owns a $500,000 kitchen and orders takeout every night.

**ARCADE.** Please invite me over if you have *Cyberball*.

**MOAT WITH MAN-EATING CROCODILES.** Security is paramount to you, the professional athlete. So why not do it with a little flair?

**DRAWBRIDGE TO CROSS MOAT WITH MAN-EATING CROC-ODILES.**

**GAME RESERVE.** I won't lie. These can be rather costly to maintain. But nothing beats the thrill of watching your South African springboks being eaten by your Siberian tigers.

**HEDGE MAZE.** Just make sure this is partitioned off from the game reserve. Mazes aren't as fun with angry polar bears stalking through them.

**MASTER BEDROOM.** I suggest buying a sleigh bed. It adds a Christ-massy touch to all your fucking.

**MASTER BATH.** A stripper pole in the bedroom is so passé. Why not put one in your dual shower? It only adds to the danger.

**SIX-HUNDRED-SQUARE-FOOT WALK-IN CLOSET.**

**WALK-IN CLOSET FOR WALK-IN CLOSET.**

**MEDIA ROOM.** I'll be honest: the other thirty-seven rooms in your house are largely irrelevant. You get yourself a 347" HD set, a Blu-ray player, the entire Sam Peckinpah filmography on disc, a Wii, a satellite dish, a Bang & Olufsen stereo, a wet bar, a regulation snooker table, and a big fucking sectional sofa, and you may as well leave the rest of the joint empty.

**ART GALLERY.** This classes up the house. I would suggest limiting the number of paintings of you to three or fewer. There's a difference between healthy narcissism and unhealthy narcissism, you know. If you play offensive line, I suggest commissioning Botero for all your family portraits.

**INFINITY POOL.** The water just falls off the side! How does it do that?

**LIVING ROOM.** You will never use this. But, if you are married, your wife will demand at least one cold, uncomfortable, formal room in the house. No one will want to spend more than five minutes in this godforsaken room. Avoid it if possible. You can actually feel the stick being inserted into your ass when you enter it.

**DINING ROOM.** Same with this room. The only purpose it serves is to get your home featured in *Town & Country.*

**HELIPAD.** If you can, try to have your helipad located on the roof of your house. That way, every time you leave, you can imagine yourself making a daring escape from a Hanoi POW camp.

**BI-LEVEL, EIGHTEEN-CAR GARAGE.** Be sure to park only seventeen cars here. The last space can be used for old boots, broken children's toys, gardening tools, and dead bodies.

**DAY CARE CENTER.** You gotta put the kids somewhere. By placing a day care center in your home, you can spend time at home with your kids without having to spend any time *near* them.

**INDOOR SHOOTING RANGE.** Indoor shooting ranges provide hours of enjoyment, especially if you turn off all the lights and play in "scuffle mode."

**GLASS CEILINGS.** A staple of some of the world's top-ranked strip clubs, glass ceilings will turn your home into one giant upskirt viewing hall. Also, you can break through the glass ceiling if you ever feel like acting out a metaphor.

**WAVE POOL.** Two giant water turbines are needed to create the eight-foot waves that shoot out from this pool. But you didn't buy a mansion just to worry about petty stuff like your ConEd bill. Or insurance. Or property taxes. Or maintenance. In fact, those additional costs probably never occurred to you at all. So crank that bitch up.

**RECORDING STUDIO.** Many athletes' home recording studios are soundproofed. If you've ever heard former Yankee Jack McDowell's music, you know why.

**GUEST HOUSE.** Smart homeowners know how insufferable most houseguests can be. That's why housing them in an entirely different mansion and never interacting with them is optimal. It's also a great place to house the children once adolescence hits.

Of course, these are merely suggestions. You may come up with all sorts of cool ideas that will allow your house to reflect your personal tastes: putting greens, vineyards,

**DID YOU KNOW?**

The laws inside your home are exactly the same as the laws that govern international waters. Or so I assume.

hostage pits, and things of that nature. The only limit is your imagination. Or, if you have no imagination, the imagination of your interior designer.

And be sure to name your estate. Jayson Williams once named his New Jersey property "Who Knew?", as in, "Who Knew I'd Blow Away My Limo Driver with a Shotgun and Then Try to Cover It Up?"

## Trophies that move! Choosing a car.

Luxury homes are impressive. The problem with luxury homes is that they aren't mobile (except in Arkansas). You have to bring people to your house in order to show it off. That's not enough. You need to let people know that you live a grotesquely opulent lifestyle while on the go as well. And that's where your ride comes in. Remember: your life is a victory parade. And your car is your float.

Or, should I say, *floats?* One car, of course, isn't enough for most athletes. You can't just drive one expensive car around all the time. Then people would assume you only have enough money to buy that one expensive car. A much better rule of thumb is to buy one car for every million dollars that you earn. At a minimum, you're going to want to own seven cars. After all, seven cars means seven times the fun, especially when it comes to emissions testing!

So, ready to drive? Let's go through each class of vehicle. You're gonna need at least one of each of the following.

# SUV

Your SUV will likely be your main traveling car. And expect to travel a lot, since your new luxury home is forty miles away from the nearest urban center. An SUV is good because it can fit all your friends, all your equipment, and 60 percent of your children. And it can do so without the giant pussy stigma of a van or a station wagon. Warning: SUVs are notorious for getting low gas mileage. So I suggest having a lackey fill up the tank for you, to avoid sticker shock.

**Suggested Models:** Cadillac Escalade, Lincoln Navigator, Hummer H2, Chevy Tahoe, Chevy Suburban, GMC Yukon, Ford Excursion, Sherman Tank

# Sports Car

Perfect for nights out with a lady. Nothing turns a woman on more than a really fast car. So hit the highway and floor it. Hit 80, 90, 100. Watch her moan in ecstasy as the wind blows through her hair. Slip your hand between your girl's thighs and move higher and higher as you go faster and faster. Don't stop. Don't you dare stop, you fucking hot rod, you. Cops in the rearview? Oh, that just makes it an even bigger turn-on, baby. Hit 150, 160, 170. Floor it until your woman can't take it anymore and jumps on top of you, attacking you like a tiger unleashed. Now your pelvic thrusts can be measured only in RPMs. Orgasm simultaneously as the car spins out of control and you roll down a steep embankment, leaving you broken and bloody in each other's arms.

God, I want a Porsche so badly.

**Suggested Models:** Ferrari GT, Porsche Carrera, Corvette, Dodge Viper, Lamborghini Diablo (Note: Don't get an Audi TT. Remember: that's ███████████████████'s car.)

# Luxury Sedan

Perfect for formal occasions, a luxury sedan lets people know you are now a man of taste and elegance. I suggest hiring a driver and sitting in the back. It totally makes you feel like Bruce Wayne.

**Suggested Models:** BMW 7 Series, Mercedes S600, Bentley Continental Flying Spur (now with 30 percent more engine trouble!)

# Pickup Truck

Preferred vehicle for Southern white athletes who want to let fans know they ain't turned city folk. Pickup trucks are made for the kinda guy who lets his Labrador ride shotgun. The kinda guy who lives to hunt and fish. The kinda guy who still thinks sushi is weird and disgusting. The kinda guy who listens to Bob Seger. In short, the kinda guy who's a pretentious, red-state asshole.

**Suggested Models:** Ford F-150, Chevy Avalanche, GMC Sierra (Note: I'll be damned if I'm putting a Toyota Tundra or some other kinda Jap truck on this here list.)

# Vintage Car

Vintage cars are great because you can send them in to be refurbished and then take credit for all the work. Why, you can even take it to a vintage car show. It's like a comic book convention for rich people! One other thing: if the film *Better Off Dead* is any indication, restoring a vintage car can really help win over a sneakily hot French exchange student.

**Suggested Models:** Chevy Camaro, Ferrari GT California, Studebaker

## Deeply Penetrating the Numbers

# $1,192,057

**The most expensive car you can buy on the market today is the Bugatti Veyron, which retails for $1,192,057. It has a top speed of 253 mph and goes from 0 to 60 in 2.5 seconds. But it can't time travel, which I find rather disappointing.**

# Motorcycle

You may have a contract clause with your team that forbids you to ride motorcycles. But if you're like Ben Roethlisberger and lack the ability to retain knowledge, that won't matter. Nothing beats owning a crotch rocket that turns your commute into one kickass game of *Excitebike*. I suggest going with a high-performance Italian or Japanese bike. Many of these bikes aren't even street legal. But who buys a motorcycle to obey traffic laws? And the helmet? Ditch it. True, a helmet can save your life. But getting in a chopper accident usually results in injuries such as severe burns and paralysis. Trust me: you don't want to live through any of that horrible shit. A helmet protects you from injury, but *not* wearing a helmet protects you from having to *suffer* through injury. See how much better the latter is?

**Suggested Models:** Kawasaki Ninja, Ducati Monster

---

Buying your new car is, of course, only the beginning. You're going to want to outfit your car with any number of options that help drive up its insurance premium and make it more attractive to car thieves. Some athletes, like the late Eddie Griffin, even have a DVD player with porn available for driver's-side viewing. If you get this feature, I strongly urge you to also invest in an E-Z Pass. It's just common sense.

## What are your thoughts on mustard?
## Choosing your wardrobe and jewelry.

Athletes used to dress in no-frills apparel such as T-shirts and jeans. But fashion-forward mavens like Michael Jordan, along with David Stern's somewhat ironic affinity for Fascist dress codes, have made today's athletes more conscious of personal style. You're a professional now. It's important to dress the part because it makes people think that you take your job seriously, even if you do not. This is a strategy that has worked wonders on Wall Street for years. Those guys get paid oceans of money, and I swear all they do is take Japanese clients to Scores and get ass shitfaced at steak houses. You see, wearing a nice suit gives you that much more leeway to be a total prick. I wrote this entire book while wearing a suit, and I think it really shows.

But you shouldn't dress nicely just for superficial purposes. Wearing the right clothes can help enhance your own self-image. When you look the part of a superstar, you're more likely to assume the confidence of a superstar, and therefore you will play better. And if there's one thing professional athletes need, it's an ego boost. Plus, if you rock a suit without any underwear, it can make you feel all tingly down under. Trust me. When you get some Egyptian cotton lightly swishing back and forth across the glans of your penis, there's no possible way you can have a bad day.

Below are some ideas for your new wardrobe, along with some suggested accessories. Now, fashion trends change by the season, of course. And each fashion season actually takes place nine months prior to the actual season. If it's fall 2009, that means it's summer 2010 on Seventh Avenue. Are you still wearing empire waists? Ugh. That is so winter 2008. God, you're hopeless.

# Fall

It's all about earth tones here. A brown, pinstriped shirt with matching argyle sweater vest makes an inviting complement to all those footballs flying through the air. The jeans? Mavi. Now, $200 for a pair of jeans may sound ostentatious, but you should see what they do for your ass. Makes it feel just like a boxing glove. Top it off with a tweed page-boy cap and cream scarf and you've got an outfit that screams, "I'm warm, friendly, and occasionally playful!" It's the kind of outfit Kobe Bryant wore for one hundred consecutive days after his rape trial was over.

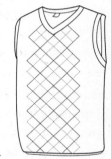

# Winter

PETA may not like the idea of a full-length mink coat. But I love what it does for your shoulders. Very regal. It's the kind of thing Genghis Khan would have worn had he played linebacker (and ancient texts say that this was indeed the case).

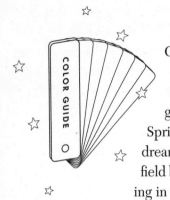

# Spring

Colors! Don't be afraid of bright colors! They don't make you look gay. They just make you look bright and extroverted, two qualities gays have had a monopoly on for far too long. Spring is a time of hope and joy, where fresh day-dreams of pitchers and catchers sprinting onto the field blossom anew. Why not incorporate that feeling in your outfits? Unless you play for the Royals, in which case I suggest you wear all black.

# Summer

You can beat the heat without resorting to tank tops and the occasional Canadian grape smuggler. It's all about breathable fabrics. Rock a crisp linen suit with matching Gucci slides, and nary a bead of sweat will cross your visage. Unbutton those top buttons on your shirt. Hit a hot LA nightclub. Stroll out onto the terrace. Catch the eye of that girl in the orange sarong nearby. Share a flirty giggle. Buy her a fruity drink. Then take her back to your private cabana. It's a scene right out of a Skyy Vodka ad, and it's the same sexual fantasy I have at least twice a week. That can totally be *your* life, man!

# Accessories

Many athletes make the mistake of overindulging in accessories, and it can have serious repercussions. What Jacob the Jeweler won't tell you about that diamond-encrusted Rolex with matching scepter is that you will need Tommy John surgery after one year of wearing it. Shaquille O'Neal owns a necklace with so much ice that, to this day, he still attributes all of his back problems to it. It's a convenient way for him to avoid diet and exercise. I suggest going with the classic diamond stud earrings. They let women know you're rich, but they also let women know that you probably have money left over to spend on *them,* and they really dig that in a man.

One other note on religious jewelry. Many people decry ostentatious religious symbols. They say it's against the teachings of Christ. Wrong. As a Christian, it's your job to spread the word of Jesus throughout the land. The bigger and more noticeable your piece of jewelry, the louder it will speak to the masses. That 300-carat carved ruby cross around your neck is like a giant billboard for God's majesty. It says to people, "I'm Christian, and I am a disgusting success." Is that spreading God's word? Fuck and yes. Who wouldn't want to accept Jesus into their lives after seeing how well it pays off? Plus, you could use the argument that doing such a great service to the Lord makes you exempt from tithing your salary. Now that's putting the "God" in "gaudy."

## The ultimate get-rich-quick scheme: a guide to free agency.

How much money can you earn over the life span of your career? You might think it depends on how good of an athlete you are. Not so. It's really just a matter of good timing. Even a mediocre athlete can earn tens of millions of dollars simply by playing the free agent market correctly. You no doubt have a clause in your current contract that allows you to opt out for free agency early if you choose. EXERCISE IT. I don't

# HEAR IT FROM A
# MINOR LEAGUER!

## Maybe I'll live like a pro one day, too!
## Oh, God. It's never gonna happen, is it? Shit.
### by minor leaguer Ray Johnson

Man, look at you! You got a bigass house, and all those cars, and a freaking speedboat! That is so cool. I can't wait to party with you when I reach the big leagues, man. It's gonna be awesome. When I get up there, man, I'm gonna buy all kinds of cool shit. I'm gonna buy my mom a house, then I'm gonna set up my sisters so they don't ever have to work again. Then, I'm gonna buy a little condo on South Beach, just for chillin' in the off-season. We're gonna party, man. It's gonna be so fucking cool. We'll compare jewelry, hang out at expensive clubs together, get laid. It's gonna be great.

Really.

I'm super excited.

I can't wait.

*(sighs)*

Oh, God.

*(buries head in hands)*

Dear God, it's never gonna happen for me, is it? I'm never getting out of Boise, am I? I'll never make it to the big leagues. Ever.

*(chokes up)*

Shit, man.

I mean, really. Jesus. Shit.

*(grabs tissues)*

You know I'm thirty-one now? Thirty-one goddamn years old. Been playing in this shithole for thirteen years. I've spent nearly half my life here, playing meaningless game after meaningless game. Shit, people don't even come out to watch the games here. They only come out for the theme nights. We had three thousand people turn out for Dress Like Larry King Night. They all left by the fourth inning. Sometimes they let toddlers run around in the outfield in the middle of the game. Christ. Shoot me in the balls.

I heard you guys travel in private planes. Is it true? Oh, God, how I'd love that. We travel in a Bonanza bus that was decommissioned in 1968. It smells like mothballs. We don't go anywhere interesting. Our most exciting road trip last year was to Billings, because they have a theater that plays first-run movies. Imagine that. Imagine spending over a decade riding a bus to nowhere. Imagine living for just one goal and never reaching it. Imagine the emptiness you feel when you realize that it's all been for naught.

I think I'm gonna be sick.

I could have had a family by now. I could have had a career in financial lending or something. Instead, I'm road-tripping it to Pullman for a day-night doubleheader that will be forgotten the moment we finish playing. We're staying at a Motel 6 that's been the scene of six different murders.

*(sticks head between knees)*

I heard you guys carry wads of $100 bills in platinum money clips. Can I see yours? Please? I just . . . I just want to smell it.

*(You pull out a wad of $100 bills in a platinum money clip.)*

Oh, wow.

*(smells it)*

God, that smells so good. Do you ever just smell your money? I'd do that all day if I were you. I'd just sit naked in my room and rub cash all over my face. Then I'd spell out FUCK BOISE on the floor with the bills and take a digital picture of it to be the wallpaper on my laptop.

*(continued on next page)*

# Men with Balls

What am I gonna do with my life? You'd think I'd be old enough by now to let go of my childhood dreams and get started on living a regular old life, but you'd be wrong. The longer I stay at this, the harder it is to give up. The closer I get to the end, the more determined I am to hold on, because I know there's nothing else after this. I envy the guys that get injured. At least their dreams are shattered right away. At least they're forced to quit cold turkey. Me? Deep down, I know I'm never making it. But as long as I'm here, it technically means there's a chance, right?

Right?

Oh, God, I'm doing it again.

I heard you're hitting Chicago next week, is that right? Take me with you. Please. Store me in your luggage. Tie me behind the plane and drag me there if you want. I'll do anything. Please. Half my teammates are eighteen years old. They punch each other in the nuts for fun. Please, I'm begging you. I can't take this.

You can't take me? Okay. That's okay. I understand, man. You got things going on. Maybe one day I'll quit and take up coaching. Plenty of managers have come up through the minors. There's no reason I can't do the same. Who knows? Maybe one day, I'll be managing you! Then we can sit on my veranda, eat some caviar, smoke some cigars, drink a little Patrón, and swap war stories. I'd like that. That would be fun. It can happen one day, right?

Can't it?

Oh, God.

care if you're the worst player in the history of the universe. The fact that you are merely *available* to other teams can increase your salary by 200 percent or more.

You see, most free agent crops are lousy because all the big stars have already signed lucrative contract extensions with their original teams. But shitty teams can't simply stand pat. That's boring and it can really piss off fans. In order to look like they are doing something, teams must sign new players, *any* players, regardless of skill level. Bringing in new players lets fans know that management is making moves, even if those moves prove detrimental to the team in the long run. That way, fans can be assured that they won't be seeing last year's shitty team, but an entirely *new* shitty team.

As a free agent, you represent the hope of better times ahead. The fact that you sucked in the past is immaterial, because there's always the faint possibility that you will find a way to stop sucking in the future. It's a long shot, but it's better than no shot at all. That's why the Knicks will happily dangle $50 million in front of you. You may not be good, but you are different, and miracles do happen, and that's all that matters. Just ask athletes like Daniel Graham ($30 million contract), Chan Ho Park ($65 million contract), or Rashard Lewis ($121 million contract). None of these players are very good. I'm not even sure Chan Ho Park can reach the plate with his fastball. But that didn't stop them from cashing in, and it shouldn't stop you.

In fact, I have come up with an ingenious plan to maximize your career revenue, and it has nothing to do with your ability or desire to win. Are you ready for it? Here it is: be an asshole. No, I'm serious. Be a total fucking asshole. Curse out coaches. Berate teammates. Bitch at fans. Hold out. It could earn you millions, and here's why.

Let's say you start out with a team that gave you a very large contract that covers four to five years. Well, that's four to five years of market prices increasing across the board, increases you aren't able to take advantage of if you stay tethered to your current contract. But if you flip out and start acting like a real prick, there's a good possibility that your team will buy out a portion of your contract, or release you outright, simply so they can be done with you.

There's always another team out there stupid enough to believe that you'll clean up your act. Usually, that team is the Oakland Raiders. Plus, your notoriety could prove useful at the box office. Suddenly, you're being signed to another lucrative contract only one year after you signed your original lucrative contract! There are endless examples of this. Steve Francis was bought out by the Portland Trail Blazers for $30 million. Terrell Owens got $5 million guaranteed from the Cowboys less than a year after being suspended by the Eagles. Hell, it even goes beyond sports. Michael Ovitz was bought out by Disney for $140 million. In all these instances, blatant assholishness paid massive dividends!

So whoever said nice guys finish last had it wrong. Not only do they finish last, they finish ass poor. It pays to burn bridges, my friend. So grab the tiki torches and get your arson on.

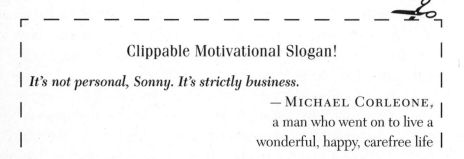

### Clippable Motivational Slogan!

*It's not personal, Sonny. It's strictly business.*

— MICHAEL CORLEONE,
a man who went on to live a
wonderful, happy, carefree life

# Chapter 11

# It's Not Whoring If You're Famous

## Endorsements and
## Extending Yourself Outside of Sports

### The great whitewashing: branding yourself.

Your team salary as an athlete is but a fraction of your potential income. Smart athletes use their playing careers to create a **brand** for themselves. What is a brand? In marketing terms, a brand is the distinctive identity or personality behind a product or company. In this case, the product is you. And your brand identity is designed to trigger a specific emotional response from consumers in the marketplace. This brand personality doesn't have to have anything to do with your actual personality. Far from it. In fact, if you're like most athletes, it should be *miles* away from your true self. Because there's a good chance that your true self is a real douche.

Case in point: Michael Jordan. When you think of Michael Jordan, you think of winning. But you also think of words like *determined, friendly, playful, elegant,* and *sophisticated.* Of course, the real Michael

Jordan is nothing like that. The real Michael Jordan can be an insufferably competitive asshole who curses a blue streak. That's not a very marketable personality, which is why Jordan carefully crafted a brand identity that was closer to that of Gandhi. And it worked. Successful brands like Jordan are ones that connect with people and establish a loyal following, like Apple, or Coca-Cola, or asspounders.com.

If you create a good brand for yourself, that brand can translate into millions of dollars. Best of all, it can continue to make you money long after you've retired. A good brand name can stand on its own and become something that exists beyond you. Since it is only an abstract concept and nothing more, it can be everlasting. Look at Arnold Palmer. What has that old fogy done lately besides split pills and gum his way through a box of Weetabix? Doesn't matter. Because every time you order a lemonade/iced tea drink (known as the Arnold Palmer), that sly coot gets a nickel. Amazing, isn't it? That's the power of a brand name. I, too, have invented my own drink. The Drewtini features six parts vodka, one part applesauce, and just a splash of warm saliva.

You might think the key to having a successful brand name is being nice and friendly. Wrong. What really matters is that your brand personality is *unique*. For example, Allen Iverson is a successful product endorser. And no one thinks of AI as being a very nice person. The irony is that he is, by most accounts, exactly that. But because white American suburban housewives take one look at Iverson and flee in terror, he made the wise decision to create a brand personality that was rebellious, dangerous, and directly from the streets. And little white kids ate that shit right up. By leveraging America's unspoken, lingering racism, Iverson is now a multimillionaire, adored by youths across the nation. See? I told you racism was your friend.

You don't even have to be *good* to become a successful endorser. I want to show you something. These were the ten highest paid athletes in

America in terms of endorsements in 2006, as researched by sports illustrated.com. Now, this list will be out of date by the time this book is published, but it serves as a valuable lesson for you.

1. Tiger Woods ($100 million)
2. Phil Mickelson ($47 million)
3. LeBron James ($25 million)
4. Dale Earnhardt Jr. ($20 million)
5. Michelle Wie ($19.5 million)
6. Kobe Bryant ($16 million)
7. Shaquille O'Neal ($15 million)
8. Jeff Gordon ($15 million)
9. Peyton Manning ($13 million)
10. Dwyane Wade ($12 million)

Look at number 5! Are you shitting me? Michelle Wie can't even beat *girls,* yet she makes more endorsement money than any other female American athlete, and more than any football or baseball player. Why? Two words: *Asian jailbait.* That's Wie's brand identity, and it has paid off quite well. Never mind that she couldn't break 80 on a fucking pitch and putt. When fifty-year-old salesmen see her out on the course in a skin-tight Lycra skirt, they're liable to buy anything, even the idea that the girl is any good. It's a fact: impulse purchasing rises 379 percent when you have your dick in your hand.

You'll also notice that the athletes listed cover a wide variety of brand personae. Tiger Woods embodies excellence. Phil Mickelson is adored by every cocky, disingenuous, lily-white, sales team douchebag at your local muni. James and Wade have the "inner-city children with unrealistic hopes and dreams" demographic covered. Earnhardt Jr. appeals to fans of his late father, but has used his looks to expand that base to people who weigh less than four hundred pounds. Jeff Gordon is loved by a surprisingly robust group of people who like both NASCAR *and* rainbows. Bryant signifies elegance and sophistication, with a dark, seamy underbelly. He's Alan Ball's favorite athlete. O'Neal appeals to the average American who is fat and cross-eyed. And Manning's got the obsessive-compulsives in his pasty grasp.

All of these athletes have used the power of branding to become small, international, one-person corporations. You can do the same. The best part: by transforming from a person into a corporation, you're free to do many of the things corporations do that regular old humans cannot, like skirt federal regulations, use questionable accounting practices, leverage overly generous tax shelters, taint lakes and ponds with arsenic,

## Deeply Penetrating the Numbers

# 27.3/0.1

The typical American household pays 27.3 percent of its income to the taxman. But, because you are now ass loaded, you can get that down to 0.1 percent for all your earnings. How? Two simple steps:

1. Filter your endorsement money through your own offshore eponymous corporation based in Monaco.
2. Own three or more domesticated alpacas.

and so much more. It's a whole other level of deviant behavior, and it makes for quite a naughty thrill.

## No, no, no, it's pronounced *AH-dee-dahs*. Know your shoe company!

Your shoe contract can be worth double or even triple your team salary. Why do shoe companies pay athletes so much? Well, for one thing, it's not like they have a very high cost of labor. Those Filipino kids are content to be paid strictly in caramel popcorn. Little angels. You, on the other hand, are paid quite a bit more (and in hard currency!) because your personality can help lend cachet to new lines of footwear and athletic apparel, cachet that can directly translate into hundreds of millions of dollars in revenue.

How? You see, when children watch you play, they become inspired. They see in you the magnificent potential of what can be achieved in life. Thus, you are the catalyst for their very first childhood dream. And the beauty of childhood dreams is that kids are too naive and stupid to realize that making it in the pros is a one in a million shot, if that. As long as children have that dream, they'll keep plunking down $150 for your signature orange cleats with real mink Velcro straps. The better you are at selling that dream, at keeping reality at bay, the more money you will make. Nice.

So how do you choose which shoe company to go with? Well, you want a shoe company with a brand personality that hews close to your own. If, say, you're a 280-pound wrecking ball of a linebacker who wads up quarterbacks and shits them out like hot diarrhea, you probably don't want to sign with Keds. Here is some basic information on each company to help you in your decision.

# Nike

**Founded:** 1972. Legend has it cofounder Bill Bowerman got the idea for starting a shoe company after making a homemade running shoe sole using his wife's waffle iron. The idea of herding Indonesian children into a crowded sweatshop and forcing them to slave over hot waffle irons, twenty hours a day, under threat of lashing? That came to him just a year later, and the company *really* took off after that.

**Logo:** The Swoosh. This legendary brand symbol is meant to convey the winged feet of Nike, the Greek goddess of victory (Note: her name is actually pronounced *nee-kay,* in case you feel like being a smartass at a dinner party). But really, I think it looks more like a lazy man's check mark. Or a ladle on its side.

**Annual Revenue:** $15 billion. And with just $50 spent per year in overhead on overseas costs, Nike is the most profitable company in the world outside of the Catholic Church.

**Slogan:** Just Do It! Coincidentally, this slogan also represents the entirety of Nike's employee handbook.

**Famous Endorsers:** Michael Jordan, Brett Favre, Derek Jeter, LeBron James, Charles Barkley, Spike Lee (white-friendly version)

**Signature Shoe:** Air Jordans. Before Air Jordans, Nike was more renowned for making running shoes. Air Jordans not only made Nike a brand that transcended all sports, but also introduced the idea that sneakers could be fashionable. Nowadays, it's not unusual for Nike to make shoes using patent leather, polyurethane, and any number of non-breathable, impractical materials.

# Adidas

**Founded:** 1949, in Germany by Adolf (Adi) Dassler. Dassler went by the nickname Adi, hence the name *adidas*. This was fortuitous, because *adidas* sounds like the name of a sneaker company, whereas *adolfdas* sounds like a company that manufactures riding boots used for kicking shooting victims to the side of the road.

**Logo:** The three stripes in the adidas logo are meant to represent each of Dassler's three sons: Gerhard, Helmut, and Ta'Quan. Company officials insist that the word *adidas* not be capitalized. No wonder they continually lag behind Nike in the global sportswear market. Show some fucking confidence and rock the uppercase, my friends.

**Annual Revenue:** $14 billion

**Slogan:** Impossible Is Nothing. The brand slogan suggests that it is not only possible to do the impossible, but that the impossible is, in fact, easily conquered. Obviously, the company has a far lower standard of what is considered outside the bounds of human ability than you or I.

**Famous Endorsers:** Kobe Bryant, David Beckham, Gilbert Arenas, DJ Run, DMC, the late Jam Master Jay (shoelace-free lines only)

**Signature Shoe:** The Samba. This classic adidas model is the preferred shoe of soccer players the world over. On the field, that is. Off the field, most soccer players enjoy the practical femininity of the Easy Spirit pump. Looks like a pump, feels like a sneaker!

# Reebok

**Founded:** 1895, as Mercury Sports. As you can see, Reebok dabbled with a Roman god name before Nike came and ruined their shit with a Greek god name. Everyone knows you only use Roman god names for planets.

**Logo:** The name *Reebok* is derived from a type of South African gazelle. So I guess it sort of looks like that. Oh, who am I kidding? It looks like a highway that's been blocked by a goddamn triangle. The Reebok logo used to include a British flag, before everyone figured out that the only sport British people excel at is darts.

**Annual Revenue:** $4 billion

**Slogan:** I Am What I Am. No doubt this slogan will have changed by the time of this book's publication, if Popeye's lawyers have anything to say about it.

**Famous Endorsers:** Shaquille O'Neal, Allen Iverson, Scarlett Johansson, Jay-Z . . . whoa, back up! Scarlett Johansson? Nice! I'm not sure she's ever played sports, but who cares? Shit, I'd buy used syringes from Scarlett Johansson.

**Signature Shoe:** The Pump. An absolute sensation upon its launch, the Pump was a high-top basketball shoe with a special air pump on the tongue that increased the cushioning around your ankle. I had a pair when I was twelve. I enjoyed pumping it up until my feet were numb and then falling down the stairs.

Those are the three main brands out there. And since adidas owns Reebok, it's more or less a two-horse race for global domination of the foot. Other brands include Converse (for basketball), And1 (also for basketball), New Balance (for runners), Airwalk (for annoying tween skaters I'd like to run over with a snowplow), K-Swiss (for no one), and Champion (for poor people who shop at Payless). All are fine companies with something to offer you, the professional. Except K-Swiss. Who the hell wears those fucking things?

---

### Clippable Motivational Slogan!

*Being a good endorser means not allowing your personal beliefs to interfere with your business relationships. After all, Republicans buy shoes, too. Usually docksiders.*

— MICHAEL JORDAN

---

## "I love this fertilizer!" The best products to endorse.

Part of being a good product endorser is knowing when to say no. It might seem like a good idea to grab a quick $100,000 for that Crazy Frog ringtone commercial, but you need to think of how that will impact your brand image in the long term. If you're seen as a shameless whore who will hawk any old product, you'll become less attractive to high-end advertisers, costing you opportunities down the road (on a totally unrelated note: have you tried new Pond's Nourishing Facial Scrub? I can really feel the deep clean!).

You don't necessarily have to be picky about what products you shill, you just need to choose products that make it appear as though you have discerning tastes. Ever seen Derek Jeter's cologne? Looks fancy, right? Wrong. It's made entirely of used brake fluid and Country Time Pink Lemonade mix. Hint of saffron, my ass.

Remember, you want to choose products that mesh synergistically with your newly established brand personality. If at all possible, you may even want to think of a line of products that bear your name. For example, Pacman Jones once trademarked a fragrance that smelled like freshly detonated C4 plastique explosive. It was a huge hit in some of the more blighted portions of the Southeast. Apart from shoes and athletic apparel, here are some other products that you can safely endorse without any danger of cheapening your image.

**SPORTS DRINKS.** Gatorade has long been a favorite product of athletes both on the field and on camera. Peyton Manning, Mia Hamm, and Michael Jordan are just a handful of the famous names that have stepped up to pitch Gatorade's patented formula of radium-infused seawater. And you can do it, too! After all, Gatorade is constantly thinking up new ways to repackage Gatorade to make it look kinda different: Gatorade Frost, Gatorade Fierce, Gatorade Ice, Gatorade Bloodbath, and such and such.

**FAST FOOD.** Fast food endorsers love to have athletes hawk their food for obvious reasons. If a world-class athlete like you can eat McDonald's, then their food has to have some semblance of nutritional value, right?

This, as you know, is not true. But here's why it's still okay to pitch products like the Double Bacon and Cheddar Ranch Pork Chopwich. Most Americans are acutely aware of the health hazards of fast food. Yet many continue to eat it anyway, due to a simple lack of willpower. These people are weak, pathetic Americans that we don't need. They drive up our health insurance premiums, drag down our economy, and are anything but aesthetically pleasing. By pitching in and making it that much harder for them to give up all that delicious, hearty food, you're helping our nation purge itself of these fat, disgusting wildebeests. And that's doing a great service to all the skinny, good-looking Americans. Kudos!

**FASHION.** Follow my fashion advice from chapter 10 and you're a shoo-in to become a part of any new Gap campaign. Because Gap never bothers to change any of the shit they sell (those 1969 jeans are *hot!*), they're in constant need of new athletes and celebrities to model them, so that people won't notice. Black pants? On a woman? That's fucking crazy!

**WATCHES.** There's no easier money in the world than popping over to a photo shoot, throwing on an Omega Speedmaster set to 10:10, and then staring into the camera with a steely look of determination. It's the basis of *all* watch advertising the world over.

**WHEATIES.** Is there a more iconic endorsement pairing in the world than athletes and Wheaties? Olympic gold medalists and championship teams have decorated the famed Wheaties box for decades. Never mind that only eighty-year-olds eat Wheaties. Or that Wheaties turn soggy three seconds after the milk hits the bowl. I'm serious. Don't even think about putting the milk back in the fridge. Don't even screw the top back on, or you'll have a bigass bowl of doo-doo brown sludge to wade through. Nevertheless, as long as Wheaties continues their time-honored tradition of marketing to the wrong demographic, you should take advantage.

**VIDEO GAMES.** Your union has licensing agreements with many prominent video-game manufacturers. As such, you'll receive a cut of the profits off the deal. And you'll be asked to appear in the occasional EA Sports ad or two, where you get to look all sweaty and grunt at the camera, "It's in the game!" Bad. Ass. Best of all, you'll have your very own video-game avatar. Designers at EA will record your movements by dressing you in a black motion-sensor suit and then having you simulate 7,500 possible game scenarios against a tennis ball on a broomstick. It's fun for the first five minutes. After seventy hours? Not so much.

Video-game companies will assign ratings to your video-game doppelgänger in categories like Speed, Hands, Strength, Intelligence, and Hair. Unfortunately, they make these ratings based on *reality,* and not on how good you think you are. This makes for many pissed-off athletes every year. No one wants a high rating in Fucktardedness. But it happened to Philip Rivers. So steel yourself now.

**BEER / LIQUOR.** As an active player, you are not allowed to endorse alcoholic beverages. Your league can and does sign all the beer endorsements it pleases, but you cannot. Why? Because having a single player endorse alcohol sends a bad message to children. Whereas, if faceless league executives do the same, kids have little to no interest. Without your explicit endorsement, kids barely notice the signage around the arena. Or the blimps. Or the branded concession cups. Or the shooter girls walking around the parking lot. Remember: stadiums aren't role models. Athletes are.

**LOCAL ADVERTISERS.** Regional businesses *love* hiring local athletes to get ~~gullible~~ enthusiastic townsfolk coming through the door. The production value and design of these ads aren't great. Most of them are shot on a Fisher-Price PXL2000. Expect the finished ad to have lots and lots of starbursts. But who needs production when you've got a handsome athlete like Randy Johnson pitching for you?

Yes, local ads are the best way for you to make a quick buck without hurting your national image. But don't take it from me.

---

 **HEAR IT FROM TWO ATHLETES!**

## Right now you can lease a new Mercury Mariner for no money down!
by Carson Palmer and TJ Houshmandzadeh

**Carson:** Hi, I am Carson Palmer.

   **TJ:** And I am TJ Houshmandzadeh.

**Carson:** And right now, Mark Randolph Lincoln/Mercury would like us to pass . . . *(throws ball to Houshmandzadeh)* the savings on to you!

   **TJ:** It is their annual clearance event, and right now you can catch . . . *(catches ball)* a new Mercury Mariner with no money down!

**Carson:** I am sorry, TJ. Did you say no money down?

   **TJ:** That is right, Carson. No money down! And 0 percent APR for qualified buyers!

**Carson:** Wow, that sounds like a real winner . . . of a deal!

*(continued on next page)*

---

**TJ:** Ha ha. It is, Carson. Provided you buy on approved credit. Excludes taxes, tags, and $289 processing fee. See dealer for details. But hurry in to Mark Randolph Lincoln/ Mercury today! This offer ends December 1!

**Carson:** December 1? Uh-oh. I had better . . . scramble in! Ha ha!

**TJ:** Ha ha. That is a very good one, Carson. *(cameras stop rolling)*

**Carson:** God, I wish I didn't have to do all these local ads.

**TJ:** No shit. This isn't worth a glass-bottom boat, man.

**Carson:** Who the fuck buys a Mercury?

**TJ:** I really hope this Randolph guy's check doesn't bounce.

# DID YOU KNOW?

That Randolph guy's check totally bounced.

## Chapter 12

# It's Like Dying in Advance!

## Retirement

### This is just the beginning—of a slow, painful death: realizing you're done.

It is often said that athletes die twice. Not so. You, the professional athlete, only die once. Usually around age thirty-five. Your actual death later on doesn't count, since the world will have long forgotten about you by then. In between, there lies the enormous expanse of time that is your retirement. If your life were a book, retirement would be the five-hundred-page epilogue that nobody reads. It is a long, agonizing period, where your past looms ever larger as it grows more distant. It is the time of life when your dreams are fulfilled but your expectations are not. You always dreamed of having all this free time to yourself. But you'll be shocked at just how dreary life can be sitting at home at 3:00 p.m. on a rainy Tuesday afternoon. I'm telling you, man, there ain't *shit* to do.

That is why I say to you: never retire. Ever. Media people love to urge athletes to retire "at their peak" and lament the ones who hold on to their careers well past their prime: Willie Mays, Johnny Unitas, Michael Jordan, etc. *Fuck* the media. You're a professional athlete. Only a tiny fraction of people on this Earth ever get to call themselves that, and the rest would kill to be included in such company. You're an icon. A rock star. A fucking demigod. Who gives that up voluntarily? Idiots, that's who.

Smart athletes are the ones who stay in the game until they have to be pried away with the jaws of life. I'm not being sarcastic. If there is one genuine piece of advice in this book, it is this: voluntarily walking away from your childhood dream is insane. Don't listen to the media. Don't listen to your wife. Don't listen to your neurologist. Play the game until no one wants you. Even if you aren't as good, you're still pretty goddamn good. And you're still living more of a life than some fuckstick walking around a golf course.

Hanging on to your career is also an excellent way of coping with the deterioration of your skills. Retire early, and you'll never know if you still had some gas left in the tank. But if you hang around for years, bouncing from team to team, you'll *know* that you suck. And you'll have learned how to come to grips with that fact. Unless your name is Evander Holyfield.

Once you begin your decline, you'll start to see the light at the end of the tunnel. Cocky new draftees will show up on the scene. At first, you'll say to yourself, "*Pfft*. These rookies don't know shit. They're all young, dumb, and full of cum." Then you'll watch them leap eighty inches up in the air and dunk with their feet. You'll hate them, and you'll hate the fact that they take it all for granted. But, secretly, you'll envy them, wishing you could be them. Congratulations. You now know how it feels to be a sports fan. Why, you're just like me now! Welcome to the Dark Side.

Eventually, your team will approach your agent and ask that you take a pay cut. You'll balk. "Fuck that!" you'll say, or words to that effect.

Then, you'll have your agent put out feelers to other teams around the league to see if any of them would be interested in your services. When they all say no, you'll go crawling back to management and accept their pay cut. Only now, they'll demand you take an even *steeper* pay cut. Fuckers, I know.

Once you take your pay cut, you'll soon find yourself eased out of the starting lineup. At first, this will come as a shock to you. But don't fret. After about thirty years, that shock kinda wears off. After that, you'll start to see the writing on the wall. Reporters will stop flocking to your locker. Your national endorsements will dry up. Younger players who once pretended to listen to your advice will, at long last, feel free to ignore you completely. And all the groupies that hit on you will be on the plus side of forty, and have that wrinkled upper lip that only comes from decades of fellating four packs of Parliaments a day.

Once the season is over, your team will cut you loose. In the ensuing couple of years or so, you'll sign with a handful of other teams, playing for the league minimum if you aren't cut in training camp. You may even do a stint or two in the minors. During this time, you'll grow increasingly disenchanted with your sport: how they build up young men only to discard them like used tissues once their skills have diminished.

*Now* you're ready to "retire." See how easy it is now to give it all up? And how dumb it is to retire from your sport when you're still good at it? No one walks away from a job they enjoy. You must first grow to despise that which you once held so dear. That way, retiring is a snap. That's how the rest of America does it, and that's how you should do it.

Ah, but what to do now that the end has begun?

# "I still got it, baby! Holy shit, my back just went out!" The art of the comeback.

Many athletes, when they retire, do so for the expressed desire of spending more time with their families. As a family man, I have to tell you: there is only so much time in each day that you can spend together as a family before all of you grow sick to death of one another. Unless you're the kind of person who enjoys being asked, "What's that?" by your children over and over again. I keep telling my kid it's a goddamn school bus, but it just won't sink in.

Anyway, once you discover just how boring life at home is, you're going to start entertaining thoughts of coming back to play. This is perfectly natural, and good for the sporting industry as a whole. Fans love comebacks. Or, at least, they love the idea of them. It's something to get overly excited about before your slow, underwhelming play becomes a day-to-day reality. Now, it may be worth coming back just for that initial burst of misplaced excitement. But I suggest you carefully consider these five case studies before doing so.

**MICHAEL JORDAN.** Jordan retired twice. His first comeback, made after playing minor league baseball, was a rousing success, resulting in three more titles. The second comeback, made after he realized that a retired Michael Jordan didn't earn quite the dicksucking that an active Michael Jordan did, was far less successful. The lesson: if you're going to be dumb enough to retire early, do it waaaaay too early. Sure, you'll waste precious years of your athletic prime. But think of the drama!

**GEORGE FOREMAN.** Upon his return to the ring in 1994, Foreman knocked out Michael Moorer to become, at age forty-five, the oldest (and many would say jolliest) heavyweight champion in history. He then used his newfound fame to transform the traditionally gay panini press into the very heterosexual George Foreman Grill, earning hundreds of millions of dollars from connoisseurs of smushed, bone-dry food. The lesson: if you're going to come back at an advanced age, make sure your sport is in such pathetic shape that you can essentially win by default. In objective terms, Foreman's victory was rather unimpressive. But winning the heavyweight title still *sounds* like a real kickass achievement. One that can move some motherfuckin' grills.

**REGGIE WHITE.** The late Hall of Fame defensive end made a brief comeback with the Carolina Panthers in 2000. His play was pedestrian, notching only five and a half sacks. But he collected a cool $1 million for his troubles. White cited God's will when he came back to play. God, as it turns out, is a rather shrewd capitalist. The lesson: can you earn a million bucks by being retired and finally getting to know your wife as a person? Fuck and no. That is *so* not what God wants.

**BJÖRN BORG.** The tennis great made a brief comeback in 1991, only to lose his first match to a journeyman player while using an old wooden racquet. He then immediately went back into seclusion. The lesson: if you're going to come back in tennis, don't be a cheap asshole. Spring for a carbon-fiber racquet. For God's sake, a Prince doesn't cost *that* much. You won't even need a shock absorber.

**MUHAMMAD ALI.** Ali returned to the boxing ring four years after being banned from the sport for refusing to serve in Vietnam. Ali regained the heavyweight crown and then retired in 1979. But a comeback fight in 1980 against Larry Holmes left Ali badly beaten. Unlike Foreman, Ali decided to come back at a time when the heavyweight division was perhaps at its strongest. If he had simply waited another fourteen

years to come back, he probably would have cleaned up. Alas, the punishment Ali took then left him unable to speak. But I have to say, the guy
can play the shit out of a tambourine.

All of these examples should offer fair warning to you. If you're going
to come back after your skills have clearly diminished, you'd better be
prepared for disappointment. Then again, you'll get to see all your old
friends, fly in private planes, make lots of money, and be treated like the
Sultan of Brunei. So really, who gives a shit if you bat .198? Being good
at the game is nice, but just being *around* it still kicks a whole lotta ass.

# DID YOU KNOW?

The oldest professional athlete to stage a comeback was Hall of Fame
hockey player Gordie Howe, who made a brief minor league appearance
with the IHL Detroit Vipers in 1997, at the age of seventy. Fans in the
stands were amazed to see Howe on the ice, rather than encased *in* it.

## "Christ, I'm bored." What to do with the rest of your life.

Once you retire for good, it's time to settle in and figure out how to pass
the time. Your life is now perfect, comfortable, and completely devoid of
conflict. But you'll soon discover that you now have nothing left to strive
for. You'll come to realize that the pleasure was in the journey and not
the destination. What's left to accomplish? Even if you did set new goals
for yourself, you now lack the physical skills to attain them. Just what the
fuck are you supposed to do?

# It's Like Dying in Advance!

Fear not, for I have a very simple solution: drink. Drink every day, without regard to your health and/or social mores. You'd be surprised at how well a scotch on the rocks at 11:00 a.m. breaks up the day. Alcohol was invented thousands of years ago by ancient tribes of people, people hell-bent on figuring out a way to numb the pain of a life devoid of television and Chap Stick. You too can use it to block out the existential dread of life's denouement. Mickey Mantle did it. Joe Namath did it. Brett Favre will almost certainly do it. Now it's your turn. I suggest getting hooked on wine. Many former athletes become oenophiles as a way of dressing up their alcoholism. Saying you have a passion for booze makes you sound like you have a disease. Saying you have a passion for wine makes you sound like a dude who races yachts.

If alcoholism isn't for you, consider these other retirement pursuits.

**BECOME A TV ANALYST.** Ever criticize someone without actually criticizing them? Then ESPN has a studio position open for you immediately. Shit, you don't even have to know proper diction. Lou Holtz works as an analyst, and I remain convinced that man has a nonvisible cleft palate.

The beauty of being an analyst is that, as a former athlete, you are presumed to have a deep knowledge of your sport. And even if you don't, even if you're like Merril Hoge and possess only a partially functional temporal lobe, you have an automatic comeback to any naysayer. And that is this: "Hey, asshole, if you never played my sport, then you can't possibly begin to understand what I'm talking about. And you certainly aren't in a position to criticize anyone out on the field, because they'd knock you on your ass." Check and mate. That is bulletproof logic that will keep you in the broadcasting chair for a very long time, no matter how asinine your commentary may be. Ask Tim McCarver.

**BECOME A COACH.** Are you fucking crazy? You saw how hard those guys work. Christ, some of them don't even shower. Look at Bill Belichick. That guy won multiple Super Bowls. Does he look happy to you? Hell no. He looks like someone just pooped in his coffee. And you don't want to fuck with those nanobots.

**PLAY VIDEO GAMES.** Video games are becoming more and more realistic with every new platform. Christ, I wish I had more time to play them. Instead, I have to do shit like work, or do chores, or host "get-togethers." Fuck. But you, my friend, are retired. You don't have to work, and you can afford a maid. So buy yourself a copy of *Hitman 2* and go to town. Or pop in *Madden 2036* years from now and play as your video-game self. After all, your avatar never ages. It's like you're still in the league, only you don't have to work hard to achieve success. That's a win-win in my book.

**HIT THE LECTURE CIRCUIT.** As a retired athlete, you can fetch upward of $10,000 for a single public speaking engagement, and some-times more than that. Why? Because Fortune 500 companies all across the country are constantly holding off-sites. What's an off-site, you ask? An off-site is when employees are torn from their families and shuttled out to a business park in some godforsaken exurb to sit in soul-crushing, team-building seminars for three days straight. It's like training camp, only with a 50 percent suicide rate.

Companies need something, anything, to help boost worker morale in between boring off-site meetings all day and getting ass shitfaced at Ruby Tuesday later in the evening. That's where you come in. You played a sport. You know how to motivate people, especially the payroll depart-ment of a local industrial grain supplier. Best of all, you don't even have to be good at public speaking. You can be a lisping stutterer and it won't matter. All that matters is that you are mildly famous, and that you're giving those folks a new person to look at after being trapped all day long in a Residence Inn conference room with the same motherfuckers they see day in and day out. You'll be greeted as a liberator.

**PLAY GOLF.** Golf is the refuge of countless ex-athletes, and it's easy to see why. Golf is extremely time-consuming, and it lets you continue to indulge your borderline obsessive thirst for competition. Best of all, golf is the kind of game in which you can work tirelessly to improve, only to experience setback after setback. It doesn't matter how many lessons you take, or what kind of driver you use. Oh, you may break ninety one day. But the next day you're right back in the shitter, five-putting from ten feet away BECAUSE THE FUCKING GREENSKEEPER DIDN'T DO A FRESH CUT IN THE LATE MORNING! THAT FUCKING IRISH COCKSUCKER!

So you see, golf continues to present new, insurmountable challenges all the way through to your death. You'll play out the rest of your life just as Sisyphus did. And that guy absolutely adored retirement.

**RUN FOR OFFICE.** Gerald Ford. Jack Kemp. Bill Bradley. Steve Largent. Heath Shuler. The list of famous athletes that went on to successful careers in politics is surprisingly robust. Former athletes make for great candidates because of one crucial trait: name recognition. Rookie candidates have to spend millions of dollars in campaign funds just to get their name out to the public. Ah, but you! People know who *you* are, my friend. They don't know anything else about you, like your character, or your ethics, or whether you'd be the kind of congressman who would use Hurricane Katrina funds to build your mistress a luxury yurt in Wyoming. But hey, at least you aren't some dipshit nobody.

As an athlete, you're also well versed in dodging questions, and giving long-winded responses that have nothing to do with the question asked, and that's important to political handlers all across the nation. Athletes are also considered by voters to be far more down-to-earth than their weaker, nonathletic opponents. Look at Hillary Clinton. I bet that frigid bitch never picked up a field hockey stick in her life.

**ACT.** Pro sports serve as a direct pipeline into Hollywood. Howie Long, Brian Bosworth, Jim Brown, Alex Karras, Lawrence Taylor, OJ Simpson: they all went into acting after hanging it up, and so can you. You'll be playing the part of yourself. And it doesn't matter if you're not a great athlete anymore. They can just CGI that shit. You'll look fucking *good*. Best of all, you'll spend the rest of your life just like all other Angelenos: casually disenchanted with everything, constantly text-messaging other people when you have company over, and flaking out on friends and family so that you can hang out at the Chateau Marmont while staring at the inside of your own rectum.

**HIT THE MEMORABILIA CIRCUIT.** Remember the autograph hounds in chapter 5? Well, how would you like to hang out with them all day long? In exotic locales such as Albany, Grand Rapids, and Spokane? With fellow autograph whores such as Pete Rose? Sound like fun? Then go for it! You're probably the kind of person who doesn't care whether you live or die anyway!

**NURSE YOUR CHRONIC PAIN.** If you played in the NFL or participated in any other sort of physically taxing sport, chances are you're not going to be able to do much of anything once you retire. You'll probably need a knee replaced. And a hip. And a shoulder. And a larynx. You may need five or more prosthetics. You may need a cane. You may need those arm brace crutch thingys that one chick on *ER* wore that make you look like you're dying of polio.

Regardless, you're probably going to play out the rest of your life tending to your chronic ailments. During the few hours a day you don't spend in a doctor's waiting room, you're going to need enough painkillers to kill Judy Garland all over again. But let me tell you something about living the rest of your life in a drug-induced stupor, with only your memories to comfort you: those drugs are *awesome*. And legal. They make you feel like you're lying on a warm down comforter. Throw in a vodka tonic for good measure and you are living the high life, my friend. Even *shitty* movies are good when you're on Percocet.

Like I said, you already won the game of life, baby. That Demerol pumping through you? That is just icing on the cake.

## Deeply Penetrating the Numbers

# 54.2

The life span of the average professional athlete is 54.2 years. Bored with your retirement? Don't worry. It's not gonna last very long.

## Death, and how it will affect your career.

Welcome to the end. This is it. You're dead. But, as an athlete, you're not quite as dead as all the other regular schmucks out there. You see, great athletes often transcend death. Their names live on long after they've shuffled off this mortal coil. They have books written about them. They get tunnels and bridges named after them. They live on in memories passed down from one generation of fans to the next. Athletes like Babe Ruth, Ty Cobb, and Ben Hogan: these men still live on in spirit. In fact, they thrive. Many of them are far better known today than they were when they were alive.

And that's the best part about being a professional athlete: even when you're dead, you're still kind of famous.

We Americans all fear death. Because we're the kind of society that forgets shit five minutes after it's happened, there's a terrible collective anxiety that our lives will get a similar kind of treatment once they have ended. I know this firsthand. I'm fucking terrified of dying. I don't believe in heaven or any of that shit. I think it all just goes to black. Forever. And man, that makes me want to wrap myself naked in a shower curtain and scream for my mommy's warm embrace. Because once I'm forgotten, then all that's left of me is gone. There's nothing there. Not a trace. It's as if I never existed. I never counted. I never meant anything.

But you! You, my friend, led the National League in RBIs in 1974. Yes, you, Willie Stargell! It says so right in this sports almanac. And, as long as they keep publishing almanacs, your name remains there in perpetuity. Your accomplishment is final. It is set in stone. And thus, so are you. Great athletes don't die. Like the characters on Keats's Grecian urn, they are forever frozen in time at the exact moment when they are at their very best. Who cares if the rest of your life is forgettable? You conquered death! You faced the Grim Reaper, and you deked the shit outta him. You live on, baby! Why rest in peace when you can still make some fuckin' noise right here on terra firma? Huh?

You are now officially an immortal. Because you, good sir, were a *man with balls*. Great, big hairy balls that made everyone sit up and take notice. I'm proud to be able to call myself your life coach. And I'm equally proud to call myself your *death* coach. In many ways, you'll always be like a son to me. An abstract, nebulous son I can't quite picture in my head, who hopefully helped earn me a shitload in royalties. I'll never forget ya, kid. You had the balls of a champion. Stuart Scott said they tasted *sublime*. I want you to be proud of those balls. They served you well.

And lest you think your journey is at an end, guess again. I've got a very special someone here to let you in on a little secret.

---

# HEAR IT FROM A DEAD ATHLETE!

## Even in heaven, my fucking leg still hurts
### by Johnny Unitas

Hoo boy. I gotta tell you, heaven is gorgeous. When I passed on from the tangible plane of existence, I expected lots of clouds and cherubs playing harps and whatnot. But it wasn't like that at all. There was this beautiful, winding, golden road in front of me, surrounded by rolling fields of glowing, amber wheat. And the sun sat hovering above the horizon, in a perpetual state of clear dawn. Never saw anything so pretty. At the end of the road was a gate. But it wasn't the ostentatious, pearly gate that you always read about. It was an old-style, carved wooden door, around ten feet high. Next to it was a rather unassuming little man who stared me down and offered me a wide smile. His nose crinkled and little crow's-feet formed around his eyes as he shouted across the way to me, "Welcome, John!"

(*continued on next page*)

---

# Men with Balls

St. Peter. Man, he wasn't anything like I expected. Yet when I saw him, everything about him felt appropriate. Felt like a brother, or someone I knew well and was finally getting to see again. Everything about this place felt warm, welcoming, like home. I wasn't scared. I wasn't daunted. I was just comfortable. So, without hesitation, I started walking along the road toward Peter.

And then, my fucking sciatica flared up again.

I tell you, even in heaven, my fucking leg still hurts. I thought I had gotten rid of this back when I died. Forty years I lived with this shit. It was like someone took a knife and tore down my leg from ass to ankle. Hell, even lying down didn't do anything. So I figured dying would probably take care of all that. I figured nerves don't feel pain when you're dead and all, and that your soul doesn't carry any of the physical deterioration you experienced during life on Earth.

But shit, was I wrong.

You can't find a decent orthopedist here. Heaven contains pretty much every person on Earth who died. Ever. You realize how many people that is? Trillions! You'd think a fair number went to hell, but you'd be wrong. Most everyone gets into heaven. They're very lenient about it. Hell only has about five people, and that's including Frank Zappa. Just finding my mother was a huge pain in the ass, let alone some doctor.

There's also the fact that most of the doctors here are from the past. Hell, one of them thought I was a warlock. What an idiot. And I thought the NFLPA had shitty medical coverage. At least they had a prescription plan down there. I'd gladly trade one night at the sumptuous buffet in exchange for a little Celebrex. One of the quacks here said chewing on milkweed would help the pain. Are you shitting me?

Most people are enjoying themselves here. I've noticed it's only former athletes who have had their pain transcend celestial worlds. Bronko Nagurski still has a knee that flaps around like a windsock. Lyle Alzado forgets every goddamn thing you tell him. And Wilt Chamberlain still has the lesions. I have a theory on this. Otto Graham thinks the wear and tear we experienced on the field was so brutal that we carried it with us to this place. But I think that's horseshit. I see war vets walking around with nary a limp.

Me, I think we traded some of our immortality in this place for a little piece of it back on Earth. I think we gave a little bit of our souls to the game in exchange for its rewards. Which I think is unfair, since I had to spend most of my playing days in Baltimore. You ever been to Baltimore? Baltimore is an elephant's asscrack.

Hang on a second. I've got to stretch my hammies. It's the only thing that soothes the pain. Ooooh! Still feels like I'm shitting lightning bolts. *Guhhhhhh.*

Anyway, what was I talking about? Oh, yeah, selling our souls. Okay, it wasn't quite like that. I don't think we made a deal with the devil. But I do think we pay a price up here for all the fun we had down there. Is that fair? Probably not. I was just doing what came naturally. I liked football and was good at it. So I played it, and damn if I didn't play it better than any son of a bitch ever played it. I didn't know that was gonna happen. Didn't ask for it. It just happened that way.

So why can't a man get some fucking Advil around here?

It's not as if I haven't paid a price for it already. When my playing days were over, I had pain. Agonizing, unrelenting pain. Sometimes the pain was so intense I couldn't think of anything else. I couldn't walk. I couldn't hold my grandkids. I couldn't just sit and *be.* Seems like God got plenty even with me for all that I enjoyed. But apparently not. Because it still feels like someone took a Garden Weasel to my hip. I'm 98 percent gristle at this point.

Sometimes, when I'm playing cribbage up here with the boys, one of

(*continued on next page*)

them will ask me if it was all worth it. Was it worth a lifetime of pain, in my life and now beyond, worth people hectoring me all the time, worth all the boring interviews with dipshit reporters, worth all the stupid bullshit that seems to get piled on top of sports year after year after year?

Well, let me tell you something. When I handed the ball off to Alan Ameche back in that '58 title game and we beat the Giants, the feeling I got was . . . well, it wasn't of this world, or even of heaven. I'm supposed to say getting married and having kids is the best feeling ever, but that's a lie. This was far better. That day, we were better men than any other men. Fuck all men being equal. That's for pussies. The purpose of sports is to prove which men are better than others. And, that day, we were better than everyone. And everyone in the stadium, and watching on TV, knew it. In that moment, I felt better than any man could ever feel at any time about anything on Earth. And forevermore, I can always go back in my mind and reenact that moment, step by step. I can refeel it. I can once again become the baddest motherfucker to ever walk the planet. And there are very few people in history that ever get to do that.

So was it all worth it?

You bet your sweet ass it was.

Ouch!

Did I just feel a twinge in my shoulder?

You gotta be fucking kidding me.

# Acknowledgments

This book would not exist without the support of the following people. In other words, it is entirely their fault.

Mrs. Drew and the Girl, the two funniest people I know ☁ My mom and dad ☁ My brother and sister and their families, all of whom are uncommonly awesome human beings ☁ My wife's family, who took me in as one of their own. If you read this book cover to cover, you know what an incredibly charitable act that is. ☁ Editor Junie Dahn, who gave me the idea to write a book before it even occurred to me (I tend to avoid books altogether) ☁ Everyone at Little, Brown, who made this process far easier than it had any right to be ☁ The outstanding Kate Lee of ICM, who helped me develop a stupid book idea into an even *bigger* stupid book idea ☁ Matt Smith, Bruce Gifford, and everyone at SmithGifford, the finest ad agency in the universe ☁ Will Leitch, to whom I owe a great deal. Not financially, but on a much more spiritual level. And that's good, because I don't like sharing money. ☁ Noted combat vet Matt Ufford of withleather.com, for helping to start KSK, and for sharing the expensive scotch ☁ Brilliant artists Christopher Brand, Kevin Richards, Dan Vail, Greg Kice at kicemetal.com, and Matt Johnson at twoeightnine.com, all of whom made enormous contributions to this book despite being paid only in prestige ☁ The Spector family ☁ Jesse Johnston ☁ Multipurpose Jew Jack Kogod ☁ Stefan Fatsis ☁ The incredibly gifted Michael Tunison, whose brilliance more than makes up for the fact that he owns a cat ☁ Reluctant Southerner Monday Morning Punter ☁ Spencer Hall at edsbs.com ☁ Peggy Freudenthal and Shannon Langone ☁ Joy

O'Meara, Dylan Hoke, and dix! Digital Prepress, Inc. ● Fine Kentuckian Reed Ennis ● Dan Shanoff at danshanoff.com ● DJ Gallo at sportspickle.com ● AJ Daulerio, for introducing me to the phrase "bologna hammer" ● Jarret Myer and Brian Brater of uproxx.com ● Wright Thompson ● Christopher Nolan ● Google, for providing imbeciles such as myself with a free, easy-to-use tool for self-publishing. All they ask in return is to scan every word I've ever written in order to create a comprehensive digital profile of me to sell to anonymous hucksters and the Chinese defense department without my permission. Not a bad tradeoff. ● Jamie Mottram and Dan Steinberg ● JE Skeets at thebasketballjones.net ● The Nation of Islam Sports Blog ● Chris Mottram ● Sarah Schorno ● Michael Rand at randball.com ● The Mighty MJD ● Finally, a very big thank-you to everyone in the KSK community and everyone in the Deadspin community: readers, commenters, fellow bloggers, etc. You folks are the *real* men with balls. I salute you. And your balls.

## Looking for some Balls online?

Visit **drewmagary.com** for reader reviews, tour dates, hate mail, bonus material, and deleted shit from the book.